4.1.80

Energy–Efficient Community Planning

A Guide To Saving Energy And Producing Power At The Local Level.

James Ridgeway
With Carolyn S. Projansky

The JG Press, Inc./The Elements

Printed in the United States of America on recycled paper.

Davis Photos by Cindy O'Dell

Book design by T. A. Lepley

Library of Congress Cataloging in Publication Data

Ridgeway, James, 1936—
    Energy-efficient community planning.

    Includes index.
    1. Energy policy—United States—Case studies.
2. Energy conservation—United States—Case
studies. 3. Power resources—United States—
Case studies. 4. Energy consumption—United
States—Case studies. I. Projansky, Carolyn S.,
joint author. II. Title.

HD9502.U52R528	333.7	79-18023

ISBN 0-932424-03-1
ISBN 0-932424-02-3 pbk.

Contents

2092450

Acknowledgements

This book was made possible by the generosity and idealism of Jerome Goldstein of JG Press. I owe him a great debt of gratitude for his support as editor and publisher and for his clear vision of what communities can achieve on their own.

I have received help and encouragement from so many people that I cannot name all of them here. They include government officials, businessmen, farmers, townspeople, researchers, environmentalists and many, many others. To all of them I express my thanks for their time and interest.

I am especially grateful to Carolyn S. Projansky, who did much of the research on which portions of this book are based. She also wrote the sections on Clayton, Burlington, Ames, and Greensboro.

Although the final responsibility for accuracy and ideas is my own, I want to thank the following for their time and kind help: In Seattle, Sam Sperry, Pete Hennault, Randy Reveille, Robin Calhoun, Robert Lamson, and Michael Hildt, along with others in the city council, the mayor's energy office and Seattle City Light; in Northglenn, Richard P. Lundahl, Director of Natural Resources, Jim McNelly, and officials of FRICO; in Hartford, John Alschuler, Assistant City Manager, Nick Carbone, Deputy Mayor, and Geraldine Pleshaw, the city's Washington representative.

In Davis I want to thank Lori and Jon Hammond; Marshall Hunt and the staff at Living Systems; Gloria McGregor; Mike Corbett; Shigamoto Yoshimine and Dave Pelz and their respective staffs; Howard Reese; Nelva Yeoman; and the Davis City Council. Special thanks go to Bob Black, the former mayor. In Clayton, New Mexico, D. Ray Blakely, editor of the *Union County Leader;* in Ames, Terry V. Sprenkel, City Manager; in Greensboro, Don Weaver and Marilyn Braun; and in Burlington, Timothy S. Cronin.

Peter Land generously gave of his time and materials. Leonard Rodberg my colleague at the Public Resource Center kindly allowed me to reproduce his valuable research on "The Solar Transition." Cathy Lerza's research, her ideas and the food plan for Hartford, helped show me what a city can do in the area of food supply. Ken Hughes of the joint Economic Committee of Congress provided helpful advice.

I want to thank Nora Goldstein, Jim Punkre, Anna Carr, and Terri Lepley for their help over the course of the project.

Building a New Energy Base

It is now clear that the oil shortages of 1973 were but the first signal in a protracted energy crisis. Six years later, in the spring of 1979, the crisis deepened with the near catastrophe at Three Mile Island nuclear power plant in Pennsylvania and with the long lines at the gasoline pumps. OPEC price rises in summer exacerbated the crisis.

Since the Arab oil boycott of 1973, three successive administrations—those of Nixon, Ford and Carter—have struggled with the energy question. None of them have achieved any real progress. Congress, for its part, has been intractable and generally unresponsive to public demands for change.

But in the last six years there have been substantial changes in the way American towns and cities use energy. While these changes are seldom noticed, they combine to make the beginnings of what could well become a national energy policy. This book is about such communities and their local energy programs.

All too often, changing the nation's energy policy is perceived as merely increasing domestic oil production, mandating the compact car, halting nuclear power, and so on. Yet an effective policy need not be only a national one. Rather, various parts of the nation can adopt the innovations that suit their needs. Thus, in the Northeast where many cities are antiquated and inhabited by people who are out of work, the most effective energy policy is aimed at improving the quality of life and reducing the cost of food. In Hartford, Connecticut, officials have worked to reorganize agriculture by revitalizing nearby farms, reintroducing growing practices that went out with the western migrations of the last century, and creating new markets. In all of this, they seek to provide jobs for the city's unemployed people.

While energy policy begins with a reassessment of agriculture in Hartford, it is centered on water policy along the eastern slope of the Rockies. To the mushrooming bedroom cities that spread from Denver across the plain, water is like gold and is taken from the farmers to supply urban needs. The contradictions are vivid: Water feeds the suburbs which are dependent on the automobile. As these energy-inefficient communities grow, they require more and more fuel, both in terms of gas for cars and energy for housing. Although natural gas has been a major source of fuel in the past, shortfalls are anticipated in the coming years. Instead, energy will come from coal-fired electric generating plants or even from coal-fed synthetic fuel plants. Mining coal necessitates the use of greater quantities of water. Thus, scarce water once reserved for the agriculture that sustained the area, now goes increasingly to feed the suburbs and the coal mines needed to maintain them.

In Northglenn, Colorado, city officials have sought to halt this ruinous cycle by developing an energy policy that is based on a sound water program. A coherent water policy means a decision to curtail growth and to move, albeit gradually, towards higher density housing. Instead of fighting the farmers for more water, citizens of Northglenn have joined with them in a remarkable plan for sharing water with a view to both answering the needs of the city and to keeping precious agricultural lands in production.

There are numerous beneficial side effects: By capturing and recycling the city's wastewater to farm land, Northglenn reduces the amount of petroleum-based fertilizers needed by nearby farmers. Recycling wastes also means reduced reliance on large, capital- and energy-intensive sewage treatment plants. Those plants, in turn, are dependent on chemicals that were produced with large quantities of energy.

Reorganization of housing is an important, immediate issue in energy policy. By building small, environmentally sound houses that are linked closely by courtyards and patio concepts, communities can dramatically reduce energy consumption. High-density, environmentally sound housing not only means less energy for space heating and cooling, but less energy for transportation. Walking and biking begin to replace automobile use. Moreover, this sort of housing can reduce construction costs because the buildings are smaller, requiring less material and labor to construct.

Even in large, established cities such as Seattle, environmentally conscious design can have a measurable effect on the energy requirements of high-rise structures existing or about to be built in downtown. After a protracted debate over nuclear power, Seattle opted for energy conservation instead. The lost nuclear power will be replaced by energy garnered from conservation measures mandated by building ordinances.

The city of Davis, California, has come to represent what a community can do on its own, across a broad range of areas, to save energy and change the way its people live.

When Davis was threatened by suburban sprawl and swarming traffic, the city council 10 years ago moved to limit growth. In 1973, before the Arab boycott, residents were troubled by rapidly rising costs of electricity and natural gas; a group of architects, professors and students persuaded the university and city council to support a study of how energy could be properly conserved in Davis buildings, many of which are apartment complexes.

The energy study showed that apartments that faced either east or west were especially hot during the summer and required large amounts of electricity to run air conditioners. In winter, apartments with south windows needed much less energy for heating than apartments facing in other directions. The survey concluded that natural heating and cooling is obtained on a north-south axis with maximum glass exposure on the south.

The city council thereupon drew up and approved an ordinance embodying a set of performance standards for building construction aimed at achieving conservation. The code regulates the amount of window area in relation to the floor area. If more glass is desired, then architects must arrange it on the south facing portions of the building, or employ thermal glass. The amount of unshaded glass is strictly limited. The code stipulates that light colors (to better withstand the sun) must be used on the roof, and it included upgraded requirements for insulation.

Plans for new buildings are carefully checked by city officials who put scale models of proposed buildings under a solar simulator. The simulator is a gadget with light bulbs canted at different angles to represent the rays of the sun on different days of the year. In this way you can get a quick idea of whether a proposed building is properly positioned on a lot, whether there is too much glass, whether the glass is properly shaded, and so on.

Since the code took effect in 1977, Davis has expanded its efforts to conserve energy. There are 28,000 bicycles in town, and Davis has built a complex of special paths and set aside lanes on public roads to encourage their use. City Hall maintains its own fleet of bikes for use of employees who need to shuttle about on the job. Bikes must be registered and youngsters are taught how to use them in special courses presented at the school by the police department.

To further cut down on the use of cars, Davis has a fleet of London double-decked buses that are run around the city as a jitney service. In addition the city is in the midst of ridding itself of big cars and trucks, and replacing them with compact or subcompact models.

Davis wants to narrow, not widen its streets, and takes pains to be sure they are well-shaded. Research has shown that neighborhoods with narrow, shaded streets are 10 degrees cooler in summer than neighborhoods with wide unshaded streets. A citizens' committee has made a careful survey of all the trees in the city, and makes sure to see that new trees are planted in accordance with a general plan.

Until recently Davis made heavy use of pesticides to control insects on trees and shrubs. Now the city sprays with water, and has introduced biological control for pests.

The City Council has designed different kinds of solar houses as models to encourage builders to formally adopt such buildings in their major complexes. There are more than 700 swimming pools in town and the City Council wants to cut down on energy by forbidding them to use gas or electricity for heating.

These are some of the fairly simple, clear-cut steps Davis has undertaken to cut energy. In the end, the city hopes to cut usage by 50 percent.

While the details of the Davis experiment in energy conservation are, of course, designed to meet the city's unique needs, the ideas and plans can be helpful elsewhere around the nation. This book sets out to investigate several different experiments in a variety of communities. But before looking at these innovations in detail, it is useful and instructive to consider the overall setting in which these experiments take place. That involves a look at the origins of the energy crisis, and political and economic factors involved in the production and use of energy.

The energy crisis can best be understood as operating on two distinctly different levels. On the first, there are the recent, sporadic and temporary shortages of fuel oil, gasoline, natural gas, exacerbated by such events as the Arab oil boycott of 1973 or the Iranian revolution of 1978-79. These temporary dislocations suggest that fuels are harder to find, are located further away from their end use and are in greater demand than they used to be. They are in reality signals of what can happen if the situation continues.

On the second level, there is a real long-term shortage of fuel that will probably become critical within the next century because the amount of fossil fuel is finite and man is using it up quickly.

The production, distribution and use of energy fuels increasingly are the business of the oil industry. Worldwide, seven companies control two-thirds of the oil and dominate the refining, transportation and marketing of petroleum and natural gas products. In the United States, petroleum companies produce a sizable amount of coal and uranium and are engaged in the manufacturing of chemicals, petrochemicals, nuclear fuel and, in some instances, in the construction of nuclear power plants. Perhaps most important, the large petroleum companies are the only sources of information available to government on the extent of mineral fuel resources.

In part, the "energy crisis" is a reflection of political and economic pressures that were exerted on the oil industry after 1950 and the industry's effort to cope with resulting changes. A major turning point in the politics of oil occurred during 1953 when the nationalist Iranian premier Mohammad Mossadeq took over the oil concessions. He was soon toppled in a CIA-sponsored coup, the Shah returned to power, and the oil companies were given back their holdings. After the Suez crisis of 1956, the Iranian parliament wrote an oil law which for the first time recognized and encouraged the concept of joint ventures between foreign producers and the producing countries in the Middle Eastern oil fields. Until that time, the big oil companies essentially had gone into the Middle Eastern countries and paid the governments a small price or royalty for every barrel of oil they removed.

When other nations followed Iran's lead, the major Anglo-American oil companies realized that the rules of the oil game in the Middle East were changing. Not only would they be called upon to pay more money, but increasingly they would also be asked to cede control of oil operations to the producing countries; those countries then would be asking for participation in the profits gained from marketing the products.

Partly because of this change the oil industry sought to diversify its holdings. The major companies spread their search for oil into Southeast Asia, in the shallow seas off Indonesia, near Indochina, and southwards towards Australia. They moved actively into Alaska, and made incursions into the Canadian Arctic. They plunged into the North Sea. Within the United States itself, there was a stepped-up campaign for increased drilling on the outercontinental shelf. Most significantly, they bought into the coal industry, took a major position in uranium and even branched out into the manufacture of nuclear power plants.

Since the 1920s, coal had been viewed as a competitor to oil, not only because it could be burned by electric power plants and industry as an alternative to petroleum, but more importantly, because a technology exists for changing coal into synthetic fuel, i.e., gasoline, oil and gas.

By the middle 1970s, the major oil companies owned vast tracts of coal reserves in the United States, and had acquired some of the major coal companies through mergers. The oil industry was producing a quarter or more of all the coal, and controlled perhaps one-third of the reserves.

The possibility of changing coal to a synthetic gas, one that could be intermixed with natural gas, became an important consideration and played a role in the energy crisis of the early 1970s. That crisis began with a shortage of natural gas.

Natural gas supplies about one-third of all energy in the United States. It is basically a clean fuel, and because of the stiff air pollution standards formulated in the late 1960s, came into great demand. In particular, electric utilities, which previously had burned air-polluting sulfurous coal, began seeking gas.

Most of the natural gas in the United States is produced by major oil companies from fields in the South and Southwest and is transported to market by interstate pipeline firms. In the future, most gas will come from wells located beneath the sea in the Gulf of Mexico off Louisiana.

The United States Supreme Court ruled in 1954 that the United States government through the then independent regulatory commission, the Federal Power Commission, must regulate the price that the interstate pipeline companies pay to the industry producers for natural gas. Subsequent attempts at regulation were resisted by the producers who claimed that their economic incentive to drill would thereby be cut off. After another Supreme Court ruling in 1968, regulation began in earnest, and by 1969, gas reserve figures published by the industry began to decline. Government efforts to investigate these figures were resisted by the industry, and the FPC subsequently accepted the industry figures as true, agreed that there was a gas shortage and an energy crisis, and said that the price of gas should be made higher so as to offer additional incentives to companies that searched for new deposits. The price began to rise. But the rising prices had a curious effect on the industry: As prices went up, reserves continued to go down, not the reverse as the industry had insisted would happen.

All through the early 1970s, staff members and Congressional investigators were issuing reports that called into serious question the reserve figures of the industry. One investigation by the Federal Trade Commission found "serious under-reporting" of gas reserves. James Halverson, then the director of the Bureau of Competition in the FTC, testified in Congress that the procedures for reporting reserves by the American Gas Association "could provide the vehicle for a conspiracy among the companies involved to under-report gas reserves."

The campaign to increase gas prices in the face of alleged shortage continued, and during the Nixon-Ford years, there was pressure from the Federal Power Commission, the White House and within Congress to formally deregulate the price of natural gas, that is, to allow the price of gas to seek its own level.

The price rise affected the structure of the industry in other ways. As the price of natural gas climbed, the oil companies took an active interest in synthetic gas made from naptha or coal. If the price of natural gas rose to a sufficiently high level, then it could become profitable for the oil corporations to launch a gasification program that would change coal into synthetic gas. This synthetic gas would supplement the supposedly dwindling supplies of natural gas. Two hundred different gasification projects were planned by the American Gas Association members west of the Mississippi. Coal gasification would require large amounts of strip-mined coal and of water, along with the construction of expensive plants. Thus it would lead to large-scale development of the largely untapped coal resources in the Western Mountain states with an attendant decline in their existing agricultural economy and a tremendous strain on the already scarce water resources of the region.

What began therefore as an effort by the oil industry to ward off federal regulation of the natural gas business had widened by the mid-1970s into a full-scale reorganization of the energy industry in general. The employment of coal reserves as a feedstock for synthetic gas would require an enormous reallocation of capital resources throughout the nation. It would mean moving the coal industry out of Appalachia, leaving behind stripped hills, impoverished people and the United Mine Workers, an important and traditional adversary. The UMW is poorly organized in the West. Billions of dollars would be required for pipelines, synthetic-gas plants, all resulting in a basic change of the economy of the Mountain states from agriculture to mining.

In 1978 the oil industry ultimately won its long battle to decontrol the price of natural gas. Almost as soon as the energy act decontrolling natural gas was enacted and signed, the much ballyhooed shortage gave way to a gas glut. The industry thereupon struggled to avoid the uncontrollable surplus, threatened by increased imports of gas from Canada and Mexico.

The Carter administration moved to decontrol domestic oil prices as well. Again they argued that domestic producers needed the incentive of higher prices to find more oil, admitting all the while that it is unlikely more can be found in the continental United States.

Increased fuel prices, achieved through policies of decontrol, have prompted oil companies and energy planners in 1979 to look forward to production of alternative fuels. By alternatives, they mean not solar energy, but synthetic fuels, based on a seemingly inexhaustible supply of coal. With prices for fossil fuels at higher levels, synthetics appear to be economically feasible.

As discussed above, the oil industry for its own narrow political reasons (pushing up natural gas prices) introduced what soon became a wide ranging debate on overall fuel shortages. This was immediately taken up by ecologists who began to argue in profound economic and political terms that the world would soon run out of fossil fuels such as oil and natural gas, and that indeed many other natural resources would soon be exhausted.

Traditionally, the argument against oil politics had come from labor unions, consumer groups, etc., who urged the federal government to establish and supervise a more equitable system for distributing energy supplies at lower prices. These voices were still heard during the early 1970s in the fight against natural gas deregulation, but they were fainter than before. On all sides, however, there was a clamor for alternatives to prevent the world from running out of scarce resources, and in the process, to change the way we live. The saving alternative was solar energy.

The energy crisis was almost always argued in technical terms, and the enthusiasm for solar energy gained momentum because it too was seen as a technical solution—safe, non-polluting and inexpensive. Solar power was used during the earlier part of the century for heating water in the southern and western parts of the country, and its proponents in the early 1970s pointed to its successful use in such countries as Israel, Australia and Japan. In 1972, a report by the National Science Foundation and NASA added official sanction to solar by stating flatly that solar-generated power could be used to replace half the energy needed to heat and cool buildings, and concluded that "solar energy is received in sufficient quantity to make a major contribution to the future United States heat and power requirements." In its narrow technical conception, the discussions over solar energy focused on heating and cooling hot water with collectors. But soon the debates became much wider, alluding to the possibilities of wind energy, biomass conversion (garbage, sewage, timber), and environmentally-attuned architecture which harked back to the Indian adobe houses.

Solar energy also was perceived as opening a new political era. Solar energy was not dominated by large corporations. Indeed, there was the prospect that by its very nature, solar would open up the prospect of a decentralized economy. A home, equipped with photo-voltaic cells and collectors to heat the water and generate electricity, was not dependent on the big energy corporations or the rate-gouging local utility. Further, it was argued that since solar energy varied in its form from one area of the country to another because of different geographic and weather conditions, no one big corporation or group of corporations could come to dominate the industry. Finally, it was pointed out that in a time of high unemployment, a change to solar power would open thousands of jobs in a new expanding and socially useful industry.

For all these reasons, solar became the focus for a political movement of sorts, comprised of factions that under other circumstances, would have been in opposing camps. There were environmentalists who saw solar energy as an alternative to nuclear power, which they had been fighting to defeat. Ecologists viewed solar as a way to fundamentally begin a reordering of the world away from growth and towards decentralization. The generation of young political activists who had grown up opposing the Vietnam war saw solar energy as a lever for a broader political reorganization. Small businessmen, and those associated with the traditional arguments of small business, began to see solar as the opening of a broad, new business category. And finally, as one might have suspected, the oil companies picked up the solar crusade, arguing for research and development, and buying up the small firms that were thought to be most technologically advanced.

Gradually the idea of a solar future wormed its way into general political discourse. In the middle 1970s, Congress adopted and the President signed a demonstration solar heating and cooling act that provided a little money and much more importantly, a precedent for future legislation. By the time of Carter's election, there literally were hundreds of bills arguing for alternative energy pending in Congress. Carter's energy program itself acknowledged the role of solar and argued for more money both in research and general aid in the form of tax incentives for those who introduced solar equipment and design into their homes. In California, Governor Jerry Brown presided over an elaborate program of tax credits, and established a solar commission at the state level to help plan the way towards a solar future. Brown enthusiastically encouraged aerospace corporations to move into solar technology.

As a practical matter, these maneuvers probably had less to do with any inherent theories of decentralized techniques or socialistic futures than with more direct political and economic imperatives. The most important of these was the rising cost of fuel, reinforced by the oil industry's successful campaign to deregulate natural gas. That campaign promised to push prices ever higher. Another factor was the relative decline of nuclear power, brought about partly because of the environmental protests but also because of the economic inefficiency of the plants themselves. The decline of nuclear power offered an opportunity for developing solar technology. And because both state and federal governments were spending more money for solar research, large aerospace corporations began to actively investigate the market. Grumman, the Long Island, New York-based aircraft corporation, opened a solar business in California. The big oil companies had purchased solar companies in the early 1970s, and through their ownership of the copper industry, stood to profit from the sale of flat plate collectors.

The major thrust behind solar energy was in the form of tax incentives, and those expenditures benefited middle class homeowners. Instead of changing the structure or organization of the housing markets, the solar incentives tended to reinforce existing inflated housing industries.

Much of the impulse in all of this has been aimed at individuals, acting alone. Where the government has involved itself, it has largely been to reinvigorate the individual initiatives of the middle class sector of the population.

At the same time, however, there has been a much slower, more deliberate move towards building a different sort of energy system within communities. This is a long, drawn-out process, which has really just begun. Over the long term, it offers the prospects for remaking communities around the nation.

This book is a detailed account of experiments in four of these communities: Seattle, Washington; Davis, California; Northglenn, Colorado, and Hartford, Connecticut. In addition, we have described different approaches to energy in other communities, such as the use of wood for creating electricity in Burlington, Vermont; wind power in Clayton, New Mexico; garbage recovery and energy production in Ames, Iowa, a scheme for energy audits in Greensboro, North Carolina. We also have looked at some ideas for financing the introduction of energy conservation, and have seen how a transition to solar energy can result in more jobs.

In sum, the communities discussed in this book are constructing a new energy base, one that leads away from a reliance on fossil fuels and towards a future society using renewable resources.

1

Seattle

Conservation Commitment

Rejecting "Cheap" Nuclear Power

City-Enforced Energy Conservation

Electric Power From Wood Burning

Solar Combined With Hydropower

After prolonged debate, the city of Seattle, Washington, in 1975 set aside—at least temporarily—plans for meeting additional electrical demand with nuclear power and instead embarked on an ambitious path towards providing needed energy through conservation.

The energy conservation scheme entails developing new building codes aimed at achieving improvements in construction and increasing densities. It also involves rethinking transport policy (installing a free bus system downtown, for example) to cut back on auto commuting into the center city, and an intensive publicity barrage to persuade citizens to adopt conservation measures in their homes.

Seattle also has begun to investigate alternative energy—such ideas as fast-growing timber that could be burned to create electric power, and combining solar with hydropower. Over the long

run, the city may try merging these technologies into its existing energy supply system.

In Seattle, the tentative moves towards energy conservation have less to do with technology, or even economics (although most of the arguments are couched in economic language), than with politics. It has not been easy to convince the officials of the city, which owns its electric system, to move away from nuclear power and investigate alternative energy. Government officials are used to the idea of cheap hydroelectric power, and like many other public power groups, keen enthusiasts for the coming era of cheap nuclear energy.

Progress has been slow, but advocates of energy conservation and alternative energy believe there is a political process under way in Seattle that will lead them away from nuclear power, open the door to technical alternatives (solar, wind, etc.), and perhaps even lead to some form of energy decentralization.

For years, Seattle has benefited from low-cost electricity generated from dams set into the High Cascades. Seattle City Light, the city-owned electric utility, is the third largest publicly owned utility in the nation. It has a long, proud tradition of providing inexpensive public power, and the utility plays an important role in city politics.

But dam sites have become scarce. In 1970, and again in 1974, the Seattle City Council authorized the utility to participate in three different nuclear power plants. The construction and operation of these plants represented the work of a regional consortium of power plants, and since the Bonneville Power Administration stood ready to take power from the nuclear stations, there was little real risk to the city.

Then, in 1975, Seattle City Light sought authority from the council to reserve an option to participate in construction of more nuclear power plants. They were planned as part of an overall scheme, Phase II of the Hydrothermal Power Program (HTPP) for meeting electrical power requirements of the Northwest through the 1980s. Washington Public Power System (WPPS) is the agency responsible for construction and operation of all public utility electric energy resources planned under the power program. WPPS also is charged with raising the capital required for construction by selling bonds on the commercial market.

Under the option agreement, Seattle would secure rights to purchase approximately 10 percent of the output of the two proposed nuclear projects, and in return, agree to pay an equivalent share of the capital and interest payments. Interim development bonds would amount to $100 million and City Light would be responsible for payments whether or not complete development and financing of the projects took place.

If Seattle entered into the final participants agreement, then it would purchase a specific share—about 10 percent—of the project's output and would agree to pay for an equivalent share of project costs, including operating and maintenance expenses, together with capital and interest payments on bonds issued to finance the projects. Total project costs then were estimated to run from $2 to $2.5 billion. Payment of the capital and interest would be required whether or not the projects were completed and put into normal operation.

At public hearings held by the City Council in March and April of 1975 to discuss the proposed nuclear project, many questions were raised concerning Seattle's future electric energy load growth, the social and economic impacts of the proposed plants, and alternative ways for meeting the city's future energy demands. Other questions had been raised earlier in connection with the City Council approval of a City Light rate increase in July, 1974, and a Citizens' Committee had recommended that a number of studies be conducted prior to any further rate increase. In addition, the Seattle Environmental Council argued that City

Neighborhood workshops are used to raise energy awareness and to promote the Seattle City Light Home Energy Checks.

Light should prepare an environmental impact statement even before it engaged in planning for the nuclear plants. Because the utility had not made such a study, the environmentalists argued that the utility might have violated federal law.

Eventually the City Council approved City Light's request to enter into an "option agreement" with WPPS but stated that before any final approval to participate in the nuclear plants was given, it wanted answers to most of the questions asked at the hearing. Those answers were to include much of the information that, under other circumstances, would be contained in an environmental impact statement, like forecasts of demand, alternatives to nuclear, and so on. The final decision

on whether or not to participate in the construction of the proposed plants had to be made by May, 1976.

The subsequent study was conducted by the utility's office of environmental affairs, under the direction of Pete Henault. Henault is a nuclear reactor scientist and an ardent environmentalist. Thus, he was respected in opposing camps. Henault began by proposing that, for purposes of the study's credibility, consultants be hired to carry forward the work and that a citizens' committee be convened to oversee the study.

In subsequent testimony before the United States Congress, Henault recalled how the citizens' committee was selected: "Organizations were first identified which had a special interest in the utility's policies and programs. This included among others, the Chamber of Commerce and groups representing the elderly, minorities and poor. Groups were asked to nominate candidates and every effort was made to select individuals who would question, voice opinions, listen and co-operate well with other members."

When complete, the citizens' overview committee included a strong representation of individuals active in the environmental movement, several economists and engineers who had an acquaintence with alternative energy systems, and experts from such well-known companies as Boeing, the telephone company, etc.

Henault continued:
"In the months that followed, this committee had a profound impact on the study and subsequent decisions by the City Council. Upon insistence by the committee, the scope was expanded substantially, the length of time to conduct the study was doubled, and funding was tripled. The committee began meeting in July 1975, and met almost weekly until May of 1976. Thousands of hours of expert assistance were donated to the project. Because funds were not available to compensate committee members for their time, something else had to be offered by the utility.

"We offered what I believe was a key ingredient to the success of any public involvement program, and anyone wishing to model their own studies after the Energy 1990 example should keep this in mind. The key ingredient was a true commitment by the utility to listen to the committee, to give the committee complete freedom to all information and facts desired, to allow all activities to be conducted openly, and to allow all conclusions, recommendations and opinions to be published as part of the final

report. While the utility reserved the right to make its own final decisions, this commitment guaranteed that nothing would be swept under the rug and won the dedication and hard work of the committee members."

As suggested above, there also were practical political considerations. If the utility had not agreed to an open and full discussion of the salient issues involved, it might well have been subjected to an embarrassing legal challenge for failure to protect the environment.

There was a second factor involved, in the eyes of some participants. During the early stages of the study, City Light was faced with a strike by its employees. The view is that the strike proved to be a distraction to the top officials of the utility, who otherwise might have busied themselves with overseeing the work of the citizens' committee in order that it not get out of hand.

In short, Henault and other environmentally-minded officials at City Light, backed up by the citizens' committee, were given pretty much of a free hand by the City Light top bureaucracy. In the past, top officials had been proponents of nuclear power, and indeed were supporting participation in the consortium that would build the plants in dispute.

Freedom of action by the citizens' committee was important in the early stages of the inquiry. It was then that the group decided which econometric model to use in projecting future electric power demand. Heretofore, utilities either did not use econometric models, resorting instead to projecting future growth on the basis of current and past trends, or if they did go in for this sort of sophisticated modeling, they employed a dependable consulting firm which could be counted on to come up with what the utility wanted to hear.

But the model adopted by the citizens' committee while the City Light officials were trying to settle their strike was not the usual sort. It had been constructed by a small Seattle consulting firm that was not close to the electric power industry. It took into account underlying factors that were in the midst of dramatic change—something that a trending forecast would not have taken into account. Those factors included rapid inflation, the rate of growth of the region, the differences in energy demand by different sorts of industries, and the world oil crisis. As a result, the model predicted a much lower demand for power than previously predicted by City Light.

Eventually the utility came to realize the implications of the model and focused attack upon it. City Light called in other economists with other models to refute the low-growth model's assumptions. But that was not until the citizens' committee was well along with its planning, based on the model's work.

The first phase of the study lasted seven months and resulted in seven volumes of detailed analysis. After a period of public comment and response, the citizens' committee came up with its conclusions and recommendations, which were published and

submitted to the City Council. In its own final recommendations, City Light had reduced its original request for a 10 percent participation to half that amount and recommended that a very aggressive conservation program funded by the Council and implemented by the utility be set into motion. The conservation target recommended by Superintendent Vickery was 250 megawatts or about 20 percent of Seattle's projected 1990 electric energy demands. The citizens' committee recommended a conservation program aimed at achieving only 193 megawatts but recommended no participation in the nuclear plant construction.

During the summer of 1976, the question of whether or not to participate in the nuclear power plant construction became a major controversial issue in Seattle. The City Council met weekly and listened to testimony on all aspects of the study. Pro-nuclear and anti-nuclear advocates debated the issue. Experts were flown in for additional testimony and the Council patiently listened and asked questions. Public hearings were held.

Henault in his description adds, "It is important to note that the real debate was not a pro/anti-nuclear debate but rather over whether or not the city of Seattle was to make a true commitment to energy conservation. Pro-nuclear members of the citizens' committee, in fact, voted against participation and in favor of conservation."

Finally in July 1976 by a narrow margin, the Council voted to meet the city's additional energy demands through

1990 by conservation. In addition to this decision, the Council passed five important resolutions:

Resolution 25257: Seeks the comprehensive revision of all City structure-related codes with an aim of institutionalizing an energy conservation and efficiency awareness in building design and construction.

Resolution 25258: Adopts policy for forecasting electrical energy demand in order to project the most likely baseline level of electrical demand.

Resolution 25259: Sets forth legislative intent to specify energy conservation policies as part of the city's comprehensive policy plan. Initial implementation involves the proposal by the Mayor of a series of programs including institution of mandatory insulation standards as a condition of conversion to electric space heating by residential customers; promotion of consumer education to encourage voluntary insulation of existing residences; promotion of City Light's technical advisory service, emphasizing assistance to commercial-industrial customers to improve efficient energy use; and energy use disclosure for residential dwellings.

Resolution 25260: Specifically outlines that generation policies be governed by elements of resource use, energy conservation, sound economics and environmental responsibility. The resolution provides for preparation of a 20-year load forecast and power generation plan to use in planning new resources.

Resolution 25271: Urges preparation of a contingency planning program to meet either unanticipated electrical energy demand or unexpected supply constraints.

Finally the Council told City Light to come back in two months' time with an implementation plan for its conservation program.

At a purely practical level, the great bulk of the 230 megawatts scheduled to be saved by 1990 will derive from the effects of proposed new building codes that were promulgated in the fall of 1978. The building codes would save up to 85 megawatts. The codes themselves were put together by a citizens' task force working through the new city energy office and will affect commercial structures, not residential. They are based on model national codes. (i.e. ASHRAE 90-75 and ERDA-sponsored model code derived from ASHRAE 90-75.)

A basic idea behind the plan is to more coherently employ land space in downtown Seattle, to intermix living and working space in a more dense pattern within the downtown, and thereby reduce energy consumed in commuting. At the same time, Seattle embarked upon free bus service for the downtown in an effort to cut down on transport by automobiles.

A second practical measure was undertaken by the utility in an effort to reduce conversions from gas and oil to electricity. This conversion standard, which pressures all those seeking to switch to electricity to install insulation and other energy-saving measures, was adopted by City Light partly as a result of the conservation program, but also because the utility was forced to conserve energy due to the 1976-77 drought in the Northwest. The regulations state:

"Prior to Residential Electric Heat service connection, the customer or contractor/installer shall obtain the necessary electric permit and submit a heat loss calculation to either the City Building Department or the State Electrical Department and forward a copy to the Utility for review. The Utility shall be notified when the new service is approved for connection."

"On Residential Electric service connection for either new or rewire conversion construction, the electric heat loss shall be limited to 10 watts per square foot of total floor area (detached garages excluded) for single family, duplex or triplex structures. The selection of electric heating equipment installed shall be to the nearest desired commercially available increment of the heat loss."

What is unusual about Seattle is the process or mechanism involved in changing the energy policies of a large city from historic reliance on cheap hydropower to first, energy conservation, and later perhaps to alternative energy technologies. It has been largely a political process, not a technical one. At the heart of the political process has been a struggle between the City Council, and the new mayor, Charles Royer, against the public utility, which has been wedded to abundant cheap electricity.

As a result of fights in the early 1970s over rate structure, the utility created an environmental affairs department to appease its critics. As a result of the City Council action on the nuclear plants, it also established a conservation department. At the same time, the Council, mindful that the city really had no source of energy information outside the expansion-minded utility, created an energy office under the Mayor. Finally, and perhaps most importantly, the Council took steps to reign in the activities of the utility superintendent so that he was made much more accountable to the Council.

The system is instructive:

The Mayor appoints the superintendent who serves not for a set period of time, but at his pleasure. He can be dismissed at any time. Moreover, from now on the superintendent must be confirmed by the City Council. The superintendent's testimony at his confirmation hearings will be under oath, with criminal penalties for perjury. This is an extreme requirement, demanded by few cities. It was required by the Council in part because it discovered that during the fight to enact energy conservation measures, the utility had been adding new large customers, thereby adding demand, and cancelling out the savings the Council had been struggling to achieve with the energy conservation program.

The utility budget is submitted to the Mayor, who can either send it on to the Council unchanged or rework it. The Council in any event has the final say.

Sale of bonds must be approved by the Council, as is the case with all contracts, sale of properties, etc. Rates must be approved by the Council.

The Mayor has a policy-planning body to oversee the activities of the

Nestled squarely in between Seattle's waterfront and Central Business District, the Pike Place Market was created by Seattle's public officials in 1907. In 1932, the heyday of the Market, over 600 farmers sold goods there daily. Currently, only about 35 make the trip from farm to Market. With the heavy development of industry, especially in the Green River Valley to the south of Seattle, King County farmland has declined from 165,000 acres in the mid-1940's to 43,000 acres today. The King County Office of Agriculture projects an acceleration of that trend, leaving less than 25,000 acres by 1990. Worse still, many local producers find themselves completely ostracized from the entire food distribution system.

But positive change may come for King County farmers. With the energy crunch looming over the city again, public officials have revived their interest in small-scale, near-urban agriculture. Last year, the King County Council proposed a $30 million bond issue to purchase development rights of county farmland. Although much debate surrounding the bond proposal stopped at growth management issues, "local self-sufficiency" — stressing the small farmers' role in an energy-efficient community — emerged as a new, regional battle cry. However, the farmland preservationists, operating out of a campaign office in the Pike Place Market, failed (barely) to gain the necessary 60 percent margin of victory.

In a continuing effort to help area farmers, a wholesale direct marketing program known as the Bulk Commodities Exchange (BCE) was begun. The BCE was co-sponsored by the King County Office of Agriculture and the Pike Place Market Preservation and Development Authority, the city-chartered public corporation which manages the seven-acre Market Historic District. More and more local farmers have joined the BCE, viewing it as a reliable, valuable outlet for their fresh produce. And the number of bulk consumers (many of whom are food co-ops and buying clubs) has tripled since the program began.

utility. And the City Council, through an energy committee, insists on a major say in policy planning for the utility.

Meanwhile, as a response to the mandates of the City Council, policies of the utility have slowly begun to change. As already mentioned an office of conservation was established. The environmental affairs department gained stature as a result of the 1990 planning. The superintendent is to be replaced. And the utility has begun an inquiry into different sources of energy.

The utility is examining, for instance, the possibility of establishing coal-fired power plants, fueled with deep mine coal reserves located in the state of Washington. It also is discussing the prospects of importing coal from the Beluga fields of Alaska, either by tanker (in which case the coal would be in the form of slurry) or in bulk. Also, there is always the possibility of buying coal from the Fort Union formation on the eastern slopes of the Rockies, and hauling it via the Burlington Northern Railroad, which has a railhead at Seattle.

More hopefully, City Light will experiment with biomass production. Here the idea is to grow Black Cottonwood and Red Alder along power line rights-of-way. These trees can be brought to maturity in four to six years, and harvested mechanically with giant scissors. The wood could be mingled with coal, garbage, etc. and burned to create electricity. And the city is investigating the possibility of using wind and solar energy.

All of this is in an early stage. But the thought is that hydropower is a natural backup power source for solar and wind

power. A solar collector has been developed by the utility and probably will be patented with an eye to later sales.

In sum, under pressure of the City Council, and now with the stated support of the new mayor, Charles Royer, Seattle has turned away from nuclear power and announced its intention of making up the energy to have been provided by the two power plants through energy conservation. Most of that energy will be saved through adoption of rather modest building standards for commercial structures.

More important over the long run, is the gradual change in emphasis within the utility itself away from generation of large amounts of cheap hydropower to conservation and alternative energy technology. And in the Seattle planning process, there is at least an inkling that a move towards alternative technology may well mean decentralization, an idea which could very well result—one day—in the reorganization of the utility itself.

But this is not a policy without problems. The planning and engineering staffs within the utility have proceeded ahead as usual, laying plans for more dams, arguing in essence that conservation won't be sufficient to make up the city's needs. Moreover, Seattle is surrounded in the state of Washington by political forces that up to now all have been arrayed against the policies it has chosen.

Since he became mayor, Charles Royer has reached out beyond Seattle to propose a regional energy program that in outline would be dramatically different from the current regional scheme, dependent as it is on coal-fired and atomic power plants. In testimony before Congress, Royer set out the basic outlines of the policy adopted by the Seattle City Council:

"First, public participation. We believe it is the responsibility of public power agencies to lead the way for public involvement in energy decision-making. Seattle's resolution on regional power—approved unanimously by the City Council and signed by me sets forth two basic policies for public participation. First, a regional energy planning commission should be established for long-range electrical energy planning; second, this commission should be publicly controlled and structured to ensure accountability and access to interested groups. Some have proposed planning by utility managers, or parallel bodies representing the utilities and region's consumers. We considered these approaches, but I believe it is important that we consolidate regional energy planning in one visible accountable public forum. Here, the opinions and expertise of utility technicians, citizens, conservation groups, and local elected policy makers can be heard and help to shape the Northwest electrical energy future. . . .

"For the region, we specifically recommend creating a publicly representative commission with members from the four Northwest states and federal government. The commission should have ultimate decision authority and responsibility for electricity planning. It would assess needs and maintain an adequate power supply at the lowest cost. The commission should be advised by groups representing utilities and local governments. Decisions should be made after thorough public review and discussion. We recommend the commission be a joint state-federal body. The group must be regionally representative, and it should represent political jurisdictions whose agencies or policies would be directly affected. This includes the federal government. . . .

"The second vital issue in regional power planning is conservation. . . . We have de-signed a detailed regional conservation program founded on three basic tenets:

1. The conservation plan should be designed to maintain an adequate power supply in the region at the lowest cost to the consumer, giving equal consideration to conservation programs and new generating supplies;

2. To maximize public acceptance and benefits, a regional conservation program should be designed to require no radical changes in behavior or comfort. Rather, a sound conservation program should concentrate on overcoming barriers to financially and environmentally beneficial conservation investments and changes in energy use; and

3. Finally, and very important, allocations of power must, in my view, reward specific conservation strategies by granting utilities the full financial benefits of their own consumers' conservation—this both prevents unfair treatment of those who conserve, and provides them with full incentives to conserve. . . .

"Seattle's resolution on regional power planning holds that Northwest preference power should be allocated to preference utilities so that they reap the full savings from their conservation efforts. I wholeheartedly support that policy and recommend that it be extended to cover all allocations of federal power. In Seattle, our model Energy 1990 conservation program, and our citizens' ten percent conservation during last year's drought can be attributed in large part to a recognition that conservation can produce real dollar savings. This incentive must be preferred."

The combination of energy conservation programs, interest in developing alternative forms of energy supplies, and efforts to maximize citizen and energy utility cooperation has resulted in a comprehensive and potentially cost-saving local energy policy for the city of Seattle.

Seattle Documents

Forecasting Electrical Energy Demand

RESOLUTION   25258

A RESOLUTION adopting a policy for forecasting electrical energy
    demand in the Seattle Lighting Department's service area.

WHEREAS, on September 4, 1973, the Seattle City Council, the Mayor
    concurring, adopted Resolution 24283, establishing goals and
    objectives for the City of Seattle for the year 2000, includ-
    ing the goal to "Reach a steady level of per capita energy
    consumption by the year 2000;" and

WHEREAS, the recently completed Energy 1990 Study included the
    construction of an econometric model which may be used in
    future years by the Department of Lighting to assess future
    electrical energy demands with greater sensitivity to chang-
    ing economic and demographic conditions than previously; and

WHEREAS, future electrical generation for the Lighting Department's
    service area is more likely to consume more non-renewable
    natural resources at substantially higher costs than hereto-
    fore using hydroelectric generation, it is increasingly
    important to base generation and energy conservation on the
    most accurate forecast of future demand available; Now, Therefore

WHEREAS, on September 4, 1973, the Seattle City Council, the Mayor concurring, adopted Resolution 24283, establishing goals and objectives for the City of Seattle for the year 2000, including the goal to "Reach a steady level of per capita energy consumption by the year 2000;" and

BE IT RESOLVED BY THE CITY COUNCIL OF THE CITY OF SEATTLE, THE MAYOR CONCURRING:

That an annual energy load forecast will be conducted which projects the most likely baseline level of electrical demand together with the probable range of statistical confidence surrounding the baseline forecast.

BE IT FURTHER RESOLVED that the forecast of energy sales and loads will be the responsibility of the Department of Lighting, prepared under the following conditions:

1.   The forecast will be prepared annually using the most current and acceptable forecasting techniques available and will be conducted and/or reviewed by an independent consultant at least every five years.

2.   The period of the long-range forecast will be 20 years to provide a projection of electricity needs at least as far ahead as the time necessary to bring new facilities on line; a short-term forecast for rate planning and financial purposes will be made as necessary.

3.   Quantitative methods shall be applied consistent with proven techniques supplemented by professional judgement.

4.   All assumptions and components should be presented explicity; major factors influencing the forecast should be isolated and explained.

5.   The forecast should allow for analysis of the sensitivity to changes in independent factors influencing the forecast.

6. The method of forecasting chosen should be flexible
    enough to apply to a wide variety of foreseeable conditions.

7. Each year the forecast report shall be made available as
    requested to the general public. The report will include
    the current baseline forecast, new data input, methodo-
    logical changes, and an ongoing comparison with actual loads.

Adopting Energy Conservation Policies

RESOLUTION   25259

A RESOLUTION adopting energy conservation policies for the City
    of Seattle and setting forth a schedule for implementing them.

WHEREAS, on September 4, 1973, the Seattle City Council (by
    Resolution 24283) adopted goals and objectives for the City
    of Seattle for the year 2000; including:

a) Reach a steady level of per capita energy consumption by
    the year 2008;

b) Use energy efficiently in providing for Seattle's demands,
    taking care to be aware of trade offs between efficient
    energy use and environmental impact; and

c) Formulate an energy policy for the City. Such a policy
    would support regional, state, and national efforts to
    formulate consistent policy. It should also encourage
    research through direct City participation or funding,
    into techniques for more efficient energy production and
    utilization and methods to reduce associated environmental
    impacts; and

WHEREAS, in October, 1973, the Citizens Policy Advisory Committee submitted policy recommendations to the Seattle Lighting Department including marketing and environmental policies which encourage more efficient use of electrical energy; and

WHEREAS, the recently enacted Energy Policy and Conservation Act of 1975 (Public Law 94-163) as well as numerous additional energy conservation measures now before Congress establish mandatory appliance efficiency standards and include numerous energy conservation assistance provisions; and

WHEREAS, in March, 1976, the Washington State Legislature enacted Engrossed Substitute Senate Bill No. 3172 which declares the policy of the State of Washington to encourage energy conservation and eliminate wasteful and uneconomic uses of energy and creates a state energy office, the duties of which include development of programs and guidelines for conservation plans for use by government, industry, and individual citizens, including the voluntary state energy conservation program provided by the federal Energy Policy and Conservation Act of 1975; and

WHEREAS, the findings of the recently completed Energy 1990 Study suggest that a substantial portion of Seattle's future electrical energy demand may be satisfied by more efficient use of present energy resources; and

WHEREAS, energy conservation measures which are economically beneficial to Seattle's energy users today also preserve energy resources and minimize energy costs for future generations; Now, Therefore,

BE IT RESOLVED BY THE CITY COUNCIL OF THE CITY OF SEATTLE, THE MAYOR CONCURRING, THAT THE FOLLOWING ARE THE ENERGY CONSERVATION POLICIES FOR THE CITY OF SEATTLE AND A PART OF THE CITY'S COMPREHENSIVE POLICY PLAN:

1. The City shall promote the wise and efficient use of all forms of energy through consumer education and technical assistance programs.

2. The City shall develop, implement, and maintain a munic-

ipal energy conservation program, including annual energy
audits of all municipally owned or leased buildings.
When practicable, new minicipal leases shall include provisions for utility payment or cost sharing of savings
realized from any conservation program implemented.
Consideration and documentation of life cycle energy costs
shall be required for all proposed municipal purchases
which involve significant energy requirements. The conservation program shall explore the uses of new energy
saving technologies or supplemental energy systems.

3.   The City shall establish and maintain an Energy Conservation Office. The functions of this Office should
include coordination, program design, research, and such
other activities as appropriate to carry out the City's
energy conservation policies. The Office shall provide
objective information about energy conservation for all
energy sources. Review or overview mechanisms shall be
provided to assure continued objectivity of such services.
The primary responsibility for electrical energy conservation activities for the City shall be the Lighting
Department.

4.   The City shall regularly review and revise, if necessary,
all existing structure-related codes to provide maximum
energy conservation consistent with the City's policies
on structure-related codes (set forth in Resolution 25011,
adopted on April 12, 1976) and justified under sound economic principles. Other City Codes, practices or policies
shall also be reviewed to insure that they do not discour-
age energy conservation.

5.   The City shall regularly review and revise, if necessary,
existing utility rates to encourage energy conservation
through voluntary consumer actions consistent with cost of
service principles and adopted City policies on utility
rates. Utility bills will be revised to fully disclose
the basis upon which the customer is charged per unit of
consumption.

6.   The City shall develop and update emergency plans for

short-term unanticipated shortages and contingency plans
in the event a failure to meet forecasted energy demand
is foreseen several years in advance.

7. The City shall encourage the establishment of efficiency
    criteria for principal energy users, and where applicable,
    shall enforce those criteria.

8. The City shall encourage research, through direct City
    participation or joint funding, into techniques for more
    efficient use of energy.

9. The City shall support regional, state, and national
    efforts to formulate consistent energy policies which re-
    inforce energy conservation goals.

BE IT FURTHER RESOLVED THAT THE FOLLOWING SCHEDULE SETS FORTH THE
INITIAL IMPLEMENTATION STEPS IN SUPPORT OF THE ABOVE POLICIES:

1. By September 1, 1976, the Mayor will submit to the City
    Council, recommended programs, necessary budgets, and
    ordinances to implement the following:

    a) Mandatory insulation standards (R-19 in attics and
        R-11 in walls and floors) as a condition precedent to
        conversion to electric space heating by any residential
        customer.

    b) An aggressive consumer education program encouraging
        voluntary insulation of existing Seattle residences,
        including performance standards to monitor results
        within two years.

    c) An aggressive technical advisory service to encourage
        and assist industrial and commercial customers to im-
        prove the efficiency of existing electrical energy
        consumption and utilize the most energy efficient tech-
        nology possible in expansions or conversions.

    d) A recommendation, budget and ordinance establishing an
        Office of Energy Conservation and/or an Electric Energy

Management Office, the duties of which will include a
Municipal Conservation Program, a technical advisory
service for customers considering installation of a
heat pump, consumer-oriented research and education
towards improved energy efficiency, promotion of clock
thermostats, water heater temperature reduction, and
other energy conservation measures which prove effective. Such an office should also be responsible for
coordinating Seattle's energy conservation program
with State and Federal programs and seek grants-in-aid
of specific programs in Seattle.

2. By December 1, 1976, the Mayor will submit to the City
Council an ordinance requiring written disclosure of the
energy use over the previous twelve months to prospective
purchasers, lessors or renters of any residential unit.

3. To take full advantage of new knowledge gained from actual
experience and changing circumstances, the Department of
Lighting together with any other City departments or offices given responsibility for energy conservation programs shall within two years from the adoption of this
Resolution and periodically thereafter report to the Mayor
and City Council results achieved and recommend revisions
in the foregoing policies and programs where appropriate.

Adopting Electrical Generation Policies

RESOLUTION 25260

A RESOLUTION adopting electrical generation policies for the City
of Seattle.

WHEREAS, on September 4, 1973, the Seattle City Council, the Mayor
concurring, (by Resolution 24283) adopted goals and objectives
for the City of Seattle for the year 2000, including:

a) Reach a steady state level of per capita energy consumption by the year 2000.

b) Select energy sources which use the least of non-renewable resources, while taking into consideration other resources such as land and minerals, and

c) Formulate an energy policy for the City. Such a policy would support regional, state and national efforts to formulate consistent policy. It should also encourage research, through direct City participation or funding into techniques for more efficient energy production and utilization and methods to reduce associated environmental impacts, and

WHEREAS, the Seattle City'Light Citizens Policy Advisory Committee submitted recommendations, including a proposed generation policy in October, 1973, and

WHEREAS, on March 12, 1976, the Washington State Legislature enacted (by Engrossed Substitute Senate Bill No. 3172) a State energy management bill, adopting in Section 2 certain energy policies, including:

The development and use of a diverse array of energy resources with emphasis on renewable energy resources shall be encouraged;" and

WHEREAS, the recently completed Energy 1990 Study provides a basis for consideration of future electrical generation alternatives; Now, Therefore,

BE IT RESOLVED BY THE CITY COUNCIL OF THE CITY OF SEATTLE, THE MAYOR CONCURRING, THAT THE FOLLOWING ARE THE ELECTRICAL GENERATION POLICIES FOR THE CITY OF SEATTLE AND ARE A PART OF THE CITY'S COMPREHENSIVE POLICY PLAN:

1. Prudent resource use, energy conservation, sound economics, and environmental responsibility shall at all times be the basic tenets governing generation planning decisions.

2. Pursuant to Resolution 25258, the Lighting Department shall maintain on a continuing basis a comprehensive 20-year load forecast and power generation plan and shall coordinate its planning with other regional utilities. Decision to construct or participate in the construction of additional generation facilities will be made on the basis of this forecast and plan. Decisions to undertake studies and environmental assessments to bring prospective projects to an advance planning stage will be made on the basis of the higher limits of statistical confidence in the load forecast and any reserve for contingencies adopted as part of the power generation plan.

3. Hydro power shall be the preferred method of generating electricity so long as hydro resources remain which can be economically developed on an acceptable environmental basis. The Lighting Department shall also consider use of other renewable energy resources in preference to fuel-consuming alternatives to the extent that such other renewable resource alternatives are practical, economical, and environmentally acceptable.   2092450

4. As circumstances make thermal generation a necessity, alternatives using abundant energy resources or resources usable only for electric power generation shall be preferred for base load generation with natural gas or oil alternatives limited, if possible, to peaking or intermediate-range generation. In undertaking thermal projects or participating in multiple ownership thermal projects, the Lighting Department will encourage the utilization of waste heat to the extent that such systems of waste heat use have economic merit and yield significant societal benefits.

5. To maximize assurance of meeting the direct utility responsibility vested in the Lighting Department, self-owned and jointly owned generation facilities shall be the preferred method of satisfying projected load. The decision to self-own or jointly own generation facilities, or to contract for the output of generation facilities owned by other entities will be decided on a case by case basis after an assessment of the costs, risks, and benefits of the various options.

6. Federal generation resources, however, will continue to be used to the extent available. The Lighting Department shall continue to participate actively in coordinated regional generation planning and system integration so as to minimize total environmental and economic costs and to optimize regional resource use and conservation.

7. The Lighting Department will use its leadership to help ensure that future regional power programs are planned in such a manner that a full range of generation and non-generation alternatives are in an advance planning stage so that the success of the programs will not critically depend upon the ability of the program participants to commence construction of any one facility.

8. The Lighting Department will use its leadership to help ensure that long-term electric energy sales by the Bonneville Power Administration fully protect the preference rights of the Lighting Department to federal power.

9. The Lighting Department will continue to minimize the expenditure of Department funds on specific generation projects while basic environmental and energy resource questions are being resolved.

10. The Lighting Department will continually strive to minimize the adverse environmental consequences resulting from the construction and operation of self-owned generation facilities, and to use its leadership to encourage extractors and processors of fuel for thermal-electric generation plants to use the most economically efficient pollution control technology and land restoration techniques.

11. The Lighting Department will use its leadership to assure that the appropriate Federal and State agencies adopt adequate health and safety standards for the construction, operation and disposal of wastes of thermal generation facilities, and that any such projects in which the Lighting Department enters into an ownership or contractual interest fully comply with these standards.

Meeting Unanticipated Energy Demands

RESOLUTION___25271___

RESOLUTION adopting a contingency planning program to meet unanticipated electrical energy demands which may occur in the
future.

WHEREAS, a majority of the Seattle City Council, after careful consideration of the Energy 1990 Study and recommendations of the
Mayor and the Superintendent of Lighting, has determined on the
basis of the Energy 1990 load forecast (increased to assure
adequate electrical energy for industrial customers) and expected energy demand mitigation from the conservation program
adopted by the City Council, the Mayor concurring, on July 12,
1976 by Resolution 25257 and 25259, that participation by the
City of Seattle in Washington Public Power Supply System Nuclear
Projects Number 4 and 5 is not necessary at this time; and

WHEREAS, prudent utility planning requires that sufficient generation
and non-generation options be thoroughly studied at an advanced
stage of contingency planning to assure adequate energy supply
should future energy demand increase at greater than the anticipated rate; and

WHEREAS, the Lighting Department has recommended (and the Mayor and
City Council agree) that the 1990 load forecast include a
"statistical confidence interval" of 175 megawatts greater or
less than the 1990 baseline load forecast of 1,349 megawatts
adopted by the City Council; and

WHEREAS, the Lighting Department has recommended (and the Mayor and
the City Council agree) that the 1990 load forecast include a
"contingency planning reserve" of 55 megawatts because future
generation projects may experience delays or start-up difficulties; Now Therefore

BE IT RESOLVED BY THE CITY COUNCIL OF THE CITY OF SEATTLE, THE MAYOR
CONCURRING THAT THE FOLLOWING IS THE ELECTRICAL ENERGY CONTINGENCY

PLANNING PROGRAM FOR THE CITY OF SEATTLE:

1. In addition to reporting conservation program results pur-
    suant to Resolution 25259, the Lighting Department (assisted
    by the Office of Energy Conservation) will submit by July 31,
    1978, a recommended program of standby conservation measures;
    including rate structure adjustments, to be implemented in
    the event future growth in electrical energy demand proves
    such measures to be necessary.

2. The Lighting Department shall submit to the Mayor and the
    City Council as part of its proposed 1977 Budget and 1977-
    82 Capital Improvement Program recommendations for under-
    taking studies of future generation alternatives as follows:

    A. By January 1, 1979, comprehensive environmental, eco-
        nomic and engineering studies of the suitability and
        feasibility of the Copper Creek Hydro Project on the
        Skagit River and hydropower developments on the North
        and South Forks of the Tolt River; and

    B. By July 1, 1977, an overall review and evaluation
        (including preliminary economic, environmental, and
        engineering studies) of undeveloped or potential
        hydropower opportunities in Washington State; and

    C. By January 1, 1979, geological, technical and economic
        studies to establish the magnitude and nature of any
        coal reserves for which exclusive mining rights have
        been or may be acquired with approval of the City
        Council, the feasibility and means of mining, alter-
        native means of using the coal for generating elec-
        tricity, and the adverse environmental impacts associated
        with the mining and use of the coal as well as appro-
        priate measures to mitigate those impacts.

2

Davis

Cutting Energy Use

Developing Energy-Saving Consciousness

Bicycle Paths

Shaded Streets

Solar Retrofitting

Davis is close to the Sacramento River, which flows into the San Francisco Bay 50 miles downstream. The terrain is flat. Big farms stretch out in all directions.

The city proper was established in the 1850s as a depot where rail lines from San Francisco met those that connected with the transcontinental railroad. Subsequently Davis became an important junction for the Southern Pacific Railroad, linking the railroad's lines running down the Valley with those going east and west. A few decades after the railroad arrived, the University of California decided to locate the state's agricultural experiment station at Davis, and that gave the community the beginnings of an important second industry.

The basic shape of the city remained much the same until the late 1950s when the agricultural school was ex-panded to become a full-fledged campus of the University of California. A medical school and liberal arts college were added to the veterinary and agricultural colleges already on the Davis campus.

With rapid growth of the city, citizens became increasingly concerned about planning. In 1968, after lengthy debate, a progressive City Council moved to curb growth.

It turned against the automobile and embraced the bicycle and bus as means of transport. After sponsoring an inquiry into energy use, the Council endorsed a series of measures aimed at reducing energy use by as much as one half. That meant regulating how a new house or apartment building is situated on a lot, what kind and how much insulation builders use, where and how much glass is to be employed, and so on. It encouraged developers and builders to begin adopting solar energy. The city obtained funds and hired consultants to design model solar buildings. It has begun to develop a program for retrofitting existing dwellings.

Davis is experimenting with energy-saving ideas in other areas. It has decided to cut back on the use of pesticides on thousands of trees and shrubs that shade the streets, opting instead for a policy of biological control for insects. The city's fleet of cars and trucks has been transformed into a fleet of compact vehicles. When a Davis employee has to get around town, he borrows a bike from the city rack. Davis even passed a law to formally and solemnly sanction the clothesline.

Two years after the city began to enforce its energy-conscious building code, the results were manifest. Figures for 1977 electricity consumption revealed a 12 percent drop in consumption per customer in the community.

Even more remarkable is that while the number of customers increased by seven percent from 11,600 to 12,500, the total consumption of electricity by all customers declined by six percent. Since 1973, the year of the Arab oil embargo and the beginning of a national energy consciousness, electricity consumption per customer in Davis declined by nearly 18 percent. (Nationwide, in 1974 with the shock of higher utility prices, there was virtually no growth in electricity consumption. Since then, however, consumption has been going up at about three percent per year.)

What follows is a collection of codes, ordinances, drawings, photographs and plans that make up the Davis experiment. It puts special emphasis on conservation of land, water, energy and other natural resources, and moves towards a general limit on growth. While many of the provisions of these papers are designed to meet Davis's unique needs, the ideas and plans will be of use elsewhere.

General Plan

Gloria McGregor, the city's community development director, explains basic features of the general plan:

California has, for many years, taken the position that it wishes local government to solve and guide its own destiny, within a very loose framework. Within that context, it has been the evolving position, as evidenced by the recently adopted General Plan, that Davis has some very distinct responsibilities to its citizens, which it accepts, but that it feels considerably less need to take up the burdens of surrounding communities, most importantly Sacramento. From this ethic sprang the policies and ordinances which circumscribe growth management in Davis.

The most important of the enabling documents is termed the Housing Development Priority Program. Its preamble calls for orderly residential development to meet the needs of the community, protection of adjacent prime agricultural land, provision of housing and services for the student body and faculty of the University of California at Davis, in an environmentally and socially responsible manner. A strong expression of the need for adequate housing in Davis for those persons of low, moderate, or fixed incomes whose work, study, or other connections with the city of Davis led them to desire to live here, threads throughout the document. This is the single most important part of the Davis General Plan which removes from it the sting and flavor of exclusion which might otherwise be present.

The method to determine the need for housing in Davis is the Annual Needs Survey, which, in as detailed a way as possible, compares the existing housing stock in the planning areas of the city with the need for new housing stock, and sets an annual needs number. This Annual Needs Survey is conducted during the summer and the allocation of approvals to build is granted in the fall for the following three years.

The Needs Survey, first completed in 1974, attempts to identify the number of low, moderate and high income single and multiple family housing units needed in each of the planning areas of Davis. Another important principle of the General Plan, of significant social and economic importance, is the direction to achieve a similar mix in types of housing available across the city, so that property values and social interaction will be maintained wherever one lives in the city. This aspect of the control of housing construction contributes a great deal to the general atmosphere of good will between the University and the city, not often present in other similarly dominated cities.

The second of these important expressions of policy is called the Amplification of Housing Development Priority Criteria. Upon the completion of the Annual Needs Survey, all those builders who wish to receive an allocation must present their plans to the Housing Review Board at the same time, to be examined in the light of the ten criteria set forth in this Resolution. (The property must be already in the right timing phase of the General Plan, and have the proper zoning; the zoning must be planned development to allow for mix of types.) These are, in order of their importance: internal growth needs, economic mix, low and moderate income housing, environmental impact, availability of public services and facilities, compactness, design diversity, economic impact, feasibility and competition. Since each application must be in the form of a planned development, over which the city has complete control, refusal of an allocation can be based on the failure to satisfactorily meet these criteria. This is the strong mechanism, for example, under which the city can assure that an adequate supply of low and moderate income housing is to be built.

The third significant feature of the adopted General Plan is the Phasing

Map, which sets forth the order in which the city shall develop, based on 21 criteria developed by the General Plan Committees and the Planning Commission and Council. Roughly speaking, Phase I and Phase II are to be completed by 1990, which would result in a population of approximately 50,000; those areas designated Urban Reserve will then be considered.

This is a capsule view of the Growth Management Plan of Davis. It is a sincere and responsible effort to state the acceptance of the city to provide the housing and services which people whose work, study or other connections need, to enable them to live in Davis. It is equally plain in its expression of disinclination to allow destruction of its attractive character and ambience by its regional location and magnetic pull for those who work elsewhere. Whether any city, without backing at the regional or state level, is able to maintain its uniqueness may be questioned, but Davis is making a strong effort in that direction.

Energy Use

In order to achieve the General Plan objective of energy conservation, a research group at the University of California, Davis, was funded to develop an energy conservation building code. The first task of the group was the collection of data on the energy use of Davis households. The goals of the research were twofold: 1) determine how design features of dwellings affect gas and electric consumption, and 2) to identify household management practices and appliance use which would reduce energy consumption.

Temperature records for apartments and houses were collected over a period of months, in summer and winter, to provide data which would contribute to understanding how design features affect energy use. In addition, utility bills were evaluated to determine actual energy use during a period of several years. The results of this data collection and evaluation formed the basis for the Davis Energy Conservation Building Code.

In the summer, the second floor rooms averaged 12°C(52°F) warmer than those on the ground floor, and north-south exposures were much cooler than east-west. The coolest units were north-south facing on the ground

---

CLIMATE

The Davis climate is characterized as mediterranean. Summers are quite dry with hot days and pleasant nights under usually cloudless skies. July average maximum temperatures are 32.2 C(90 F) with mean minimum temperatures of 14.5 C(58 F). The absolute maximum temperature for July was 45.5 C(114 F) while the absolute minimum for July was 8.3 C(47 F). Rainfall during the summer months is almost zero.

Winters in Davis have periods of cool or cold and foggy weather depending upon the number and intensity of rain-bearing storms entering the area from the Pacific. These winter storms, lasting only a few days each, increase in frequency as fall turns to winter, and become more sporadic as the spring months give way to the dry summer. Average annual rainfall is 45.7 cm(18 in.) with a range from dry years to wet years from 11.9 cm(4.7 in.) to 92.2 cm(36 in.).

Summer winds affecting Davis are usually from the south; cool air flows into the southern Sacramento Valley through the Carquinez Straits. Spring and fall winds alternate between dry northerly winds channeled southward down the Sacramento Valley and southerly winds associated with winter storms.

Top. *Skylight of house under construction in the Corbett development.*
Left. *Sundance, built under the Davis Code by Arthur &*
Russell.
Above. *Longview School solar cylinders which hold*
water to cool and heat the school.

floor, reaching a maximum of 24°C(75°F), perfectly comfortable in hot summer weather. The hottest apartments were those facing east-west on the top floor. The results of the temperature tests were perfectly paralleled by the actual electrical use of the apartments.

In the winter, the south facing apartments performed significantly better than those facing north, east, and west. On several occasions, south facing apartments had high temperatures in the 80s F on sunny winter days, with a maximum of 87 F. During several days the high temperatures were 24°F above ambient, and 17°F above apartments with north, east, or west exposure. These high temperatures occurred in selected vacant apartments built with solar exposures that were far from ideal. By comparison, a specially constructed research room with nearly ideal south window exposure registered an interior maximum temperature 48°F above the maximum ambient.

Tests on single family detached houses provided less clear results than apartments. However, it was evident that the houses in the core area used less electricity for cooling per square foot than other dwellings. This was attributed to the shade trees in the area which prevented the hot summer sun from reaching the dwellings. West Davis homes had the best insulation and this accounts for their superior performance in both summer and winter.

Research on building in the Central Valley climate has continued for more than thirty years at the University of California, Davis. Most of this work on design with climate has been carried out by L. W. Neubauer, F. A. Brooks, and Richard Cramer. Their achievements provided much of the background for the Davis Energy Conservation Ordinance, and supported the contention that it is possible to achieve good thermal performance by providing proper orientation and shading windows.

Precise answers to the second question of how household management practices and appliance usage affect energy consumption were more difficult to obtain because of the high degree of variability from household to household. Data was collected from household interviews and from gas and electric bills. Analysis of the data show that electric consumption is positively correlated with the number of children in the household, the hours of television watched, and the number of washloads per week. Electric consumption in the households is also highly related to the number of appliances owned.

Building Code

The basic idea of the Davis Energy Conservation ordinance is that new housing built in Davis shall not experience an excessive heat gain in the summer nor excessive heat loss in the winter. The requirements vary de-

Construction in Davis's Corbett development.

pending on the size of the housing unit and are expressed in BTUs gained or lost per square foot of the house each day. Thus, the thermal efficiency of all housing designs presented to the city's building inspection division must be tested against conditions assumed to exist on typical summer and winter "design" days. The designated design days are August 21 and December 21. The conditions considered include the angle of sunlight at Davis' latitude at different times of the day, the intensity of sunlight, wind speed (assumed to be 15 miles per hour) and outside temperature (45 degrees F as a 24-hour average in the winter, hourly variation in the summer ranging from 59 to 100 degrees).

Maximum permissible amounts of heat gain/loss are shown in the following table, taken from section 10 of the ordinance.

Detached Group 1 Dwelling Unit Thermal Standards

Floor Area (sq.ft.)	Winter Heat Loss (BTUs/sq.ft./day)	Summer Heat Gain (BTUs/sq.ft./day)
500	363	118
1000	239	103
1500	208	98
2000	192	95
2500	182	93
3000	176	91

The methods used to meet the requirements set forth above include the following:

Infiltration. All swinging doors and windows opening to the exterior or to unconditioned areas such as garages shall be fully weather-stripped, gasketed or otherwise treated to limit infiltration.

Loose Fill Insulation. When blown or poured type loose fill insulation is used in attic spaces, the slope of the roof shall be not less than 2½ feet in 12 feet and there shall be at least 30 inches of clear headroom at the roof ridge. ("Clear headroom" is defined as the distance from the top of the bottom chord of the truss or ceiling joists to the underside of the roof sheathing.)

Pipe Insulation. All steam and steam condensate return piping and all continuously circulating domestic or heating hot water piping which is located in attics, garages, crawl spaces, underground or unheated spaces other than between floors or in interior walls shall be insulated to provide a maximum heat loss of 50 BTU/hr. per linear foot for piping.

Walls. All exterior walls (excluding windows and doors) shall use R-11 batt insulation between studs. Group H structures must have lightly colored or shaded walls.

Roof/Ceilings; Ceiling/Attics. All roof/ceilings and ceiling/attics must use insulation achieving a minimum resistance of R-19 for the insulation itself. Group H occupancies having roof surfaces unshaded on August 21, at 8:00 a.m., 12:00 noon, or 4:00 p.m., shall be no darker than No. 6 on the Munsell chart.

Floors. Suspended floors over a ventilated crawl space or other unheated space shall have insulation with a minimum resistance of R-11. Concrete slabs on grade require no insulation.

Glazing Area. In Group H occupancies, exterior single-pane glazing (windows, skylights, etc.) may not exceed 12½% of the floor area. Exterior double-pane glazing may not exceed 17½% of the dwelling unit's floor area.

Glazing Shading. All glazing which is not oriented to the north must be shaded to protect it from direct solar radiation for the hours of 8:00 a.m., 12:00 noon, and 4:00 p.m. (P.S.T.), August 21. In Group H occupancies, the total accumulated amount of unshaded glazing may not exceed 1.5% of the dwelling unit's floor area. The use of approved shade screen systems may be employed to demonstrate compliance. Tinted, metalized, or frosted glass shall not be considered self-shading.

The regulations are expressed in two forms, Path I and Path II. Path I is a set of prescriptive standards and Path II is a set of performance standards. The city provided two versions so that a builder with a standardized product might have a routine means of compliance, while those using innovative techniques and materials might have additional scope.

Builders can follow Path I and conform to these provisions:

• A light-colored roof with a Munsel rating of six to ten.

• Six-inch insulation (R-19) as a minimum in the roof.

• Three and a half-inch insulation (R-11) in the walls between the studs.

• Light-colored or shaded exterior walls, with a limit of 15 percent dark allowed for trim.

• Glazing limited to 12.5 percent of the floor area for apartments, with an additional 20 square feet of window area allowed for single family homes, intended to benefit especially small houses.

• Unshaded glazing limited to 1.5 percent of the floor area.

The code includes more detail and some additional provisions, but these have the most significant effect on construction.

Or a builder can follow Path I "with exceptions". Essentially, credit is given when standards are exceeded in one part of the dwelling which can then be applied to another portion. Thus, if the builder improves insulation in the floor or wall, applies heat storage concepts or adds double-paned glass, the area of glass in the house may be increased.

Under Path II the builder presents a design which he certifies meets the standards for winter and summer heat loss.

The three different paths involve different fee structures. For plans conforming to Path II, the building inspection division adds $20 to the permit fee.

Once the builder has selected the path he proposes to follow, he then decides which of several possible plan check methods he will use. The city has produced a workbook which leads the builder through the energy-plan check process. The most important variable to be checked at this point is the amount of glazing permissible in the proposed

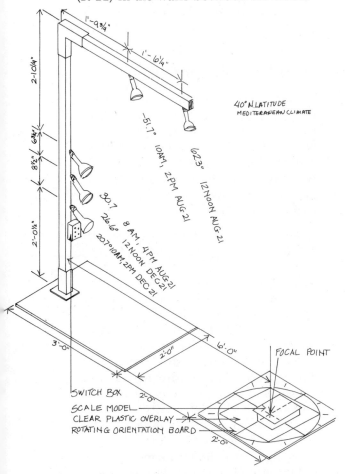

Solar Simulator designed by Jon Hammond, Loren Neubauer and Dennis Long.

home, since glass has a very low degree of thermal resistence.

The builders choosing prescriptive standards may elect to have their plans checked in any one of three ways. The simplest approach, the "math method," asks the builder to make a few easy arithmetic calculations to determine how much glass is allowable considering building square footage and other variables. In general, window areas may not exceed 12.5 percent of the building's floor area; but the true amount of glazing permissible may be much greater if the windows are properly shielded from the summer sun.

A second method of checking the glazing requires the builder to make a scale model of the building for examination under a solar simulator which is kept in the building inspection division office. The simulator reproduces the position of the sun at different times on the summer and winter design days.

A third, more complicated approach (profile angle method) requires analysis of windows according to shading angles cast by roof overhangs.

Builders choosing performance standards must also submit their designs for a plan check and may, if they desire, simplify the analysis of glazing by using either the solar simulator or profile angle methods.

The building code does not in any way require the use of solar energy, although it is one way to meet its requirements. Davis, however, is concerned about retrofitting existing and new houses with solar systems. To that end, it now requires that all new houses be equipped with plumbing stubs for solar hot water heating.

The construction ordinance is one formal step in the Davis energy conservation program. Another step involves adoption of design standards for subdivisions and city circulation systems. These standards have not been adopted, but they are used in an informal manner in the design of planned developments. Since Davis has a housing development priority program which allows for residential construction by permit only, the city has considerable control over the type and design of construction.

Builders' Response

One major reason for the success of the Davis building code program was the support by local builders. In November, 1976, three Davis builders testified before the California Energy Resources Conservation and Development Commission on their reactions to the code. Excerpts follow:

Michael Corbett: I build houses in Davis and have been building for ten years, about 100 houses. The last five years I have been building energy-efficient houses, and of course the last eight months under the Davis Energy Ordinance. Building under the Davis Energy Ordinance has been no difficulty. I was doing basically the same thing prior to the Ordinance. It has caused a few minor changes, but it has still allowed a lot of diversity in design. In fact, we are just beginning to find a lot of new ways to design houses working within the Ordinance.

I think the 12 percent glass, unearned glass, in Davis, works well. Sometimes we do houses that would have 20 or 22 percent glazing and still fall into the Ordinance. In one case we had 28 percent glazing and still fell under the Ordinance. So it's not really a limitation. It just means if you put more glass on, you have to have the appropriate designs to utilize that glass as passive solar heating.

Question: *What is the aspect of the* Code *that allowed you to go over the 12½ percent limit?*

Mr. Corbett: I basically relied on using additional mass or the mass of the building and having the glazing on the south side shaded in the summer and then available for solar collection in the winter. I have been working in passive solar design and shuttering and experimentation with two by six walls versus two by four walls. . . .

I'd like to make one other comment. We have found that we have been able to sell about 70 percent of our houses without air conditioners, and this was unheard of through the '60's and early '70's. Based on compliance with the Energy Ordinance, the houses are naturally cool enough that we can have a sales pitch to sell them without air conditioners and the people that have lived in them now for the first summer are not objecting at all and are happy that they are saving that amount of energy and still living in a quite comfortable temperature.

John Whitcombe: I have been building ten years. I have built about 1000 units, 750 apartments and 250 homes. Every unit (in a 138-unit apartment complex) is oriented north-south to meet the Davis Energy Ordinance. It is almost impossible to meet it unless you do, particularly with apartment units. And it is a very energy-efficient kind of apartment complex.

The problem we have with it is number one, the spaces. The interior space is one of the tradeoffs you have. The interior spaces aren't as nice as they are in a complex that you can design on a pinwheel kind of basis.

When you begin talking about multi-family complexes, apartments and condominiums, you are not just talking about a single lot that has a fence around it. Orientation becomes more difficult from a design point of view.

I am not saying your values shouldn't ride towards energy, but at the same time you should recognize the kind of tradeoffs that you are talking about with the Davis Energy Code.

I'd concur with the comment that 16 percent glass is probably satisfactory. We should probably have two percent unshaded. The fact that you have a 40 degree angle and an east-west wall just means for a typical window you might have to have an 8 or 10-foot overhang rather than one 14-foot overhang from a practical basis. You are going to have either a very substantial overhang or you're not going to have a window there. And many designs you might have a bathroom, for example. You might be able to get your bedrooms north and south on a north-south lot, but even on a north-south lot, you might have a bathroom, and that precludes a window in that bathroom.

A lot of people talk about costs, and the costs of the Energy Ordinance are really subjective. You have to get a handle on lot yield on a given piece of land and that's very difficult to do without a specific situation.

But, once again, it is a subjective kind of thing. You are concerned about both life cycle costs and about pricing out moderate and low-income people. I think there is a conflict there, because when you go on a life cycle analysis, you are looking at it from an investment point of view. You are saying you are going to put up some money now; we are going to lose some money for a while; and then we are going to gain more money back here and then in the total we are going to make money.

But lower-income people don't have the money to make investments.

Ron Broward: I am a builder and I have been a builder for 16 years. I have built approximately 500 houses; 178 apartment units, and a little over 300 houses.

First of all, I was opposed to the Ordinance when it was adopted because I felt the estimated added cost to meet the requirements would not result in a like amount of energy saved. I also felt that after having built several hundred homes during the past sixteen years I knew how to build energy-conserving homes better than the young men who proposed the Ordinance. I was wrong and now believe the Davis Energy Ordinance should be a model for all homes being built.

The added cost is minimal. The average cost for the twenty-one homes we have built since the Ordinance was adopted was approximately $60 per home.

The Ordinance does work and I would like to list some of the reasons why I believe so.

The single most important factor is proper lot orientation. A lot which faces north or south and has proper window placement will permit the cooling night breezes to penetrate a home.

Going hand in hand with lot orientation is the reduced glazing allowed. We have had no difficulty in meeting this requirement.

When the Davis Energy Ordinance was first proposed the unshaded glazing allowed was 1.5 percent of the total floor area. Through compromise with builders, this was upped to 3.5 percent. I believe the less unshaded glazing permitted, the more energy-efficient the home will be.

During this past summer we built four homes on lots with a lot orientation of 18'55"N. These homes had a 2'6" overhang and were insulated with R-11 wall insulation and R-19 ceiling insulation. The windows permitted the night breezes to penetrate the homes. Thermostats were placed in the homes after they were drywalled and were checked daily in the late afternoon.

I might add that I did this not to prove the Ordinance out. I put those thermostats on there because I thought that what the consultants, the people that proposed the Ordinance, wanted wasn't going to work and I was going to try to prove just the opposite.

When the outside temperature was in the high 90s to over 100°, the inside temperature was 72° to 75°F. This was without any exterior or interior window screening. If screening had been installed, the temperature would have been lower.

In conclusion, I would like to stress the importance of early adoption of the standards in the Davis Energy Ordinance. The planning stage of proposed lot development is the single most important part of energy conservation. Planners should be encouraged to design streets which have as many north and south facing lots as possible.

The Davis Energy Ordinance does work, and I am firmly convinced that the result will be less energy consumption and lower utility bills for the consumer.

I'd like to pass these out. This was a study that I had Living Systems do for me on a seven-unit apartment that was going to be built in Davis. And after I presented my program to FHA, they did say that we could redesign the heating and cooling systems to reduce it from a central heating and air conditioning system, a zone system, and in

this study we will show calculations of what the monthly utility bills are going to be.

We have calculated that, in the winter, the utility bill, the total utility bill for the five months' season, is about $11.95, and in the summer months, $7.90, and in the spring and fall, $6.76. Averaging this out over the year, the total utility bill per month per apartment is going to be about $9.30.

Now, these apartments were designed with the Davis Energy Ordinance in mind and tried to utilize several energy conservation materials.

And I might add that by being able to redesign the heating and air conditioning system for these apartments, we are going to save approximately $500 an apartment, which amounts to about $35,000 over the project. The standards increased the costs of my houses on an average of $60 per house and my houses range in square footage from 1,600 to 2,000 square feet.

Energy Conservation Retrofits

The Davis building code applies to new structures, but there has been a good deal of interest within the city for developing a method of dealing with existing dwellings as well. Davis has taken two different tacks to meet this problem.

First, the city enacted an ordinance that requires inspection of all homes when they are put up for sale to ensure that existing codes are met. If a home fails to meet the dictates of the requisite

laws, then the buyer would be required to bring it up to standard. This is an unusual ordinance for in most cities homes are inspected because of complaints or at the request of the buyer or seller. Inspection usually is not mandatory on sale.

This ordinance was adopted in part with a view towards providing a mechanism for administering a retrofit program. Consultants were then engaged to draw up a scheme by which existing dwellings could be made to meet certain basic energy conservation standards. A point system was developed, a plan outlined. The idea is that in expectation of receiving a sizeable amount of cash, the seller of a house will be in a position to make the required changes at the time of sale. The "Proposed Energy Conservation Retrofit Ordinance," prepared by Sedway/Cooke for the city, is included in the Document Section at the end of this chapter.

Solar Houses

An important aspect of the Davis energy conservation project was to develop designs of innovative energy-conserving buildings which would demonstrate to local builders and developers methods for complying with the new building code. Several prototype buildings were designed which include various schemes for solar heating and cooling. Some of these designs have been tried out in houses outside Davis, others in the city itself. Living Systems, the city's consultants, carried out this work under a HUD grant.

Before the buildings could be designed, general goals were set forth:

• Develop a 80- to 90-percent solar heated and 100 percent naturally cooled dwelling.

• Reduce the total cost of the dwelling through the use of conventional construction techniques, the reduction of built square footage consistent with the provision of a comfortable living environment, and the maximum use of simple efficient solar technology.

• Develop a system of landscaping that would improve the thermal performance of the building by allowing both solar access in the winter and shading in the summer.

• Create outdoor spaces that extend and enhance interior spaces and provide usable space for year-round outdoor activity.

• Promote an efficient and integrated use of natural and artificial lighting to provide a high quality visual environment at low energy-use levels.

• Utilize high-efficiency appliances: low water-use fixtures, solar hot water heating, and a "solar clothes dryer."

• Provide full handicapped access to all rooms and services.

Living Systems then designed two prototype buildings to meet these goals. The first of these, called the Alice Street house, was planned for a lot owned by the city adjacent to a junior high school. The second building, Sun Catcher, was a solar duplex. The city was granted funds from the Farmers Home Administration and HUD for construction of the projects. The buildings will be used in part as residences for farm workers.

Both the solar projects employ pas-

Swimming is a popular pastime in Davis where summer temperatures can reach 114°F., but heating pools in cooler weather is an expensive and energy-consuming luxury. Here is the Casitas del Valle pool which, like an increasing number in town, is heated by solar energy.

sive systems because of low cost and adaptability to both heating and cooling.

Collecting energy in a passive system is a fairly simple proposition. First, you aim your house south with large window exposure. However, storage and distribution can be problems. The solution lies in providing mass within the building structure—dense interior materials with high heat holding capacity such as masonry, adobe, concrete, stone, water. These are materials that absorb surplus heat from sunlight entering the windows and radiate it back into the room after dark. The term "mass" is used in its most literal meaning. Thick walls are a crucial part of the passive system. Water can be the medium for storing heat. In drums or columns facing the sun, it picks up heat faster and stores more of it than any other common material. Insulation is used to trap the heat in the structure. By manipulating heat flow and storage it is possible to take advantage of those parts of the daily and weekly temperature fluctuations that drive the temperature of the building above or below the average outdoor temperature.

The first of the building projects, the Alice Street house, involved designing a home for a large family or a group of students on a city-owned lot located in the outskirts of Davis. That meant providing three or four bedrooms, two bathrooms, a sizeable dining area, large kitchen with space for storage, laundry and general storage. The house is to be set on the lot to take advantage of southern exposure, and the design calls for vegetable gardens, a garage, and patios.

The Alice Street house is to be of wood frame set on a concrete slab. It has 2″ x 6″ exterior walls to allow for R-19 batts in the walls, and the ceiling insulation is R-30 batts. There is no slab edge insulation. The 235 square feet of south glass act as a solar collector during the winter months. Only 79 square feet of glass face other directions to reduce unwanted heat gain and heat loss. There are 13 solar cylinders in the house, which hold 320 cubic feet of water for a total of 20,000 pounds of water or about 85 pounds of water per square foot of collector. Solar cylinders are vertically upright steel tubes. They are painted dark colors on the south to absorb the solar energy coming in through the south windows in the winter. In the summer, the sun is blocked by overhangs, awnings, and special insulated draperies made with aluminum foil bonded to a cloth substrate. The solar cylinders absorb internal heat gain on summer days and release this heat at night.

One sunny day in January should provide heating carryover for one to two cloudy days. Carryover for other months would be slightly better due to higher average temperatures. The greater number of days of successive sunshine, the greater the carryover of the heat storage.

The Alice Street house design calls for a small backup system (gas heater 35,000 BTUs), but requires no backup cooling system. Calculations by Living Systems indicate a thermal performance 3.5 times better than a typical Davis Energy Conservation Code house in the winter with full natural cooling during the summer. It is estimated that between 70 and 80 percent of the heating will be provided by the solar passive system during an average winter in Davis.

The estimated gas heating budget for an average year is 14,150,000 BTUs (assuming 2,189 heating degree days), while there is no cooling energy demand. Water heating is mostly achieved with a flat plate solar water heater which saves 150 therms of natural gas per year. The estimated electrical use is 250 KWH per month, or 3,000 KWH/year, and 342 therms per year of natural gas. These figures are computed for a family of four with typical lifestyle.

The projected energy use for the Alice Street house is compared with average Davis figures for 1973-1975 (from PGE) and average California figures for 1975 (from Rand).

The Davis climate is not typical of California, and the average energy use per household is greater. The Alice Street house nevertheless should use

	A.S.H. estimate	1973	Davis Av. Use 1974	1975	CA. Av. Use 1975
KWH/hr	3000	7210	6800	6744	6370
THERMS/yr	342	1044	946	1024	793

less than half the energy consumed by the average California household.

The second solar building project, the Sun Catcher solar duplex, is based on concepts similar to those of the single family Alice Street house. Here, however, Living Systems was anxious to develop a design that did not rely heavily on solar devices built into the south-facing portion of the building. After all, what could be done with lots or buildings that did not necessarily afford large openings to the South?

Living Systems wanted to integrate the solar collectors and water heaters more directly into the shape of the building as a whole. Thus, it set out to create a basic plan that could be employed in "worst case" sites, those lots that were hopelessly oriented away from good southern exposure. The specific program for the duplex included:

• Provide a duplex of two identical three-bedroom, one-bath units for use by a family or a group of students.
• Provide cooking facilities, laundry facilities, a dining area to seat six people, and adequate storage.
• Provide a one-car garage for each unit.

An attempt was made to both maximize winter radiant heat gain and minimize summer gain. Various cone configurations were studied for their performance in both summer and winter. After investigation it was decided that a south facing cone of 19°, rotated 22° from horizontal, satisfied these requirements.

To test the graphic studies a scale model was built and tested. Through light meter readings, Living Systems determined that the effect of the reflective cone could double the amount of light entering the house. For example, if the ambient level outdoors was 7,000 Fc., then the readings just inside the glass would be 14,000 Fc.

By placing the glazing at the end of a cone, the amount was reduced to, in this case, 4'0". This further reduced heat gains and losses through the glass. The need for shutters and curtains was likewise reduced.

The architectural implications of the Sun Catcher cone on a dwelling could be beneficial. To begin with, it reduces dependence on the south facade. When used as a clerestory on the roof, it is less likely to be shaded by nearby houses, trees, etc. Secondly, the clerestory allows the penetration of light and heat into the center of the house, allowing for a more even distribution of the solar heat. Thus, more of the water cylinders could be placed away from the south windows.

Davis resident Dorothy Cecil hangs her wash on a "solar dryer." Like many other communities, Davis once had banned clotheslines as unsightly. These prohibitions had popular support—but not any more.

Solar Dryers

In April, 1977, Davis passed Ordinance No. 876 nullifying regulations that banned the use of clotheslines and establishing requirements for clotheslines in new multi-unit dwellings. The Ordinance states:

The City Council of the city of Davis does hereby ordain as follows:
Section 1.Purpose: It has been determined
　　(a) Clotheslines are economical and are the most energy efficient method of clothes drying:
　　(b) Concern for aesthetics has occasionally resulted in subdivision restrictions or landlord rules and regulations banning the construction and use of clotheslines;
　　(c) Energy required to operate electric and gas clothes-dryers has become increasingly expensive and may in the future become less available; and
　　(d) The desirability of permitting the use of clotheslines outweighs the

aesthetic disadvantages.

Section 2: Section 29-169.1 is hereby added to Chapter 29 of the Code of the City of Davis, 1971, as amended, to read as follows:

Section 29-169.1 Clotheslines:

It shall be unlawful and a nullity to establish any private covenant or restriction which prohibits the use of a clothesline in any residential zone, except that all multi-family developments (three-family and greater densities) requiring Design Review Commission approval shall require suitable space or facilities except where such space would preclude good project design, to enable residents to dry their clothes using the sun. Such clotheslines shall be convenient to washing facilities and oriented so as to receive sufficient sun to dry clothes throughout the years.

Pools

There are perhaps 700 swimming pools in Davis, many of them heated by gas. To increase the temperature of a swimming pool from 70 to 80 degrees can cost $40 to $60 a month in gas bills.

The city is switching its pools to solar heat. It requires that pools in apartments and motels be solar heated. There is discussion of proposals requiring existing pools to be retrofitted with solar heating devices and the city council has been considering a new ordinance to ban pools heated by any means other than solar. That proposed ordinance reads as follows:

"New swimming pools, hot tubs or similar devices, installed after _____ _____ shall not be heated by gas, electricity, oil, propane, kerosene, gasoline or butane. Such existing heaters utilizing gas, electricity, oil, propane, kerosene, gasoline or butane shall become non-conforming by this ordinance and shall be abated within 10 years of the date of adoption of this ordinance."

Fences & Hedges

Davis is gradually moving to a new approach in setbacks—the arrangement of houses in relation to sidewalks and fences or hedges. If houses are to have large south-facing windows to take advantage of the winter sun, they must also have adequate space between the window and fence to allow the low angled winter sun to enter the window. That means fences must be set back closer to the street when the house faces south.

If zero lot lines (i.e. attached "townhouses") are encouraged, less energy loss will occur because there will be fewer outside walls to heat or cool. In addition, if front yards are allowed to be fenced close to the street, there will be a great deal more private yard space which can be utilized by the occupants. Here again, we see a return to private inner courtyards.

Set forth below are a variety of measures undertaken in a city ordinance to cut down on the use of energy through standards on the location of fences, walls, and hedges:

Fences, walls and hedges may be located in required yards as follows:

(1) If not exceeding at any point four feet in height above the elevation of the surface of the ground at such point, they may be located in any yard or court, except for a corner lot.

(2) If not exceeding at any point six feet in height above the elevation of the surface of the ground at such point, they may be located in any required rear yard or interior side yard.

(3) On a corner lot, a fence or hedge over three feet in height, measured from the curb gutter grade, shall not be located in a triangular area measured twenty-five feet along the inside face of the sidewalk in either direction from the sidewalk intersection. Where no sidewalk exists, the measurement shall be made along the right-of-way line.

(4) Fences not exceeding six feet in height may be located at the 10-foot setback in the front yard.

(5) The Community Development Director may issue a permit to allow a fence to:

(i) Be located at the five-foot setback for the street side provided that such fence will not conflict with public utility easements; or

(ii) exceed the six-foot height limitation up to a maximum height of eight feet for side and rear yard fences only if such proposed fence design will not have an adverse effect upon adjoining properties.

In 1977, the city council added a requirement for landscaping in commercial zones. In such areas landscaping must cover 10 percent of the site. Trees are to be distributed throughout parking areas, and landscaping is to be provided to assure screening of loading, storage, refuse and other unsightly areas. Native drought resistant trees are to be used wherever feasible.

Work At Home

One way to reduce the use of energy is to work in the neighborhood where you live. But in many cities, zoning prohibits development of work places in residential areas. In addition, housing is often owned by individuals and organizations outside the community who are engaged in real estate speculation.

Davis is attempting to encourage people to live and work in their neighborhoods with two different ordinances. One requires the purchaser of a house in certain zones to live there. The ordinance (No. 917) does not cover apartments, duplexes or commercial real estate. But in residential zones, buyers must sign a declaration that they will move into the house they are purchasing within six months and live there for one year. The declaration is sworn and must be filed within 10 days of the sale. A false declaration is a misdemeanor. Repeated violations may be subject to injunction.

If the new owner does not take up residency within six months and live in his house for one year, he is considered in violation of the law unless it can be shown "that the purchaser's circumstances changed after execution of the sworn declaration so as to prevent such intended occupancy. Examples of good cause would be a job change, a change of marital status, a change in family situation such as ill health of the purchaser or related persons, or other circumstances which raise practical or economic difficulties relating to occupancy of the unit." The ordinance does not apply to foreclosures due to default, or to acquisitions by inheritance or bequest.

A second ordinance backs cottage in-

In addition to encouraging cottage industry, Davis supports the creation of farmers' markets in the different city neighborhoods.

dustry within the home by allowing home owners to operate small businesses. In effect, this law gives formal sanction to home-industry. In April, 1977, the city council set out these definitions of "home occupation" in Ordinance 875:

Home Occupation. A home occupation is an accessory use of a residential dwelling unit which shall be conducted entirely within the dwelling. It shall be conducted by the inhabitants of the dwelling, and one non-familial employee, if desired. A home occupation shall be clearly incidental and secondary to the primary use of the residential dwelling; shall not change the character thereof or adversely affect the uses permitted in the residential district of which it is a part; shall create no additional traffic or require additional parking space; and shall not have outdoor storage of materials, equipment supplies visible from outside the premises other than materials equipment and supplies necessary for domestic purposes.

Criteria. The following criteria shall be employed by the Community Development Director to determine a valid home occupation:

1. No employment of help other than the members of the resident family and one assisting non-familial employee.
2. No external use of material or equipment not recognized as being part of the normal practices in the residential district.

3. No direct sales of products or merchandise from the home.
4. The use shall not generate pedestrian or vehicular traffic beyond the normal to the residential district.
5. It shall not involve the use of commercial vehicles for delivery of materials to or from the premises.
6. The home occupation shall not involve the use of advertising signs on the premises except that one nameplate (name/occupation only) is permitted not to exceed 0.5 square feet in area. The nameplate is to be located flat against the building wall only.
7. No more than 25 percent of the area of one floor of the residence shall be used for such purposes.
8. In no way shall the appearance of the structure be altered or the occupation within the residence be conducted in a manner which would cause the premises to differ from its residential character either by the use of colors, materials, construction, lighting, signs, or the emission of sounds, noises, vibrations.
9. There shall be no use of utilities or community facilities beyond that normal to the use of the property for residential purposes.
10. No storage or display of materials, goods, supplies, or equipment related to the operation of a home occupation shall be visible from outside the premises.
11. No equipment or process shall be used in such home occupation which creates noise, vibration, glare, fumes, odors or electrical interference detectable to the normal senses off the lot, if the occupation is conducted in a single

family residence, or outside the dwelling unit if conducted in other than a single family residence. In the case of electrical interference, no equipment or process shall be used which creates visual or audible interference in any radio or television receivers off the premises, or causes fluctuations in line voltage off the premises.

12. Persons with demonstrated physical handicaps may be permitted special review by the Planning Commission. The applicant may request waiving of one or more, or a portion thereof, of requirements (1) through (9). This special request shall be reviewed by the Planning Commission, at a Public Hearing, involving the notification of property owners within 100 feet of subject property. In reviewing the request, the Planning Commission shall consider any waivers based solely on the applicant's physical inability to function within the requirements of (1) through (9).

13. In cases where the Community Development Director is undecided about the compatibility of the use with the neighborhood, the Director may issue temporary approval for a specific time period. After the stated time period, the Community Development Director shall review this use, and shall consider adjacent property owner comments and any other information regarding the conduct and operation of the use. After such review, the Director may approve such use permanently but must notify originally surveyed property owners.

Exclusions. The following uses are examples of those uses which are specifically prohibited: (1) Schools of any size or type. (2) Boarding or lodging house as defined in Zoning Ordinance. (3) Antique shop. (4) Barber shop, beauty parlor. (5) Funeral chapel or home, mortuaries. (6) Gift shop. (7) Medical or dental clinic or hospital, animal hospital or grooming facilities. (8) Day care centers or nursery schools. (9) Private clubs. (10) Restaurants. (11) Auto or motorcycle, boat or trailer, similar type repair shops. (12) Kennels. (13) Office of a health care provider when special mechanical equipment is required.

Application and Procedure. Application for a Home Occupation shall be made to the Community Development Department on a form provided by the Community Development Department, and shall be accompanied by the appropriate filing fee. The decision of the Community Development Department shall be final unless an appeal is filed within 15 days of the decision. Any appeal shall be reviewed by the Planning Commission.

Voiding of Permit. The Community Development Director may void any Home Occupation for noncompliance with the criteria set forth in this section.

Time Limit. All Home Occupations shall be valid for a period of two years from initial date of approval. Request for a time extension shall be submitted to the Community Development Department in writing, accompanied by the appropriate fee and one month prior to expiration.

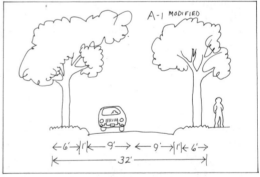

Narrow streets save space and use less asphalt. They also may contribute to slower auto speeds, thereby enhancing fuel efficiency and safety. Drawing shows a proposed access, one- or two-way street, serving less than 20 units.

Streets

In Davis there has been a move towards narrower streets. The widths of streets are determined primarily by the width of fire trucks, with a minimum acceptable width of a street being equal to two times the width of a fire truck plus some clear space to allow for passing.

Narrow streets are less energy-consuming in several ways. They cost less and savings in land and site development could be as high as $1,000 per lot.

They use less asphalt. They probably contribute to lower speeds by autos, thereby enhancing fuel efficiency. If use of alternative transportation systems such as buses, walking or bicycles become important enough, wider streets would be less and less needed anyway. The reduction of local streets from 34 to 28 feet is contemplated, with a possibility of further reduction in width in conjunction with neighborhood parking bays.

Recycling

The recycling effort in Davis dates back to 1972, when a small group of volunteers formed a non-profit organization called the Resource Awareness Committee of Davis (RCAD). They got permission from the UC-Davis campus to set up a recycling center at a publicly convenient location on university property near the downtown area and started accepting glass, aluminum, bi-metal cans, and newsprint. A full-time employee was hired to keep the center clean, and to make sure that the various commodities being brought in by the public were properly sorted: volunteer employees pitched in as well. Hauling to market was basically handled by the various commodity buyers (Coors for aluminum, Owens-Illinois for glass, a large Sacramento garbage company for paper).

In July 1974, the Davis City Council passed an ordinance requiring the separation of newspapers from garbage, and ordered the Davis Waste Removal Co. (DWR) to collect the separated papers at the curb along with the garbage. Cognizant of some of the problems that other companies had experienced with putting newspaper racks under their garbage trucks, DWR decided to run a separate scooter for newspapers only.

DWR's president Charles Hart describes the recycling program:

"The community's response was quite good; in fact many citizens requested that we extend the recycling pick up service to include cans and glass as well. Unfortunately, considerable friction had developed between DWR and the paid help at the

The Davis recycling center handles newspapers, cans, oil and organic wastes. Profits aside, the center has played an important role in making Davis residents conscious of waste.

RACD's recycling center. (The employee felt that we were in direct competition.) Even though the founders of the RACD didn't share this view, to defuse the situation we agreed to furnish the RACD with our collection scooter fully maintained and insured, so that they could go house-to-house and collect cans and glass as well as newspapers. Furthermore, we put our own 50-cubic-yard drop boxes over at the recycling center (the Sacramento garbage company removed its boxes), and, because the price of newsprint was plummeting (from $30 per ton to $2 per ton), we agreed to haul for RACD at no charge.

"Between furnishing the collection scooter and furnishing drop boxes and hauling, our contribution to the RACD was worth $900-1,000 per month. This continued for many months, until newsprint (the backbone of the recycling effort) began to rise again in price. Then the RACD agreed to pay us $50 for each load of newsprint or cans that we hauled to market, and although this did not meet our costs, our subsidy to recycling dropped to $500-600 per month.

"In April 1976, DWR received permission from the Davis City Council to build a combined shop/office/recycling center which included a concrete pit so that recyclables could be easily and efficiently top-loaded into our drop boxes. It was intended by mutual agreement between the RACD, UC-Davis, DWR, and the Davis City Council that DWR would take over the community recycling effort upon completion of its facility. However, construction suffered several lengthy delays; meanwhile, DWR ran afoul of the Public Utilities Commission because we were charging RACD lower rates for hauling than those authorized by the PUC. Moreover, the RACD was having a tremendous problem with employee turnover, abuse of our collection scooter, and lack of daily route supervision. Consequently, with the blessing of the RACD, DWR took over complete management and control of the recycling effort on December 1, 1976.

". . . We intend to continue actively in this field, whether it makes us a buck each month or not, and to handle this operation as efficiently and conscientiously as possible. We feel that recycling is important in making the public conscious of its waste, and hope that through this awareness the public will waste less. Although this line of reasoning—coming from a garbage company—may surprise you, it is our conviction that recycling is an integral part of professional waste management, and we consider ourselves professionals."

Shade Trees

As part of its far-ranging energy conservation efforts, the city council organized a street tree committee, made up of five citizens, to advise them on matters pertaining to maximizing benefits from the trees. The committee meets quarterly and all gatherings are public.

The committee originally prepared an ordinance which was made law in 1963. The committee and the park superintendent put together a master list of every tree in the city, and then laid out a plan for planting of trees. A complete inventory and card system of every tree has been established. The basic idea of the ordinance is to develop and maintain a comprehensive plan for planting and maintaining trees and other plants, and to set up rules for planting, maintenance and care of the trees.

The city's basic tree policies are that all planting is done by city crews. One tree is required per lot (on corner lots one on each street front) and is planted in the 10 foot easement behind the sidewalk. Planting is done only after homes are occupied. The street tree committee designates a tree for each street. When it comes to pruning, this too is done by city crews.

In the older section of the city there are about 3,000 trees of various kinds, in the newer areas there are about 6,000, and the city is planting about 700 additional new trees each year. The total tree population is about 17,800. There are some 80 different kinds of trees, and the tree committee has set limits on the numbers of any one kind of tree by establishing use categories.

The planting program calls for evergreen trees to be planted on major streets and either evergreens or deciduous trees on the embounded streets. Evergreens on the major streets reduce the problems of leaf pickups in the fall, provide good scale and give the appearance of a city of trees year around.

Cooling shade trees can help to reduce energy use during the hot Davis summers, when temperatures of streets and walls go as high as 140 degrees Fahrenheit. The city is taking measures to protect streets, homes and commercial buildings wherever possible from the sun by trees. And since there is little rain from May through October, the trees must be drought resistant.

Transport

Like many suburban communities in California, Davis has been dominated by the automobile. Over the last decade the city has consistently sought to reduce the importance of the car, and establish other modes of transport. As a result, many citizens use bicycles for getting about town, or take a double-deck bus run by university students.

In 1978, the city contracted with the Sacramento, the bus service may help to for hourly service between Davis and the state capital. The city, in effect, subsidizes the opening of the bus route. Since many Davis residents work in Sacramento the bus service may help to cut down auto commuting. Amtrak has reopened passenger service twice a day from Davis to Oakland, servicing the bay area. Train service may reduce the auto influx bringing professors and other employees to the university from Berkeley and San Francisco.

The city itself has moved towards a more fuel-efficient transportation system. It maintains a fleet of bicycles for employees. In addition, the fleet of cars and trucks maintained by the local government has been changed to meet fuel efficiency standards. Thus, in fiscal 1973-74, the city owned eight full-size sedans, 35 one-half ton pickups, four compact cars. In 1977, it owned seven regular sedans, 22 one-half ton pickups and 19 subcompacts. In effect, the one-half ton trucks were replaced by subcompact cars.

Bicycles

Davis has 28,000 bicycles. Considering that the city has a population of only 36,000, probably no other city in the United States has as high a proportion of its citizens owning bicycles and using them as a regular means of transportation.

In their paper, "Bikeways in Action," Robert Sommer and Dale Lott describe Davis' unique transportation situation:

A number of factors produced this situation—the presence of many young people attending the Davis Campus of the University of California, the flat terrain, the mild weather, and the many wide streets. When the campus was

There are nearly as many bikes (28,000) as people in Davis. Together with the popular student-run bus service, they provide an alternative to cars.

expanded and the population in the area grew rapidly in the early 1960s, the streets became much busier. About the time the first stop light was installed, people riding bicycles began to feel crowded. At the local bicycle shop, it was common to see bikes appearing with damaged front wheels when riders were forced onto the curb by passing cars. Competition, both for space on the streets and for opportunities to cross at intersections, grew between bicycles and automobiles. It was a lopsided competition at best—bicycles are small and frail, automobiles large and sturdy. It became clear to a number of concerned Davis citizens that, if bicycles were to remain a viable part of the city transportation system, they would have to be given a place of their own in city traffic planning.

What was needed was some way to separate bicycles from automobiles, and the plan adopted was the bicycle lane or bikeway—a strip of pavement or concrete from which automobiles would be excluded. At first this suggestion was rejected by the city council; it was considered to be visionary, impractical, potentially dangerous, and its proponents were regarded as cranks. However, as the debate continued, it became apparent that there was widespread support for bicycle lanes. A citizens group circulated a petition asking the city council to establish bicycle lanes along principal streets and rights-of-way as an integral part of the city's transportation system. This petition was signed by 90 percent of the several hundred voters approached. Bike lanes became the central issue in a city election of 1966 and the pro-bikeway candidates won. Soon after that, the first bike lanes were established along the sides of existing wide streets.

Since that time, Davis has been developing a bicycle lane network that is probably unique in the United States. New housing tracts in the city are required to set aside space for bicycle lanes separated from traffic, and a special act was passed by the California Assembly to enable the city to formulate traffic regulations for bicycles. It is important to realize that the bicycles are not merely owned, stored or used for recreational purposes; they are an important part of the transportation system. On one heavily trafficked street, traffic counts during the summer (with few university students in town) show that bicycles represented 40 percent of all traffic. During the rush hour, 90 percent of all riders are adults. The emblem of the city shown on many municipal vehicles is a gay nineties two-wheeler. Many business leaders in the community are strong proponents of bike riding, and admit that this is a matter of self-interest. The bicycle has also helped preserve the central city core as a viable shopping district, since parking is not a serious obstacle to shopping downtown. The university and high schools have been able to set aside less space for parking lots than they would ordinarily. The acceptance of the bicycle as a viable means of transportation by virtually all segments of the community provides the unique opportunity to learn the structural and social requirements of safe, efficient and pleasurable bike riding.

The potential of bicycle transportation cannot be realized without the necessary environmental support system. Just as one cannot have a railroad without tracks, or a bus system without highways, so one needs special facilities and regulations for bicycle traffic. This means planning which must rest on firm knowledge of the special requirements of the bicycle. One simply does not design highways for automobiles and sidewalks for pedestrians, leaving bicyclists squeezed in between moving automobiles, parked cars and pedestrians.

First let us review the history of the Davis bicycle lane network. About eight years ago a group of concerned citizens formed the Bike Safety Committee which investigated bicycle traffic problems in the city and made various suggestions about how to alleviate them. The city public works department became interested and made traffic counts to determine the streets most heavily used. There was very little precedent to follow in developing bike lanes. The city public works department believed that the most feasible plan was to create bike lanes on the outsides of the streets over 50 feet wide. Where this contradicted the California Motor Vehicle Code a special bill relating to bike lanes was passed with the help of the state assemblymen. This bill permitted the Davis City Council in 1967 to pass Ordinance 442 creating bike lanes and regulating bike traffic.

The city now operates programs in bicycle education, safety, and enforcement, through the police department. Under this program an officer visits each grade three or four times a year. A specially prepared curriculum intro-duces bikes in the kindergarten and continues on up through the ninth grade. The curriculum includes a talking bicycle, films, slides, lectures and hand-out materials.

A bike rodeo held on the school's grounds during the school day tests the rider's ability to balance, turn, stop and signal for turns. On bike safety check day, each bike at school is inspected for safe use. Bolts, nuts, pedals, etc. are checked and minor repairs done by a police officer.

Bike licenses are sold for a three year period at a cost of $4.50 each. The license information is put on a computer, so that lost or stolen bikes can be identified.

All uniformed patrols of the Davis police department can issue citations to individuals, regardless of age, who are in violation of the bicycle ordinance. The "Bike Enforcement Officer" rides a 10-speed bike in uniform and he checks to make sure riders are obeying the bike traffic laws. In addition, the bike aide is responsible for retrieving stolen or abandoned bicycles. He maintains the bike files, assists with licensing at rush times of the year and conducts bike auctions. Abandoned bicycles must be held 90 days prior to being auctioned off. About four auctions are held each year.

Buses

Ian Ross, general manager of the Davis University Transport System (Unitrans) describes the city's bus system:

Bus service at Davis began as a campus-oriented transit service on an experimental basis by the Associated Students of the University of California, Davis (ASUCD) in 1967. In April 1967 ASUCD decided to buy two London double-deck buses in hopes that their distinctive appearance would increase transit usage.

Through the years, as patronage increased, more vehicles were purchased. In 1977 we had 13 operational buses, seven 56-passenger London double-deck buses, and six single deck standard diesel 45 or 48 passenger buses. Two other buses, one of each type, are kept for parts, as all equipment in service is over 20 years old.

Normal transit service is provided primarily by the double-deck buses, while the standard diesels are used to provide additional service on rainy days when patronage increases.

Double-deck buses are used not only because of their distinctive appearance, but because of their efficiency. They get twice the fuel mileage of our single decks. They have a greater seating capacity, and are shorter, more suitable for Davis' somewhat narrow streets. Also, a conductor located in the passenger section is available to collect fares and help in safe loading and unloading of passengers.

Davis Documents

Davis City Code: Housing

Sec. 12A-1. Purposes

The city council hereby finds and determines:

(a) The city has adopted a comprehensive general plan which calls for refined planning and residential development review in order that suburban growth meets the needs of the community and proceeds in a logical, orderly, efficient and environmentally sound manner.

(b) The city is located upon and adjacent to prime agricultural land which is a limited resource of statewide significance.

(c) The city derives much of its social and cultural character from its historical development as a "university town" which provides housing and services for a large segment of the student body, faculty and employees of the University of California, Davis campus.

(d) Inadequately planned speculative residential development has sometimes created in the past and unless controlled in the future will create or aggravate the following conditions:

(1) Wasteful construction of public facilities on a crisis basis.

(2)   Overburdening of municipal services and utilities.

(3)   Increases in tax costs in excess of tax gains.

(4)   Unavailability of adequate low cost and moderate cost housing to serve the needs of students, the elderly and persons of low and moderate incomes.

(5)   Premature and inefficient commitment of prime agricultural lands to urbanization.

(6)   Environmentally detrimental development patterns.

(e)   There are many persons of low, moderate or fixed incomes whose work, studies or other connections with the city have led such persons to desire to reside in the city. Many such persons cannot locate adequate housing within the city within their economic means and this fact may have a disproportionate exclusionary impact upon disadvantaged citizens. The only effective means to prevent such exclusion is the provision of ample low and moderate income housing. Additional federal subsidies may or may not be presently unavailable and traditional zoning has been ineffective in this regard. Thus, only through residential development reveiw is there any likelihood of securing such housing.

(f)   Zoning ordinances alone cannot provide the comprehensive types of development review procedures which will ensure a high level of environmental protection, encouragement of the construction of low and moderate income housing, sequential orderly development and achievement of other goals set forth in the general plan.

(g)   The public welfare requires the establishment of a housing development priority program and housing development review board, hereinafter referred to as the "board," to accomplish the following:

(1)   Prevent premature development in the absence of necessary utilities and municipal services.

(2)   Coordinate city planning and land regulation in a manner consistent with the general plan.

(3)   Facilitate and implement the realization of general plan goals which cannot be accomplished by zoning alone.

(4)   Provide significant incentives to developers to include low and moderate income housing in their undertakings.

(5)   Prevent unplanned capricious growth which has no relationship to community needs and capabilities.

(6)   Encourage and facilitate development proposals which accomplish the objectives of the general plan.   (Ord. No. 765, & 1.)

Sec. 12A-2.   Applicability

(a)   Except for a single-family or duplex residence on a lot legally in existence before November 6, 1974, no building permit shall be issued for single-family or duplex residential construction, including mobile homes, within the city; unless such construction has been approved in accordance with the standards and procedures provided for by this chapter.   A lot will be deemed to be in existence if a final subdivision map has been submitted to the city for approval prior to November 6, 1974.

(b)   In the event that the city council, by resolution, declares the necessity for inclusion of other types of residential development within the housing development priority program, such other types of residential development shall be subject to the restrictions and procedures of such program during such time period as is specified by such resolution.

(c)   The foregoing notwithstanding, residential lots legally in existence before November 6, 1974, may be divided into a maximum of four lots through the appropriate parcel map process, and building permits may be issued for the construction of residences thereon without regard to the requirements of this chapter.   (Ord. No. 765, & 2; Ord. No. 774, & 2; Ord. No. 845, & 1.)

Sec. 12A-3.   Housing development review board generally.

(a)   Composition.   The duly appointed members of the planning commission shall serve as the housing development review board.

(b) Meetings. The board shall meet on or before September 15 of each year and thereafter for so long as is required to rate all projects for the next ensuing construction season and later seasons. The board shall complete its report no later than November 15 of each year.

(c) Staff. The community development department of the city shall serve as the staff of the board. (Ord. No. 765, Sec. 3,4,6; Ord. No. 845, Sec. 1.)

Sec. 12A-4.   Development proposal--Applications.

Upon the written application filed with any required environmental impact reports by a developer, the housing development review board shall consider any residential development proposal which is within an appropriate phase or phases as shown on the general plan's time phasing maps and which has zoning or prezoning appropriate to the development proposal. Such an application and proposal shall be filed with the city office of community development prior to October 1, 1975, and September 1 of each subsequent year for apartment projects and August 15 of each year for all other projects. The proposal shall be submitted on a form provided by the city and shall contain all data and information as called for therein.

As used in this chapter the term "proposal" shall include the developer's application and any and all maps, schematics, written information and data submitted by the developer in support of his or her application. In addition, the application shall state the minimum number of units acceptable to the applicant. (Ord. No. 765, Sec. 5.)

Sec. 12A-5.   Same--Hearings.

The housing development review board shall conduct a separate hearing on each proposal. The sole issue at such hearing shall be the rating of the project. The board shall have no authority to disapprove or remand an application. All hearings shall be public. The developer and all interested persons shall be entitled to appear and testify. After the conclusion of the hearings, the board shall render a decision rating the project on the basis of the criteria set forth in section 12A-6. (Ord. No. 765, Sec. 8.)

Sec. 12A-6. Same--Ratings.

(a) All proposals shall be preliminarily rated by the housing development review board staff in accordance with the criteria set forth in subsection (b) of this section. The developer shall be furnished with a copy of such rating and any supporting data at least five working days prior to the board's hearing thereon.

(b) The following criteria shall be used to rate projects which are in conformity with the city general plan:

(1) Internal growth needs.

(2) Economic mix.

(3) Low and moderate cost housing.

(4) Environmental impact.

(5) Availability of public services and facilities.

(6) Compactness.

(7) Design diversity.

(8) Economic impact.

(9) Feasibility.

(10) Competition.

These criteria shall be applied and evaluated in accordance with the amplification of criteria contained in city Resolution No. 1604, Series 1974, adopted December 18, 1974, and any subsequent amendments thereto. (Ord. No. 765, Secs. 7, 9.)

Sec. 12A-7. Same--Approvals--Generally.

When all rating hearings are completed, the housing development review board shall determine, on the basis of comparative ratings, projects which are eligible for approval based upon the number and

types of units to be allowed in accordance with section 12A-8.
(Ord. No. 765, Sec. 10.)

Sec. 12A-8.   Same--Same--Number per three year period.

Prior to August 15, 1975, and June 1 of each subsequent year, the
city council shall meet and determine the number and types of residential
units which should be approved during the subsequent three year period.
This determination shall be based upon:

(a)   The general plan of the city.

(b)   The number of units approved and actually constructed in
prior years.

(c)   Availability of utilities and public services.

(d)   The goals, purposes and objectives contained in section
12A-1.

(e)   The three year residential needs report which shall be
annually reviewed and adopted as prescribed in the city housing action
program.   (Ord. No. 765, Sec. 11.)

Sec. 12A-9.   Same--Same--Partial or Conditional.

If a development involves more than twenty units, the project
may be considered in segments. If the segments are interdependent,
the board may approve the entire plan or a portion of the entire plan
subject to the requirement that a limited number of units will be
constructed each year but approval shall not be given for more than
a three year period.

The board shall have discretion to approve a portion of the
housing units proposed and to disapprove or differentially rate the
balance of the housing units proposed in any particular project. In
granting partial approvals, the board shall evaluate economic feasibility
and cost factors in small projects.

The board shall impose such conditions as may be determined
necessary or desirable in order to implement the city general plan

and the purposes and objectives of this chapter. (Ord. No. 765, Sec 12.)

Sec. 12A-10. Same--Same--Modification.

Notwithstanding any other section of this chapter, the city council may at any time increase the number and types of approvals determined pursuant to section 12A-8. Such modifications shall only be made when unforeseen circumstances occur which justify such modification based upon those factors listed in section 12A-8.

In the event of a modification of the number or types of approvals, the board may increase the number of approved units in a project or it may accelerate the phasing of a project. (Ord. No. 765, Sec. 13.)

Sec. 12A-11. Same--Same--Effect.

The approval of units pursuant to the procedures and provisions of this chapter shall not exempt nor affect the developer's obligation to obtain all required zoning environmental, subdivision and other approvals as are required by statute or ordinance as a prerequisite to the application for building permits. (Ord. No. 765, Sec. 14.)

Sec. 12A-12. Same--Same--Revocation, etc.

The board may approve development proposals upon condition that construction shall commence and be carried out in accordance with an established development construction schedule. Failure to comply with such development or construction schedule shall be good cause for the revocation or modification of approval. Approved single-family and duplex units shall be deemed to have been completed for purposes of this section upon the date that a final subdivision or parcel map pertaining to such units has been approved.

Failure to comply with conditions imposed pursuant to section 12A-9 of this chapter shall be good cause for the revocation or modification shall be made by the board only after conducting a hearing into the causes of such noncompliance upon ten days written notice to the developer. The developer and all interested parties shall be entitled to appear and testify as to the reasons for noncompliance with the requirements of the board.

Revocation of approval may permit reallocation of units to other projects. (Ord. No. 765, Sec. 15.)

Sec. 12A-13. Appeals from decisions.

(a) Any member of the city council, upon the majority vote of those present and voting, or any applicant for a development aggrieved by any action of the housing development review board may file written notice of appeal with the city clerk, which notice shall be filed within fifteen days of the action and shall set forth in general terms the alleged error which is the basis of the appeal. An appeal shall suspend the effect of the board's approval as to all applications for which the fifteen day appeal period has not expired as of the date upon which the notice of appeal is filed. Upon receipt of the notice of appeal, the city council shall schedule a public hearing and shall publish notice of the time and place of such hearing in a newspaper of general circulation within the city, which notice shall be published at least ten days in advance of the hearing date. Notice of the hearing date shall be mailed to all applicants whose applications are affected by the appeal. Mailed notices shall be addressed to the applicant as shown upon the written application provided for in this chapter. Failure to actually receive such mailed notice shall not affect the validity of the appeal proceedings.

(b) Upon conclusion of the public hearing, the council shall affirm, overrule or modify the action which is the subject of the appeal. The action of the city council shall be final.

(c) Any legal action to challenge any decision, procedure, approval or denial of the city council must be filed in a court of competent jurisdiction within thirty days after the act challenged. (Ord. No. 765, Secs. 16, 17.)

Sec. 6-8. Severability.

If any section, subsection, sentence, clause or phrase of this chapter is for any reason held by a court of competent jurisdiction to be invalid, such a decision shall not affect the validity of the remaining portions of this chapter. The city council hereby declares that it would have passed this chapter and each section or subsection, sentence, clause or phrase thereof, irrespective of the fact any one or more sections, subsections, clauses or phrases be declared invalid. (Ord. No. 725, Sec. 2.)

Article II. Energy Conservation Standards for Residential Construction.

Sec. 6-9. Definitions.

For the purposes of this article, the following words and phrases shall have the meanings respectively ascribed to them by this section:

(a) Floor area. The total habitable area of a dwelling unit, expressed in square feet, which is within the exterior face of the insulated shell of the structure and which is heated or cooled.

(b) Summer design day. A day upon which it shall be assumed, for purposes of structural heat gain calculations, that all of the following climatological conditions exist:

(1) The sun's path and resultant angles of direct sunlight shall be those which occur on August 21 of each year at latitude 38° 32' north. These angles can be approximated by using latitude 40° north.

(2) The sun's intensity through glazing shall be calculated for August 21 of each year at latitude 38° 32' north; this can be approximated by using latitude 40° north data.

(3) The outside temperatures on August 21 shall be assumed to be, at each hour, Pacific Standard Time, as follows:

Time A.M.	Temp. °F	Time P.M.	Temp. °F
1:00	66	1:00	95
2:00	64	2:00	99
3:00	61	3:00	100
4:00	60	4:00	99
5:00	59	5:00	98
6:00	59	6:00	95
7:00	67	7:00	91
8:00	72	8:00	87
9:00	78	9:00	81
10:00	82	10:00	77
11:00	87	11:00	73
12:00	91	12:00	68

(4)   For the sake of determining the exterior air film co-efficient, the wind speed shall be 15 m.p.h. in accordance with ASHRAE procedures.

(c)   Winter design day. A day upon which it shall be assumed, for purposes of structural heat loss calculations, that all of the following climatological conditions exist:

(1)   The sun's path and resultant angles of direct sunlight shall be those which occur on December 21 of each year at latitude 38° 32' north. These angles can be approximated by using latitude 40° north data. (See Table 1.)

(2)   The sun's intensity through glazing shall be calcualted for December 21 of each year at latitude 38° 32' north; this can be approximated by using latitude 40° north data.

(3)   The 24 hour average outside temperature is 45°F.

(4)   For the sake of determining the external air film coefficient, the wind speed shall be assumed to be 15.0 m.p.h. in accordance with ASHRAE procedures. (Ord. No. 784, Sec. 2.)

Sec. 6-10.   Minimum performance standards--Adoption.

The city hereby adopts minimum standards for the thermal performance of buildings to be constructed within the city. In order

to achieve maximum thermal performance, the performance standards
have been carefully adjusted to the special problems and opportunities
of the city climate. These standards shall apply to all residential
structures designated Group H and Group I in the Uniform Building
Code.

   (a) Winter performance standard. For a winter performance
standard the total day's heat loss per square foot of floor area
during the winter design day shall be as follows: For single-family,
detached structures designated U.B.C. Group I, see table 2; for multiple dwellings, U.B.C. Group H, the total day's heat loss shall not
exceed one hundred twenty BTU's per square foot of floor area.
Commonwall Group I structures shall meet Group H standards. The
resolution establishing methods of compliance with the performance
standards will allow for numerically increasing the permissible
standard on the basis of surface areas in common in order to equitably
deal with the variability which occurs in this class of dwelling units.

Table 2

Detached Group I Dwelling Unit
Thermal Standards

Floor Area (sq.ft.)	Winter heat loss (BTU's/sq.ft. day)	Summer heat gain (BTU's/sq.ft. day)
500	363	118
1000	239	103
1500	208	98
2000	192	95
2500	182	93
3000	176	91

   Note: Direct interpolation shall be used for floor areas not
          shown. Infiltration and internal heat production are
          not considered under the requirements of these standards.
          These are very important considerations in the real
          performance of a building and must be estimated when
          sizing heating and cooling devices whether conventional
          or solar. However, for the present purpose they are too
          variable to be standardized.

(b) Summer performance standard. For a summer performance
standard, the total day's heat gain per square foot of floor area
during the summer design day shall be as follows: for single-family,
detached structures, U.B.C. Group I, see table 2; for multiple
dwellings U.B.C. Group H, the total day's heat gain shall not exceed
forty BTU's per square floor area. Commonwall Group I structures
shall meet Group H Standards. The resolution establishing methods
of compliance with the performance standards will allow for numerically increasing the permissible standard on the basis of surface areas
in common in order to equitably deal with the variability which occurs
in this class of dwelling units. (Ord. No. 784, Sec. 3.)

Sec. 6-11. Same--Methods of compliance to be established by resolution.

Standard methods for calculating the performance of a proposed
structure to determine compliance with the standards of this article
shall be adopted by resolution of the city council. (Ord. No. 784,
Sec. 4.)

Sec. 6-12. Administration and enforcement.

(a) The provisions of this article and the resolution establishing the methods of compliance shall be administered by the building
official of the city.

(b) No building permit shall be issued by the building official
for any new structure subject to this article unless such structure
is found to be in compliance with the winter and summer performance
standards hereby established. (Ord. No. 784, Sec. 5.)

Sec. 6-13. Partial exemptions.

(a) Structures designated U.B.C. Group I to be built on lots
which are unimproved with structures and for which a tentative subdivision map has been approved prior to September 1, 1974, shall be
exempt from requirements adopted by resolution pursuant to section
6-11 of this article. To the extent that the exemption from requirements causes a structure to exceed the performance standards
established by section 6-10 of this article, such incremental excess
shall be permitted.

(b)   Structures designated U.B.C. Group I to be built on lots
which are unimproved with structures and for which a tentative subdivision map has been approved prior to January 1, 1976, but after
September 1, 1974, and which lots front upon a portion of street
having an axis between 292.5° and 067.5° true (N67.5°W and N67.5°E)
and 247.5° and 112.5° true (S67.5°W and S67.5°E), shall be exempt
from glazing shading requirements adopted by resolution pursuant to
section 6-11 of this article. To the extent that the exemption from
glazing shading requirements causes a structure to exceed the performance standards established by section 6-10 of this article, such
incremental excess shall be permitted. (Ord. No. 784, Sec. 6, 7;
Ord. No. 787, Sec. 1.)

Sec. 6-14. Variances.

(a) Purpose. The purpose of a variance is to allow variation
from the strict application of the requirements of this article and
implementing resolutions where, by reason of the exceptional narrowness,
shallowness or unusual shape of a specific piece of property, or other
extraordinary situation or condition of such piece of property, or of
the use or the development of property immediately adjoining the property in question, the literal enforcement of the requirements of this
article would involve practical difficulties or would cause undue
hardship unnecessary to carry out the spirit and purpose of this
article. In most cases, the variance shall only relate to the allowable area of unshaded glazing permissible under the resolutions
implementing this article.

(b) Application. Application for a variance shall be made by
the property owner or the board of building appeals or the community
development director on a form prescribed by the city, and shall be
accompanied by a fee as prescribed by resolution adopted pursuant to
City Code section 29-12.1, no part of which shall be refundable. No
fee shall be charged if the variance is initiated by the board of
building appeals or the community developemnt director.

(c) Maps and drawings. Maps and drawings required to demonstrate
that the conditions set forth in this article apply to the subject
property, together with precise and accurate legal descriptions and
scale drawings of the property and existing buildings, and other data
required, shall be submitted with the application for a variance.

(d) Grounds for granting. The board of building appeals may grant a variance only when all of the following conditions are found:

(1) That any variance granted shall be subject to such conditions as will assure that the adjustment thereby authorized shall not constitute a grant of special privilege inconsistent with the limitations upon other similarly situated properties which were developed under the limitations of this article.

(2) That because of special circumstances applicable to the subject property, the strict application of this article is found to deprive subject property of privileges enjoyed by other similar properties which were developed under the limitations of this article.

(3) That the authorizing of such variance will not be of substantial detriment to adjacent property, and will not materially impair the purposes of this article or the public interest.

(4) That the condition or situation of the subject property or the intended use of the property for which the variance is sought is not so general or recurrent in nature as to make reasonable or practicable the formulation of a general regulation for such conditions or situations.

(5) That there are not available reasonable alternative construction methods which will bring the proposed structure into compliance with the performance standards of this article.

(e) Examples of grounds for granting. The following types of physical or topographical factors are examples of conditions which may justify the grant of a variance from the glazing shading requirements to be established by resolution as provided by section 6-11 of this article:

(1) Overriding off-site view considerations which are determined to add appreciable incremental value to the subject property.

(2) Minimum size lots with fixed and adverse orientation problems.

(3) Adverse lot orientation dictated by street or utility

improvements or similar physical limitations where such limitations are in existence prior to the adoption of this article.

(f) State standards. No variance shall be granted under this section which will result in a structure which exceeds the then existing state residential energy conservation standards.

(g) Notice of variance hearing. Upon the filing of an appeal, the building official shall provide written notice of the filing of the appeal to all persons interested in the matter and shall cause notice of public hearing to be published in a newspaper of general circulation.

(h) Review of the decision. The decision of the board of building appeals to grant or deny the application shall be subject to appeal in accordance with the resolution establishing the board of building appeals. (Ord. No. 784, Sec. 8.)

Sec. 6-15. Appeals.

Any person aggrieved by a determination of the building official in the application of this article may appeal such determination to the city board of building appeals. Such appeal shall be in writing and shall be filed with the building official within fifteen days of the determination appealed. All appeals shall be accompanied by payment of a fee in the amount set forth in the city's community development fee schedule.

Upon the filing of an appeal, the building official shall provide written notice of the filing of the appeal to all persons interested in the matter and shall cause notice of public hearing to be published in a newspaper of general circulation.

In consideration of an appeal, the board of building appeals shall have authority to determine the suitability of alternate materials and methods of construction and to provide for reasonable interpretation of the provisions of this article and implementing resolutions, provided, that no alternate material nor method of construction shall be approved which results in a reduction in the performance standards established by this article for both summer and winter conditions.

The decision of the board of building appeals shall be subject to appeal in accordance with the resolution establishing the board of building appeals. (Ord. No. 784, Sec. 9.)

Resolution No. 1833, Series 1975

Resolution Adopting Procedures for Compliance with the Energy Conservation Performance Standards for Residential Construction Within the City of Davis

WHEREAS, the City of Davis has, by ordinance, established certain energy conservation performance standards for new residential construction within the City of Davis; and

WHEREAS, the ordinance which establishes energy conservation performance standards provides that standard methods for determining compliance of proposed buildings shall be established by resolution;

NOW, THEREFORE, BE IT RESOLVED by the City Council of the City of Davis as follows:

Section 1. Application.

Compliance with the energy conservation performance standards established by the City of Davis shall be determined by reference to the provisions of this resolution and any amendments thereto.

Section 2. Definitions.

For purposes of this resolution and the energy conservation performance standards ordinance of the City, the following words and phrases shall have the meanings respectively ascribed to them by this section:

A. R Values. (1/U = R) Thermal Resistance (R) is the measure

of the resistance of a material or building component to the passage
of heat. The units of measurement are: (Hours) (Degrees Fahrenheit)
(Square Feet)/BTU. The resistance value (R) of mass-type insulations
shall not include any value for reflective facing. (NOTE: For
reflective foil insulation, use ASHRAE procedures only. Calculate
both the winter and summer composite resistance value and use whichever is less.)

B. Composite Thermal Resistance. (R_t) is the sum of each of
the resistance values of the parts of an assembly of materials which
together form an external skin element of the structure. For example,
a commonly used wall is one which has an interior air film, one-half
(1/2) inch thick plaster board, three and one-half (3-1/2) inches
batt insulation, stucco, and finally, an exterior air film, all of
which have R values which are added together to derive the R_t value
for the wall element.

C. Orientation. The compass directions are designated as
follows when the attached tables are used:

North	337.5° - 022.5°
Northeast	022.5° - 067.5°
East	067.5° - 112.5°
Southeast	112.5° - 157.5°
South	157.5° - 202.5°
Southwest	202.5° - 247.5°
West	247.5° - 292.5°
Northwest	292.5° - 337.5°

D. Exterior Surface Area. The area for each dwelling unit of
walls, ceilings, suspended floors, glazing, doors, etc. enclosing
conditioned spaces and exposed to ambient climatic conditions.

E. Heavy Exterior Building Elements. The walls, suspended
floors and/or ceilings which contain a heat storage capacity of 30 BTU's/
Day for each square foot of surface area are considered to be heavy
(see definition K). Only those materials located on the interior side
of insulation materials may be counted. (An eight(8) inch thick
lightweight concrete block wall with exterior insulation slightly
exceeds these requirements.)

F. <u>Color.</u> Surfaces with a Munsell lightness value of 6.0 to 10.0 are to be considered <u>light in color</u>. Surfaces with a Munsell lightness value of 9.0 to 10.0 are to be considered <u>very light in color</u>. Unpainted wood surfaces are to be considered <u>light in color</u>. The Building Inspector shall prepare two (2) representative collections of materials and surface covering materials, one with Munsell lightness values greater than 6 and one of materials with Munsell lightness values greater than 9. These collections shall be available for inspection by the public.

G. <u>Glazing.</u> All vertical, horizontal, and tilted translucent or transparent exterior building elements shall be considered glazing with a thermal resistance and daylight transmittance as specified by the manufacturer or as calculated by ASHRAE methods or other reliable references or procedures.

H. <u>Shading Coefficient.</u> The ratio of the solar heat gain through a shading-glazing system to that of an unshaded single-pane of double strength window glass under the same set conditions.

I. <u>Hour's Solar Heat Gain.</u> The amount of energy transmitted through an area of glazing oriented to a particular direction in one (1) hour. The following formula is used for calculation:

$$HSHG = (SC)\ (SHGF)\ (A)$$

Where:

HSHG = Solar Heat Gain through the glazing for one (1) hour (BTU's/hour)

SC   = Shading Coefficient

SHGF = Solar Heat Gain Factor for the hour from attached Table 1 (BTU's/square foot of glazing) using December 21 for winter and August 21 for summer.

A   = Area in square feet of glazing exposed to the sun (square feet).

J. <u>Solar Heat Gain Factor.</u> The number of BTU's of solar energy transmitted through one (1) square foot of clear 1/8-inch glass in one (1) hour. This is determined by using the attached Table 1 which applies to 40° North latitude and the eight (8) compass orientations (see definition C).

K. Heat Storage Capacity. The mass located inside the insulated shell of the structure that fluxes through a temperature cycle each day in summer and winter, absorbing heat during overheated periods and storing it for release during underheated periods. Heat storage capacity shall be estimated by the following procedure:

$$HS = (WM) \ (SH) \ (\Delta T)$$

Where:

HS = Heat Storage Capacity (BTU's/Day)

WM = The weight of the materials (lbs.) inside the insulated shell of the building to a depth yielding a resistance of R-1, except in the case of slab floors where only the slab itself is credited.

SH = Specific Heat of those materials (BTU's/lb. degree F)

ΔT - Temperature flux; 5°F will be the maximum allowable for calculation purposes, except that light weight frame construction will be allowed to flux 10°F. (In order to determine the heat or cold available for storage, see Path II, Section 5.)

This total stored heat may be subtracted from the day's heat loss or gain to yield the adjusted Total Day's Heat Loss or Total Day's Heat Gain. Mass located in exterior elements to which the Equivalent Temperature Differential Method (E.T.D.) is applied to calculate summer heat gain shall not be included in the summer heat storage capacity credit.

L. Floor Area. Total habitable area of a dwelling unit (expressed in square feet) which is within the exterior face of the insulated shell of the structure and which is heated or cooled.

Section 3.   Standard Methods of Building Performance Calculation.

A.   There are hereby adopted two (2) alternative standard methods of determining compliance with the City of Davis energy conservation performance standards. The two (2) alternative standard methods shall be referred to as Path I and Path II approaches.

B.   Structures utilizing either Path I or Path II shall comply with the following:

(1) Infiltration. All swinging doors and windows opening to the exterior or to unconditioned areas such as garages shall be fully weatherstripped, gasketed or otherwise treated to limit infiltration. All manufactured windows and sliding glass doors shall meet the air infiltration standards of the 1972 American National Standards Institute (A134.2, A134.3 and A134.4), when tested in accordance with ASTM E 283-73 with a pressure differential of 1.57 lbs./ft,^{2} and shall be certified and labeled.

(2) Loose Fill Insulation. When blown or poured type loose fill insulation is used in attic spaces, the slope of the roof shall be not less than 2-1/2 feet in 12 feet and there shall be at least 30 inches of clear headroom at the roof ridge. ("Clear headroom" is defined as the distance from the top of the bottom chord of the truss or ceiling joists to the underside of the roof sheathing.) When eave vents are installed, adequate baffling of the vent opening shall be provided to deflect the incoming air above the surface of the material and shall be installed at the soffit on a 45-degree angle. Baffles shall be in place at the time of framing inspection. When loose fill insulation is proposed, the R value of the material required to meet these regulations shall be shown on the building plans or calculation sheet.

(3) Pipe Insulation. All steam and steam condensate return piping and all continuously circulating domestic or heating hot water piping which is located in attics, garages, crawl spaces, underground or unheated spaces other than between floors or in interior walls shall be insulated to provide a maximum heat loss of 50 BTU/hr. per linear foot for piping up to and including 2-inch and 100 BTU/hr. per linear foot for larger sizes. Piping installed at depth of 30 inches or more complies with these standards.

Section 4.   Path I (Prescriptive Method).

Buildings meeting all of the following criteria will fulfill the required energy conservation aspects of this code with no overall performance calculations required.

Calculations using the applicable methods outlined in Path II may be employed to demonstrate compliance of alternatives to any particular section of Path I. Thermal trade-offs between sections of Path I must be done by using Path II or by referring to approved thermal trade-offs table developed by the Building Inspector.

A. Walls. All exterior walls (excluding windows and doors) shall use R-11 batt insulation between studs. Group H structures must have light colored walls or shaded walls. Fifteen percent (15%) of the wall area may be dark colored to allow for trim and color accents. (Group I structures have no wall color requirement.)

Exceptions:

(1) All exterior walls shall achieve a composite resistance value (Rt) of 10.52 if the insulation is not penetrated by framing, and Rt of 12.50 if the insulation is penetrated by the framing or furring. (California Administrative Code, Title 25, Chapter 1, Subchapter 1, Article 5, Section 1094a.)

(2) Heavy walls with exterior insulation not penetrated by furring or framing shall have an Rt of 7.36, and Rt of 8.75 if the insulation is penetrated by furring or framing.

(3) Group H structures with dark colored walls shall increase their applicable Rt requirements by twenty percent (20%).

B. Roof/Ceilings; Ceiling/Attics. All roof/ceilings and ceiling/attics must use insulation achieving a minimum resistance of R-19 for the insulation itself. Group H occupancies having roof surfaces unshaded on August 21, at 8:00 a.m., 12:00 noon, or 4:00 p.m., shall be no darker then No. 6 on the Munsell color chart. Unshaded roof areas on Group I occupancies shall be no darker than No. 4 on the Munsell color chart. Roofs having unshaded areas and color darker than No. 6 or No. 4 respectively must increase the total insulation to yield R-25 for the insulation itself.

Exceptions:

(1)   All Roof/ceilings and/or ceiling/attics sections shall achieve a composite resistance value (Rt) of 16.67 if the insulation is not penetrated by framing or furring and Rt of 20.0 if the insulation is penetrated by the framing or furring. (California Administrative Code, Title 25, Chapter 1, Subchapter 1, Article 5, Section 1094c.)   Blown insulation (loose fill type) shall be considered to be penetrated by the framing.

(2)   The roof/ceiling and/or ceiling/attic sections of the dwelling unit as a whole may be insulated to values greater and/or less than required in (1) above if the resulting heat loss equals or is less than that which would occur if the values required in (1) above were met, or if the thermal resistance values of the ceiling areas satisfy the following equation:

$$1/Rt \text{ required} = (\text{Area A/Total Area}) (1/Rt \text{ achieved})$$

$$+(\text{Area B/Total Area}) (1/Rt \text{ achieved})$$

$$+...+(\text{Area N/Total Area}) (1/Rt \text{ achieved})$$

(3)   In Group H occupancies, roof/ceilings or ceiling/attics located beneath dark colored roofs shall achieve composite resistance values (Rt) 30% greater than the values in (1) and (2) above, i.e., Rt. = 21.67 and Rt = 26.00 respectively.   In Group I occupancies, roof/ceilings or ceiling/attics located beneath roofs that are darker than Munsell Color No. 4 shall achieve composite resistance values (Rt) 30% greater than the values in (1) and (2) above, i.e., Rt = 21.67 and Rt = 26.00 respectively.

C.   Floors.   Suspended floors over a ventilated crawl space or other unheated space shall have insulation with a minimum resistance of R-11.   Concrete slabs on grade require no insulation.

Exceptions:

(1)   Suspended floors over an unheated space shall achieve a composite resistance value (Rt) of 10.52 if the insulation is not penetrated by framing, and Rt of 12.50 if the insulation is penetrated by framing.

(2) Heavy suspended floors with exterior insulation shall achieve a composite resistance value (Rt) of 7.36 for insulation not penetrated by framing members, and Rt of 8.75 for insulation penetrated by framing members.

D. Glazing Area. In Group H occupancies, exterior single-pane glazing (windows, skylights, etc.) may not exceed 12-1/2% of the floor area. Exterior double-pane glazing may not exceed 17-1/2% of the dwelling unit's floor area. In Group I occupancies, a glazing constant of 20 square feet in single-pane glazing and 28 square feet in double-pane glazing may be added to the percentage figures allowed above.

Exceptions:

(1) A combination of single and double-pane glazing may be used so long as the area of the single plus the area of the double glazing divided by 1.4 is not greater than 12-1/2% (plus 20 square feet for Group I occupancies) of the dwelling unit's floor area.

(2) A combination of single and/or double-pane glazing with interior shutters may be used to increase the allowed glazing provided that:

(i) The interior shutters are of a permanent construction and installed so that they are operable, and tight fitting or weatherstripped so that a seal is created.

(ii) The areas in each treatment do not exceed those allowed by the following procedure.

$$GC + (FA) (.125) = Area_s + (Area_D) (.64) + (Area_{shut})/Rt$$

Where:

GC   = Glazing constant (square feet) taken at 20 square feet in Group I and zero in Group H occupancies.

FA   = Floor Area (square feet).

$Area_s$ = Area in single-pane glazing (square feet).

$Area_D$ = Area in double-pane glazing (square feet).

$Area_{shut}$ = Area in interior shuttered glazing (square feet).

Rt   = The composite resistance of the shutter-glazing systems.

    (3)   When the area of glazing allowed by application of (1) or (2) is exceeded, the excess area will be considered justified if all the following conditions are met:

    (i)   Glazing must be south facing. If it is mounted other than vertically, it must be tilted at least 30° up from the horizontal to face south.

    (ii)   It must be clear. (Shading coefficient numerically greater than or equal to .80 for the glazing itself.)

    (iii)   It must receive full direct sun from 10:00 a.m. to 2:00 p.m. (P.S.T.) on December 21.

    (iv)   For each square foot of glazing being justified, the building must contain a heat storage capacity (HS) equivalent to 750 BTU's/Day, located inside the insulated shell of the structure, and not covered with insulation materials such as carpet yielding an Rt of 1.0 or greater. The following will allow a quick method for calculation of mass needed for each square foot of exempted glazing:

    59 Square feet of interior stud partition wall
        (2" x 4"s - 16" o.c. with 1/2" gypsum two sides).

    117 Square feet of exterior stud wall or ceiling
        (2" x 4"s - 16" o.c. with 1/2" gypsum inside,
        insulation, and various external treatments).

    21 Square feet of 8-inch lightweight concrete
        block masonry exterior wall insulated externally,
        cores filled for structural support only.

    15 Square feet of concrete slab floor provided with
        a steel trowel finish, exposed aggregate, tile
        (vinyl, asbestos, or ceramic), terrazo, or
        hardwood parque not greater than 1/2-inch thick.

(Note: Lightweight stud frame walls are assumed to flux 10°F; heavy walls are assumed to flux 5°F. Dee Definitions E and K.)

E. Glazing Shading.

(1) All glazing which is not oriented to the north must be shaded to protect it from direct solar radiation for the hours of 8:00 a.m., 12:00 noon, and 4:00 p.m. (P.S.T.), August 21. Glazing facing SE or SW must also be checked for shading at 10:00 a.m. for SE and 2:00 p.m. for SW in addition to the standard three hours. For each check hour the area of glazing not shaded is calculated and accumulated. In Group H occupancies the total accumulated amount of unshaded glazing may not exceed 1.5% of the dwelling unit's floor area. In Group I occupancies the total accumulated amount of unshaded glass may not exceed 3% of the dwelling unit's floor area. Shading shall be demonstrated to the satisfaction of the Building Inspection Division of the Community Development Department. Drawings showing shadows cast by shading systems, or scale models suitable for use in the solar-ranger setup by the Building Inspection Division, or the use of approved shade screen systems may be employed to demonstrate compliance. Tinted, metalized, or frosted galss shall not be considered self-shading.

(2) Interior mounted shutters meeting the following specifications may be utilized to meet the shading requirements:

(i) The exterior oriented side must be very light in color (Munsell of 9.0 or greater) and flat.

(ii) The shutters must be tight fitting or all cracks or edges in the system must be weather stripped to create a seal.

(iii) The shutters must be opaque.

(iv) A composite resistance value of $R_t = 1.0$ for the shutters must be achieved.

(3) Exterior mounted shading systems meeting the following specifications may be utilized to meet the shading requirements:

(i) They shall be of permanent materials and con-

struction.   A permanent frame with sheathing having a life expectance
of five years minimum must be provided and guaranteed by the builder.

(ii)   For the required design hour, the shading device
must be capable of intercepting 100% of the direct beam solar
radiation, or provide a minimum shading coefficient of 0.2 or less.
If the shading system at a design hour does not perform to these
standards, then the portion of the glazing which is left exposed is
to be calculated and added to the accumulated unshaded glazing total.

(4)   Other types of shading systems are allowed if they
comply with either of the following:

(i)   All on-site and off-site obstructions to the
sun, providing 80% attenuation of the direct solar beam, may be
considered as external shading devices and may be accounted for in
the summer shading calculations. (NOTE: If during the life of the
structure the off-site obstructions to the sun used to achieve shading
standards compliance are modified or removed, then the structure may
be found to be in violation of the Code if other compensating obstructions to the sun or shading devices have not been deployed.)

(ii)   A shading system may be temporary, provided
that it is designed and constructed to function to the standards above
and built to last until its function is replaced by plantings. Plan
and elevation drawings must show expected plant configuration and
accurately state the number of years required for the projected plant
growth.   Final occupancy permits shall not be issued until the specified plants are in place.

F.   Ventilation for Summer Night Time Cooling. Where design
of the dwelling unit is such that openable windows may only be provided along one elevation, mechanical cross ventilation must be installed to provide 15 air changes per hour ducted to the exterior.

Section 5.   Path II (Performance Method).

Buildings regulated by the Residential Energy Conservation
Code that do not meet the criteria of Path I must be calculated by
a registered architect, engineer, building designer, or other qualified person to show that the proposed building will not exceed the

standards set forth in Section 3 of Ordinance No.   . The required calculation schedule is outlined below. (NOTE: More precise calculations may be submitted using ASHRAE or other comprehensive methods provided that the same design days are used.)

Commonwall U.B.C. Group I dwelling units may increase the permissible thermal standards for Heat Loss or Heat Gain using the following equation:

$$TS = TS_H + (TS_I - TS_H) (L - SAC/1.5 FA)$$

Where:

TS = The Thermal Standard which is applicable to the dwelling unit (BTU's/sq. ft. Day)

TS_H = The Thermal Standard for Group H structures (BTU's/sq. ft. Day)

TS_I = The Thermal Standard for a detached Group I dwelling unit of the same floor area (BTU's/ sq. ft. Day)

SAC = The Surface Area in Common with other dwelling units such as ceilings, walls, and floor (square feet)

FA = The dwelling unit's Floor Area (square feet)

A. Winter Calculations.

(1) The Total Day's Heat Loss shall not exceed the standards set in the Residential Energy Conservation Ordinance, Section 3.

(2) Winter heat loss calculations shall be based on the following formula:

$$TDHL = (DHL - SHGC)/(FA)$$

Where:

TDHL = Total Day's Heat Loss (BTU's/sq. ft. Day)

DHL = Day's Heat Loss (BTU's/Day)

SHGC = Solar Heat Gain Credit (BTU's/Day)

FA   = Floor Area of dwelling unit (sq. ft.)

(3)   The Design Day for sun angle considerations is December 21 at latitude 40°N or 38° 32'N. The outside daily temperature average for December and January is 45°F, yielding a 23°F difference between the inside (68°F) and the outside (45°F) average daily temperatures. The number of degree hours in the design day is the temperature difference times 24 hours or 552 for Davis. This figure is used as described in Paragraph (4) (i) below. (NOTE: This design, outdoor condition, is not intended to be for equipment sizing, but rather is meant to serve the purpose of performance design for energy conservation by more closely predicting the long term average conditions and energy use of the structure. Equipment sizing will require additional standard peak load calculations.)

(4)   Calculation of Day's Heat Loss (DHL): Winter heat loss is determined by the composite resistance (Rt) of the exterior building surface to heat transfer to the outside air from the heated interior spaces.

DHL = HL & SHL

Where:

DHL = Day's Heat Loss (BTU's/Day)

HL = Heat Loss from outside surface elements
      (except slab) (BTU's/Day)

SHL = Slab on grade Heat Loss (BTU's/Day)

(i)   The heat loss for all surfaces (except slabs on grade) facing the outside air or unheated spaces may be determined by the following formula:

$$HL = (A_1/Rt_1) \ (552) + (A_2/Rt_2) \ (552)$$
$$+ \ ... \ + (A_n/Rt_n) \ (552)$$

Where:

HL = Heat Loss from exterior surface element except
       a slab on grade (BTU's/Day)

A   = Area of the exterior surface element (sq. ft.)

Rt = The element's composite thermal resistance
       ([hours][Deg. F][sq. ft.]/BTU)

552 = Davis Design Day Degree Hours
       (Deg. F., Hours/Day)

All exterior elements (walls, ceilings, doors and suspended floors) which are exposed to unheated enclosed or partially enclosed spaces shall be calculated as if they are exposed to outside conditions, or the temperature difference may be altered according to accepted ASHRAE procedures for surfaces adjacent to unheated spaces.

(ii) Concrete slab floors on grade lose heat in direct relation to the perimeter dimension in linear feet. The following formula applies:

SHL = (F) (P) (552)

Where:

SHL = Heat Loss from Slab (BTU's/Day)

F   = The thermal conductivity of the edge of the
      slab with F = 0.81 (BTU/foot, hour, Deg. F)
      where no insulation is used and F = 0.55
      where   slab is insulated with edge insulation
      of R = 4.5 minimum. The insulation shall come
      within one inch of the top of the slab and ex-
      tend sixteen inches below grade.

P   = Perimeter dimension (feet)

552 = Davis Design Day Degree Hours (Deg. F, hours/
      Day)

(5)   Calculation of Solar Heat Gain Credit (SHGC). Direct use of solar energy is dependent on the day's Solar Heat Gain (DSHG) through the glazing, the Heat Storage (HS) characteristics of the building, and the Solar Climatic Variable (SCV). The following steps are to be followed to calculate the SHGC:

(i)   Calculate the Day's Solar Heat Gain (DSHG), by adding up the Solar Heat Gain for each daylight hour of December 21 design day for each square foot of glazing receiving sun.

$$DSHG = (HSHG_1 + HSHG_2 + \ldots + HSHG_n)\ (SCV)$$

Where:

DSHG = Day's Solar Heat Gain (BTU's/Day)

HSHG = Hour's Solar Heat Gain. HSHG is found according to the procedure described in Definition I. The number of hours added depends on the hours of sunlight on the glazing surface in question. (BTU's/hour)

SCV = Solar Climatic Variable (no units). SCV = 0.56 for Davis. This was determined by averaging the mean fraction of possible sunshine available for each month of the winter heating season (November, December, January, February, March).

(ii)   Calculate the Heat Storage capacity of the building (HS).   (See Definition K for calculation procedure.)

(iii)   Then the Solar Heat Gain Credit (SHGC) (BTU's/Day) equals:

SHGC = DSHG or HS, whichever is less.

B.   Summer Calculations.

(1)   The Total Day's Heat Gain (TDHG) shall not exceed the standard set in the Residential Energy Conservation Ordinance, Section 3.

(2)   Summer heat gain calculations shall be based on the following formula:

$$TDHG = (DHG - HS) /FA$$

Where:

TDHG   = Total Day's Heat Gain (BTU's/(sq.ft.) (Day)

DHG   = Day's Heat Gain (BTU's/Day)

HS   = Heat Storage (BTU's/Day)

FA   = Floor Area of the dwelling unit (sq. ft.)

(3)   The calculations below are based on the design day cited in the Residential Energy Conservation Ordinance taken at the five hours of 8:00 a.m., 10:00 a.m., 12:00 noon, 2:00 p.m., and 4:00 p.m.

(4) The Day's Heat Gain (DHG) is based on the weighted sum of calculations done at each of the five heat gain calculation hours (see equation (a) below). Structures without elevations oriented to the intercardinal directions may delete calculations for 10:00 a.m. and 2:00 p.m. and equally weigh the remaining three calculation hours by multiplying them by four (see equation (b) below). The following two weighted sun equations hold respectively.

(a) $DHG = ([HG_{8:00 \text{ a.m.}}]\ [3]+[HG_{10:00 \text{ a.m.}}]\ [2]$
$+[HG_{12:00 \text{ noon}}]\ [2]+[HG_{2:00 \text{ p.m.}}]\ [2]$
$+[HG_{4:00 \text{ p.m.}}]\ [3]$

or

(b) $DHG = ([HG_{8:00 \text{ a.m.}} + HG_{12:00 \text{ noon}} + HG_{4:00 \text{ p.m.}}]$

Where:

DHG = Day's Heat Gain (BTU's/[Day])

HG = Heat Gain at the hour calculated (BTU's/hour)

(NOTE: More detailed analysis of Heat Gain may be done by calculating each hour's heat gain for the daylight hours. The digits "2", "3" and "4" in equations (a) and (b) above have the units of hours.)

(5) The Heat Gain (GH) may be calculated by using the following formula:

$$HG = WHG + OHG$$

Where:

HG = Heat Gain (BTU's/hour) at one of the design hours

WHG = Heat Gain through Windows (BTU's/hour)

OHG = Heat Gain through Opaque surfaces (BTU's/hour)

(i) Heat Gain through Opaque surfaces. Calculations will be based on the Total Equivalent Temperature Differential Method (TETD) as described in ASHRAE Handbook of Fundamentals 1972, Chapter 22, pages 411-417. The TETD appropriate for the wall or roof section is found in attached Tables 2 and 3. Since the average Davis design day temperature is 5°F less than that used by ASHRAE, 5°F should be subtracted from the TETD values given in attached Tables 2 and 3 in accordance with ASHRAE procedures, as shown in the calculation below. (The interior temperature is assumed to be 75°F in accordance with ASHRAE.) The Heat Gain through Opaque surfaces is calculated as follows:

$$OHG = A_1(TETD-5)/Rt_1 + A_2(TETD-5)/Rt_2$$
$$+ \ldots + A_n(TETD-5)Rt_n$$

Where:

OHG = Heat Gain through opaque surfaces at the calculation hour (BTU's/hour)

A   = Area of the outside surface element (sq. ft.)

Rt = The element's composite thermal Resistance ([hours] [Deg. F] [sq. ft.]/BTU)

TETD = The element's Total Equivalent Temperature
Difference from attached Tables 2 and 3.

(ii)   Glazing.   Summer Heat Gain through windows (WHG)
shall be calculated using the following formula:

$$WHG = ([A]\ [SC]\ [SHGF]+[\Delta T]\ [A]/Rt)_1 + (A...)_2$$

$$+ ... + (A\ ...)_n$$

Where:

WHG = Direct solar heat gain plus conducted heat
gain through windows at the calculation hour
(must be done for each wall or roof section
with glazing).   (BTU's/hour)

A   = Area of glazing surface being calculated (sq. ft.)

SC   = Shading Coefficient (see Definition H). (Unitless)

SHGF = Solar Heat Gain Factor at the hour being calculated
(BTU's/[hours] [sq. ft. of glazing])

Rt   = Thermal Resistance of the glass (0.9 for single
weight glass and 1.7 for double-pane).
([hours] [Deg. F] [sq. ft.[/BTU's)

ΔT = Difference between the outside and the inside
temperatures, with 75°F being taken as the
inside temperature.   (Deg. F)

(6)   Heat Storage Capacity (HS).   Where the building design
provides for ventilation in minimum conformance with Section 4F, credit
can be taken for the Heat Storage capacity of the structure.
(NOTE: When calculating the heat storage capacity for the summer, no
credit may be taken for exterior elements.)

Section 6.   Fees.

The following schedule of fees shall be applicable for the checking

of plans for conformity with the performance standards of the Residential
Energy Conservation Code:

Path I	(No Exceptions)	No Charge
Path I	(Exercising Exceptions)	$20.00
Path II		$25.00

PASSED AND ADOPTED by the City Council of the City of Davis on
this 15th day of October   , 1975.

"Proposed Energy Conservation Retrofit Ordinance"

An ordinance amending the Housing Code for the City of Davis to
establish energy conservation standards for existing residential
structures within the City of Davis.

The City Council of the City of Davis does hereby ordain as follows:

SECTION 1.   FINDINGS

A. The electrical and natural gas energy used to power the climate
control and habitability systems of residential structures is essential to the health, safety, and welfare of the people of the
State of California. The cost of energy is rapidly rising due to
uncertainties about present and future supplies of natural gas,
and the inability of powerplant construction to keep pace with the
rising demand for electricity. Rising residential energy costs are
becoming an increasing economic burden for lower and middle-income
families and persons.

B. Almost all existing residential structures in the State of
California were constructed during a period of relative energy
abundance. Therefore, most of these structures employ climate
control and habitability systems which consume energy at levels
exceeding those which are possible if recently developed and previously existing energy conservation technologies are employed.

Significant opportunities exist for energy conservation through
the application of appropriate technologies to existing residential
structures. Conservation of energy in this manner would result in
decreased residential energy bills and would diminish the threat
to the health and welfare of residents of this state which is
posed by potential future energy shortages.

C. The Housing Code of the City of Davis presently does not
address energy conservation in existing residential structures.
The climate control and habitability systems employed in many of
these structures consequently consume energy at rates which exceed those which could be obtained if the Housing Code did provide
standards requiring the installation of appropriate energy conservation technologies. These excessive rates of energy consumption,
in the face of rising energy prices, adversely affect the present
and future ability of the occupants of these residences to purchase
the energy necessary to adequately maintain the climate control and
habitability systems essential to their health and welfare. Amendment of the Housing Code to establish energy conservation standards
as part of the housing resale inspection program is therefore
necessary to protect the health and welfare of the occupants of
housing within the City of Davis.

SECTION 2. PURPOSE

The purpose and intent of this ordinance is to prescribe, by
regulation, standards which increase efficiency in the use of
energy by residential structures. These standards accomplish
this goal by requiring the application of appropriate energy
conservation technologies to the climate control and habitability
systems of these structures.

SECTION 3. DEFINITIONS

ECT: An energy conservation technology, as specified in this
ordinance.

Unit: A dwelling unit in a single-family, two-family, or multi-
family residence building, motels, hotels, rooming and boarding
houses, fraternities, sororities and similar living accommodations.

(This definition is contained in the Davis Housing Code and is repeated here only for clarity.)

Unit Type:

A: A dwelling unit with a slab-on-grade floor, a flat roof, and plywood siding;

B: A dwelling unit with a slab-on-grade floor, a flat roof, and stucco siding;

C: A dwelling unit with a floor raised above grade over an accessible crawl space, a flat roof, and plywood siding;

D: A dwelling unit with a floor raised above grade over an accessible crawl space, a flat roof, and stucco siding;

E: A dwelling unit with a slab-on-grade floor, an accessible attic space, and plywood siding;

F: A dwelling unit with a slab-on-grade floor, an accessible attic space, and stucco siding;

G: A dwelling unit with a floor raised above grade over an accessible crawl space, an accessible attic space, and plywood siding;

H: A dwelling unit with a floor raised above grade over an accessible crawl space, an accessible attic space, and stucco siding;

Accessible Crawl Space: A space between the floor and finished grade below in a residential building having a vertical clearance of at least thirty (30) inches from the top of the finished grade to the underside of the subfloor. A raised-above-grade floor which is not atop an accessible crawl space shall be considered to be a slab-on-grade floor.

Accessible Attic Space: A space between the roof and ceiling next
below in a residential building, such that the roof slope is not
less than two and one-half (2-1/2) feet in twelve feet and the
vertical clear height from the top of the bottom chord of the
truss or ceiling joist to the underside of the roof sheathing at
the roof ridge is at least thirty (30) inches.

Single-Family Residence Building Equivalence Factor: That number
which is calculated by multiplying six (6) by the total number of
units located in a multi-unit residential building which contains
a particular unit.

Multi-Unit Residence Building Opportunity Factor: That number
equal to the sum of the weather-exposed exterior surfaces of all
units located within a multi-unit residence building. For the
purpose of determining this factor, exterior surface means either
a roof, floor or outside wall, and no unit shall have more than
four (4) outside walls.

Multi-Unit Residence Building: Any residence building other than
a single-family detached residence building.

SECTION 4.   EXEMPTION

Any unit constructed pursuant to the City of Davis Energy Conservation
Performance Standards Ordinance No. 784, adopted October 15, 1975,
is specifically exempted from the amendment of the Housing Code which
is established by this ordinance.

SECTION 5.   AMENDMENT OF THE HOUSING CODE

The Housing Code for the City of Davis is hereby amended by the
following additions:

A.   SECTION 506(a): Energy Conservation Standards. Every unit
shall be provided with any ECT or any combination of ECT's selected
at the discretion of the owner of the unit, whose point value(s),
as specified below, at least equal(s) the standard applicable to
the unit.

Unit Type	ECT Points Required Per Unit	
	Electric Hot Water Heater	Gas Hot Water Heater
A	27	19
B	33	26
C	41	33
D	48	40
E	48	40
F	55	47
G	62	54
H	69	61

B.   SECTION 506(b):   Adjustment for Units Located in Multi-Unit Residence Buildings.   This section shall apply only to units located within a multi-unit residence building.   The Energy Conservation Standard specified in Section 506(a), which would otherwise be applicable to a unit subject to this section, shall be adjusted by multiplying it by the ratio of the single-family residence building equivalency factor to the multi-unit residence building opportunity factor applicable to the unit.

C.   SECTION 506(c):   ECT Point Values and Specifications.

   1.   Attic Insulation. Forty (40) points are granted for the installation of either cellulose, glass or mineral fiber insulation with a minimum thermal resistance rating of R-19 over the entire attic area of one unit.   Points shall be awarded for insulation installed prior to the effective date of this ordinance by multiplying 40 points by the ratio of the thermal resistance of the existing insulation to the thermal resistance of R-19 (R existing ÷ R19 x 40).

   2.   Exterior Window Shading. Thirty (30) points are granted for installing exterior window shading with a shading coefficient of 0.36 or less on all windows of one unit which are not oriented between 337.5°T to 022.5°T.

3. Solar Swimming Pool Heating. Twenty-eight (28) points are granted for each indirect thermal (active) collector solar water heating system which is used exclusively to heat a swimming pool. Eighteen (18) points are granted for each system which assists in the heating of a swimming pool. Each system shall comply with Title ____, Sections 2601-2608 of the California Administrative Code.

4. Solar-Assisted Domestic Water Heating. Twenty (20) points are granted for each integral collector/storage (breadbox) solar water heating system which serves a unit with electric water heating and six (6) points are granted for each system which serves a unit with gas water heating. Each system shall comply with Title ____, Sections 2601-2608 of the California Administrative Code.

5. Flat Roof Insulation. Ten (10) points are granted for the insulation of the entire flat roof area of one unit with cellulose fibers to a minimum thermal resistance of R-19. Points shall be awarded for insulation installed prior to the effective date of this ordinance by multiplying 10 points by the ratio of the thermal resistance of the existing insulation to the thermal resistance of R-19 (R existing ÷ R19 x 10).

6. Floor-Insulation. Eight (8) points are granted for the installation of either mineral or glass batts or layered, enclosed air-space, reflective metal foil insulation with a minimum thermal resistance of R-11 over the entire floor area of one unit. Points shall be awarded for insulation installed prior to the effective date of this ordinance by multiplying 8 points by the ratio of the thermal resistance of the existing insulation to the thermal resistance of R-11 (R existing ÷ R11 x 8).

7. Wall Insulation. Eight (8) points are granted for the insulation of all exterior walls of one unit with either urea formaldehyde synthetic foam or with cellulose fibers to a minimum thermal resistance of R-11. Points shall be awarded for insulation installed prior to the effective date of this ordinance by multiplying 8 points by the ratio

of the thermal resistance of the existing insulation to the thermal resistance of R-11 (R existing ÷ R11 x 8).

8. Low-Flow Showerhead. Eight (8) points are granted for each installation of a low-flow device in a showerhead supplied with hot water which is heated electrically, and four (4) points are granted for each installation of a device in a showerhead supplied with water heated by gas. The low-flow device shall have a maximum rated flow of three gallons per minute. The same respective number of points shall be granted for each showerhead which has a maximum rated flow of three gallons per minute, regardless of whether a low-flow device is installed.

9. Water Heater Insulation. Six (6) points are granted for each installation of a water heater insulation blanket with a minimum thermal resistance of R-6 in an electrically heated system. Two (2) points are granted for each R-6 insulation blanket installed in a gas heated system. The same respective number of points shall be granted for each existing water heater equipped with integral insulation with a minimum thermal resistance of R-12.

10. Solar-Assisted Hot Tub Heating. Four (4) points are granted for each integral collector/storage (breadbox) solar water heating system which serves a hot tub. Each system shall comply with Title ____, Sections 2601-2608 of the California Administrative Code.

11. Fluorescent Lights. Two (2) points are granted for each fluorescent lamp installed as a principal fixture. (Principal fixture supplying the major light source in a living or utility area of the unit.)

12. Door Weatherstripping. Two (2) points are granted for each door equipped with pressure-type neoprene gasket weatherstripping.

3

Northglenn

Wastes Into Resources

Water Reuse Program

Agricultural Land Preservation

Fertilizer From Waste Water

Earthworm Production

Northglenn is a small (pop. 32,000) bedroom city in the northern suburbs of Denver, Colorado. An outgrowth of rampaging land development that has accompanied Denver's own rapid growth, Northglenn is hemmed in on all sides. Twenty miles to the west, the peaks of the Rockies jut through the dense yellow smog that oozes across the plain from Denver, spreading a noxious cloud over the land.

Northglenn was built in the mid-1950s, a model community planned by the Perl-Mack Corporation. At the time, it was widely celebrated as an example of what a new city could become. The company sold lots and houses, but retained ownership of the profitable shopping mall with its sizeable amounts of commercial footage. Perl-Mack holds these properties today but the city as a whole is self governing. It was incorporated in 1969.

Water is scarce along the eastern slope of the Rockies, and there is a continuing battle over its use by agricultural interests on the one hand and spreading urban communities on the other. Under Colorado law, domestic water uses (urban) prevail over agricultural ones so that as the urban bedroom communities reach out across the plain from Denver, agricultural use declines and farmers close up shop. The precious water is diverted from farms to cities which fight tooth and nail for it. Land development, tax base, economy—all depend on acquiring sufficient amounts of the scarce water reserves.

From its inception, the water and sewerage facilities in Northglenn were provided to homeowners through individual contracts with a private utility firm, Northwest Utilities. Then, in the late 1950s, the next-door city of Thornton acquired Northwest Utilities and assumed the contracts. These contracts remain in force today, and the residents of Northglenn to all intents and purposes are dependent for water and sewerage, not on their own government, but on the government of a nearby city whose interests often are in competition with those of Northglenn.

To obtain water for its customers, the city of Thornton buys from different "ditch" companies. These companies are organized by farmers who have rights to water that runs off the Rockies to their land. But cities also can be stockholders in the ditch companies and exercise influence over their affairs. Thornton owns stock in one such ditch company, the Farmers Reservoir and Irrigation Company (FRICO).

Thornton, which by the 1970s had surrounded Northglenn on three sides and was apparently intent on continuing expansion out into the plain, needed a source of increasing water to meet the needs for land development. Thus, through condemnation proceedings, it sought to lay claim to a large supply of water held by FRICO. The proceeding was based on the theory that domestic uses had prior rights over agricultural uses. The additional water it sought from FRICO would be taken from farmers who were using it to irri-

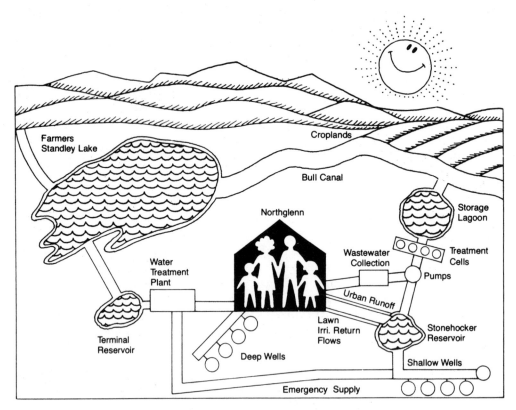

Northglenn Water Management Program.

$29,000,000 refinancing of Northglenn Water Project bonds
in offices of Goldman, Sachs & Co. in New York, Sept., 1978.
Former New York Mayor John Lindsay (center) and Stuart
Fuchs (left), both of Goldman, Sachs & Co., congratulate
Mayor Al Thomas. Looking on are City Manager Stan
Bender, City Clerk Shirley Whitten and Director of Natural
Resources, Richard Lundahl.

gate 40,000 acres of land. It was a clear battle between urban and agricultural interests. Thornton's move incurred the wrath of the farmers, who had seen their land and water steadily eroded by expanding cities. Thus to counter Thornton, agricultural interests sought unsuccessfully to gain approval within the state legislature for measures that would slow urban claims to water. But Thornton wanted the water, for without it, the city's expansion could not continue, and in the battle for prestige, growth, tax base, etc., it would lose ground.

The residents and officials of Northglenn were worried by what they considered to be Thornton's fumbling efforts to obtain more water. Hemmed in on all sides, Northglenn itself had taken

a basic no-growth line. The most its population could grow would be 42,000. The city had no territorial ambition. Thus, on the issue of growth, it was headed on a collision course with Thornton.

Since Northglenn was built there had been little love lost between the two communities. Residents of Thornton, some of whom lived in poorly constructed homes, looked with envy on their neighbors ensconced in lovely new homes in Northglenn. Those that could afford to make a switch sold and moved to the new city. Others, who lived in brick homes built on unstable clay soil, were not so lucky. Their homes gradually deteriorated and were unsalable. They were stuck in Thornton, and watched with envy as the new city took shape. So there may have been certain relish with which the city of Thornton held fast to the water and sewer lines of the upstart neighbors in Northglenn. Whatever the reason, Thornton consistently refused to sell Northglenn the lines to its own sewer and water system.

Then, during the early 1970s, the Denver Council of Regional Governments, a body charged with planning a coherent land and water use policy for the Denver metropolitan region, published a report that revealed for the first time that Thornton did not have requisite water supply to meet its current demands. This excited the residents of Northglenn. If Thornton did not have available supplies of water, then the city would have to buy expensive water on the open market (probably importing water from the western slope of the Rockies through a canal drilled into the mountains). Sewage was another problem. Northglenn and Thornton along with other communities discharged sewage to a Denver municipal sewage treatment plant. That plant did not provide adequate treatment, and there were ominous reports of nitrites and nitrates beginning

to appear in some of the water supply of both Northglenn and Thornton. The pollutants apparently had infiltrated underground acquifers which fed deep wells used as a partial source of water supply. A proposed, much improved regional sewage treatment plant for Denver would mean higher sewerage charges, and as with all of the advanced sewage treatment plants, there was no real assurance it would work. All of these factors helped to persuade officials of Northglenn that they must act to secure their own supply of water and arrange for sewage treatment.

Northglenn began to push harder on Thornton to sell it the sewage and water lines in the city. It then employed the engineering firm of Sheaffer & Roland, Inc., of Chicago. This firm was expert in handling wastewater schemes, and had devised the plan for Muskegon, Michigan whereby sewage effluent was pumped back on land and used as a fertilizer. Together Northglenn and the engineers began to lay out an ambitious program that would both provide water for the city, and in the process, provide farmers with continued backing so that they would remain on the land.

The Northglenn Plan

As the snow melts in the Rockies, water flows down into Clear Creek. Currently the waters of this creek are diverted and stored by, among others, FRICO at Lake Standley, about 25 miles West of Denver, for later domestic or agricultural use by the members.

(FRICO is the Farmers Reservoir and Irrigation Company.) FRICO has the right to divert certain of Clear Creek's waters because of rights long ago attached to members' individual landholdings.

It works like this: If a farmer-member

Above right. *Church Ditch
is a 26-mile long,
man-made earthen canal
which delivers water from
Clear Creek upstream of
Golden, Colorado to about
200 users.*
Above left. *Bull Canal is
owned by FRICO and is
the principal delivery
system for Standley Lake
water. Much water is lost
(25 to 35 percent) through
evapotranspiration with
this type of ditch. The
four-way agreement
will result in the entire
Bull Canal Delivery System
being lined with concrete
to virtually eliminate water
losses.* Left. *Thompson
Ditch, also owned by
Northglenn, is used to
deliver water from Big Dry
Creek to farmers.*

of FRICO bought or inherited land that was settled in earlier times, those land-holdings might well carry with them water rights to a certain portion of Clear Creek's annual flow. Indeed, these rights might specify how much and at what times of the year the particular farmer could take up the water.

When individual farmers banded together and formed a ditch company the members, in essence, agreed to exercise these water rights through the ditch company. Normally FRICO's members would draw down water from Standley Lake via the Bull Canal, a primary irrigation ditch. Once the water was used, it was to all intents and purposes gone for good.

Under the proposed plan, a portion of the water from Standley Lake would no longer flow directly to the farmers. Rather, the water would be piped first to Northglenn for municipal use and then recycled for agricultural uses. Storm and wastewater would be collected, treated, stored and given back to the farmers for irrigation purposes. About 60 percent of the water borrowed in this manner from the FRICO reservoir and used by the city could be returned. The other 40 percent would be obtained from deep wells and storm runoff. For use of the water, Northglenn would pay FRICO 10 percent interest, payable in water, not money. If, for instance, the city borrowed 5,000 acre-feet of water, it would return to the farmers 5,000 acre-feet plus 10 percent or 500 acre-feet for a total of 5,500 acre-feet.

Ths water from Standley Lake would be piped to a Northglenn treatment plant via a 7.5 mile, 36-inch pipeline. The water would be metered as it leaves the lake dam in order to record the exact amount diverted. This pipeline would be sufficient to provide peak water demand for Northglenn's anticipated maximum population—42,500. Just in case this line is damaged and put out of service, the city would construct a reserve pipeline from a well field near the South Platte River.

Before the water from Standley Lake was introduced into the municipal system, it would be treated in a plant to be constructed in the northwest corner of the city. The proposed treatment facility would meet standards set both by the Colorado Department of Health and by the federal government under the Safe Drinking Water Act. Northglenn expects to surpass the standards.

After it is treated, the water would be stored in municipal reservoirs. This storage would be sufficient to provide adequate supplies for peak needs and fire protection. The storage area would be elevated so that a minimum amount of pumping would be required to send water through the mains. And since the original Northglenn water lines were designed to move water from east to west—the opposite direction from the new flow—the city would build new pipelines to maintain even pressure throughout the city.

Under the agreement, all the water borrowed from FRICO plus 10 percent must be returned to the farmers. Since 40 percent of the water taken from Standley would be lost, where would Northglenn obtain the requisite amount of make-up water?

After extensive engineering analysis,

the city proposes to make up the water in a variety of different ways. It plans to produce 2300 acre-feet of high quality water from wells drilled into acquifers lying far below the earth's surface. That water could become an integral part of Northglenn's water supply. Another set of wells sunk into shallow alluvial fields nearby would be another source of water, although of somewhat less quality. After treatment it could either be pumped into the Northglenn system, or sent directly to the farmers for agricultural use.

Then, the city proposes to capture storm run off waters and store them along with water from some of the wells in a new reservoir. Finally the city would use the lower quality well water for irrigating public lawns and other open space, thereby saving the high quality water borrowed from the farmers. And it would attempt to recover waters used in irrigation within the

city, i.e., water for lawn sprinkling and so forth.

The heart of the Northglenn plan lies in its program for handling wastewater in such a way that properly treated sewage effluent could be returned to the land. This system would work as follows:

Wastewater would be conveyed through existing sewer lines to a central pumping station with a capacity of 9.6 million gallons per day. From there the water would be transmitted by pipeline to a treatment facility located adjacent to the winter storage reservoir. The treatment would be somewhat better than secondary treatment. Use of aerated lagoons would ensure removal of harmful bacteriological organisms and suspended organic and inorganic solids. The city says, "State of the art technology can effectively eliminate both aesthetic objections and health

Comparison of Untreated Northglenn Sanitary Wastewater with Final Treated Effluent

Parameters	Units	Untreated Wastewater	Aerated Lagoon Effluent	Renovated Water Discharged From Storage Lagoon
BOD_5[1]	mg/l	175	40	10
Suspended Solids	mg/l	175	52	25
Nitrogen	mg/l	30	25	20
Phosphorus	mg/l	7	6	5
Fecal Coliform Organisms	#/100ml	1,000,000	200,000	200

[1]BOD_5 is quantity of biochemical oxygen demanding organics.

hazards that are posed to man and livestock. The resulting water quality will surpass all applicable health standards, and will be perfectly suited for agricultural purposes."

Following treatment the water would be retained in the winter storage reservoir until the farmers need it. With a designed capacity of 3300 acre-feet, the reservoir would be capable of storing Northglenn's sanitary wastewater flows for the nine month period, running from September through May. The reservoir also would serve to provide additional treatment by providing further opportunity for stabilization and aeration.

While Northglenn is a relatively small community situated within the overall Denver area, nonetheless its water reuse scheme can have several important and different environmental effects.

There is, of course, concern over application of treated municipal wastewater, much of it sewage, to agricultural land. In their report, the engineers say the following:

"Application of treated municipal wastewater to agricultural land raises questions about the effects of possible toxic substances and pathogens potentially present in the wastewater. The fact that Northglenn is principally a residential community makes it highly unlikely that significant quantities of toxic substances will be found in the wastewater. Laboratory analysis of Northglenn's effluent have also conformed that heavy metals are not present in any significant amounts. A strong industrial waste control ordinance, coupled with a continuous monitoring program to detect possible toxic substances, will be implemented to prevent the occurrence of health related problems in the future.

"The insignificant amounts of toxic substances identified in Northglenn's effluent indicates that there is very little basis for concern about the accumulation of toxic substances in soils or crops. However, in order to ensure that problems do not arise in the future, continuous monitoring of water quality, crops, and soils will be carried out."

Benefits from Northglenn's reuse program accrue to urban and agricultural interests alike. Principal urban benefits are an inexpensive supply of high quality water and substantially reduced wastewater treatment costs. Principal agricultural benefits include conservation of precious irrigation water supplies and added nutrient value of the treated effluent. Hopefully the added nutrient value of the water may allow farmers to reduce the amounts of chemical fertilizers they now employ. Of course, the most significant benefit is shared by farmers and city-dwellers alike: In an age of soaring populations and shrinking food supplies, *essential agricultural land will be preserved in production.*

Looked at another way, the Northglenn plan is one measure for shaping and controlling urban growth. Since 1940, Denver has been a rapidly growing metropolitan area. From 1940 to 1970, the population increased at a rate of from three to 4.6 percent a year. Between 1970 and 1975 the rate was 3.7 percent a year. While the city of Denver has 56 percent of the region's jobs, only 36 percent of the population resides within Denver proper. Most of the pressure to house the workers is occurring in suburban cities and counties.

Colorado Governor's office, May 4th, 1979. Principals after signing the agreement which drops all water condemnation suits pending against FRICO and ushers in a new era of cooperation are, from left to right: Adolph Bohlander, president of FRICO; Northglenn Mayor Alvin B. Thomas; Governor Richard D. Lamm; Westminster Mayor Vi June and Thornton Mayor Tony Richter.

Adams (home of Northglenn) is one of three counties receiving the bulk of the population growth. Urban sprawl is expected to continue with a 60 percent population increase for the region during the 25 year period from 1975 to the year 2000. According to a regional environmental impact statement prepared by the federal EPA, this trend will result in increasing conversion of agricultural land to urban uses, and the decline in recreational or park lands.

But the Northglenn plan can result in shaping, even containing growth. In essence existing open space will be used for tertiary treatment of city-generated sewage effluent. Thus, in terms of urban planning those spaces are committed to non-urban uses. Open space becomes a real, viable part of urban planning. Parks also can be incorporated into this setting.

By providing an alternative to the condemnation of agricultural water, millions of dollars worth of direct and indirect costs have been avoided by

Northglenn. Condemnation or direct acquisition of a water supply for a city of Northglenn's size would cost, according to the engineers, between $6 and $9 million. Coupled with the loss of farm investments, jobs and crop incomes, the costs of condemnation would be staggering. The ripple effect from these losses would have a devastating impact on the urban economy as well.

Clean water is another dividend to be reaped from the project. Low-cost secondary treatment of wastewater, followed by land application, guarantees that 1985 federal water quality goals will be met at a substantial savings over the cost of conventional treatment methods.

There are other more subtle effects. The current water quality of the South Platte River, into which the main Denver sewage treatment plant pours its wastes is poor. In fact, the South Platte is little more than an open sewer. Sixty-to-seventy percent of the river flow during the winter and 40 percent during the remainder of the year is sewage effluent from the Denver plant. Under its proposed scheme, Northglenn will ease the load now being pumped into the Denver plant. Indeed its wastewater will be exchanged for fresh water.

The Northglenn water management program also will improve the air quality of the region. Denver has a severe air pollution problem, and cannot meet standards for ozone, particulates and carbon monoxide. Improved air quality is achieved in two ways, as the result of preserving 80,000 acres of farmland. First, about 40,000 acres of

land will be maintained in highly productive agricultural use. The vegetation and the soils of the land will act as a sink for the air pollutants generated from nearby urban areas.

Second the land will not be converted to low density residential development. Low density residential developments encourage widespread use of the automobile which in Denver as elsewhere is the largest contributor to air pollution. If the lands in question were converted to residential lots, automobile usage by the residents is estimated to be 98 miles per day or 260 percent of the usage for a similar residence located in the urban service area. It will also encourage higher urban densities to improve the feasibility of other transportation control measures in designated urban service areas. These reductions in vehicle usage will further reduce the generation of air pollutants from the automobile.

The project should result in several different sorts of savings in terms of energy. The Denver metropolitan region contains 57 percent of the state's population, but is responsible for 64-68 percent of its energy consumption. About three quarters of the region's consumption of petroleum products is for transportation, compared to the national average of 50 percent. Natural gas supplies 41 percent of the Denver region's energy needs.

Within five years, natural gas shortfalls are expected to be 15-20 percent. That will hurt rural areas especially hard since they are dependent on liquid propane and nitrogen fertilizer.

Both are made from natural gas. This situation, it is argued, will result in increasing reliance on coal-fired power plants, with a concomitant increase in air pollution, and increased water demand for mining and processing.

Wastewater treatment plants consume energy in the manufacture and transportation of chemicals. Because land treatment systems do not employ chemicals to achieve the desired levels of treatment, the overall energy use of such a system can be less than one half of the entire use of an advanced waste treatment plant. And, of course, it can result in reduced need for manufactured fertilizers in irrigated areas. Energy is further conserved when these petrochemically derived fertilizers do not have to be manufactured, transported and applied to the crops.

Since the Denver area is expected to experience energy shortages over the next several years, the Northglenn water reuse system amounts to an important, structural step towards energy conservation.

Beyond these widescale and generalized potential energy savings, Northglenn has begun to develop plans which would result in putting waste, both animal and human sewage, to work in creating energy.

Within the city itself, a dairy farm and an adjacent public school have experienced substantial pollution problems. The dairy farm has a backed-up holding pond, full of smelly wastewater from the cows. The school puts its sewage into a septic area, which has backed up onto open land, creating the effect of an open sewer. The city proposes to har-

ness the wastes from both dairy and school for the production of methane gas, electricity and sludge in commercial quantities.

The farm, Karl's Farm Dairy, milks up to 400 cows, and has difficulty in disposing of both manure and wastewater from milking operations. The manure from barns and lots is scraped up and hauled to a field where it eventually is sold off at 50 cents a ton. The milking parlor and bottling operation use up to 12,000 gallons of water a day for cleaning and flushing. The wastewater is collected in a basin adjacent to the main building and from there drained into a holding pond. From this pond, the effluent is pumped to a tank trailer and spread on the 60 acre pasture used for dry cows.

But this process is both costly and inefficient. The holding pond is often allowed to overflow since the winter snow makes spreading difficult.

Meanwhile, at nearby East Lake School 4,500 gallons of wastewater from 275 students, teachers and workers drains into a septic field, which is full, and backs up onto open land.

Under a plan developed by the city's consulting engineers, manure from the barns and lots will be scraped into a centrally located manure collection sump, and from there pumped into a digester. At the same time, wastewater from the school will be pumped from the school to the manure collection sump, mixed with the cattle manure. Eventually the combined wastes of school and dairy will be pumped into a digester.

This digester will provide the

anaerobic digestion of the water, pathogen control, odor control, and produce three acre-feet of water per year for reuse. The sludge will be stored in an effluent holding pond from which it will be pumped to tank trucks, or onto Karl's farm irrigation system, and used to fertilize the fields.

The manure from Karl's Farm Dairy will provide sludge containing approximately five times the quantity of nitrogen required for his 60 acres. The City of Northglenn will use the remainder on playgrounds and parks.

As a result, the wastes of both school and dairy will be turned into methane gas, which in turn, will be used to create electricity for the farm. Heat produced as a byproduct of the digester operation can be used to pre-heat the feedwater lines. Excess gas can be used to create hot water in the dairy. For its part, the school eliminates pollution without costly pumping of waste through pipelines to sewage treatment facilities. The city obtains fertilizer for its park.

The Karl's Farm digester scheme is a pilot project that could be used elsewhere around Northglenn. In addition, Northglenn has been considering an intriguing idea: Harnessing excess wastes from Karl's Farm and other parts of the city in the large scale production of earthworms and earthworm eggs for sale as a protein supplement to animal and fish feed.

The idea, developed by Jim McNelly, a young environmentalist who lives nearby, is roughly as follows:

For some time, the city has been attempting to collect grass clippings from lawns, composting them on a big empty lot outside town. The compost then would be sold. McNelly now wants to take the grass clippings, which over the course of a year amount to many thousands of tons, and combine them with surplus manure from the dairy-school project. The combined manure, wastewater effluent and grass would be fed into a digester, along with shredded newspaper also collected from Northglenn residents.

The watery mixture would then be fed to hundreds of thousands, indeed, millions of earthworms. They would prosper in the muck. The production of worms might well produce considerable revenue for the city if sold within the Denver area, simply for gardens and small farming. (This prospect is less than certain because the earthworm market has been flooded with get-rich-quick worm-growing schemes. As a result, there is a surfeit of earthworms in certain parts of the country.)

McNelly, however, is less interested in producing earthworms for sale than he is in developing a scheme for massive production of earthworm eggs. Eggs are tiny and lightweight, and hence can be shipped cheaply in sizeable quantities. Moreover, they can be frozen and stored against poor market conditions. If he can produce enough eggs, quickly and inexpensively, McNelly believes Northglenn could become a factor in supplying protein in the form of earthworm eggs to the livestock industry for feed. The earthworm eggs, McNelly believes, would compete successfully against other protein sources, such as fish and other animal sources. Or more suitably, earthworm eggs could become feed for

Table 1
Daily Energy Available From 400 Cows

Season	Manure $\left(\dfrac{lbs}{day}\right)$	Straw $\left(\dfrac{lbs}{day}\right)$	Biogas Production $\left(\dfrac{BTU}{day} \times 10^6\right)$	Potential Energy From Biogas		Karl's Farm Dairy Usage	
				Electrical (kw)	Waste Heat $\left(\dfrac{BTU}{day} \times 10^6\right)$	Electrical (kw)	Gas $\left(\dfrac{BTU}{day} \times 10^6\right)$
Summer	36,800	-	12.8	53[a]	3.2	42	7.7[b]
Winter	36,800	2,000	17.8[c]	73[a]	4.5	42	10.2[b]

[a] Assumes maximum electricity production. Heat may be produced by burning gas directly, at the expense of electricity production.

[b] Heat gained from gas is approximately 65% of this figure.

[c] The fact that straw is weighed dry and is 80% cellulose accounts for the seemingly large increase in biogas production. The manure consists of 13% solids; the rest is water.

Table 2
Yearly Energy Benefits From Biogas Production

	300 Cow Operation		400 Cow Operation	
	Gas (BTU x 10^6)	Value ($)	Gas (BTU x 10^6)	Value ($)
1. Electricity[a]	3,631	12,600[d]	3,631	12,600[a]
2. Waste Heat to Preheat Water[b]	905	2,050	905	2,050
3. Gas to Heat Boiler Water[c]	530	780	886	1,300
	5,066	15,430	5,422	15,950

[a] Assumes electricity cost is $0.035 KWH or $3.47 per million BTU's at 30% engine/generator efficiency. This takes advantage of the fact that about 13% of the energy must come from diesel fuel.

[b] Assumes 25% of engine heat recovered; valued at $2.26 per million BTU's.

[c] Assumes 65% efficiency when burned; valued at $1.47 per million BTU's.

[d] Karl's Farm Dairy currently uses $12,600 worth of electricity. As electrical needs increase, this value and Item 2 would increase at the expense of Item 3.

Table 3
Summary of Annual Benefits

	300 Cow Operation ($)	400 Cow Operation ($)
Benefits to Farm		
1. Reduction in purchase of electricity	$12,600	$12,600
2. Reduction in purchase of natural gas[a]	2,050	2,050
3. Reduction in purchase of natural gas[b]	780	1,300
4. Reduction of manpower	9,000	11,000
5. Reduction of equipment operation costs	9,000	11,000
6. Sale of fertilizer	(3,000)	(4,000)
7. Elimination of pollution	-	-
8. Elimination of odor	-	-
Sub Total	$30,430	$33,950
Benefits to School		
1. Elimination of pipeline ($30,000 @ 20 years)	$ 3,000	$ 3,000
2. Elimination of need to pump wastes (power & maintenance)	300	300
3. Elimination of sewage treatment fees	1,100	1,100
4. Elimination of pollution	-	-
5. Elimination of odor	-	-
Sub Total	$ 4,400	$ 4,400
Benefits to City		
1. Fertilizer supply for parks	$ 7,200	$ 9,600
Total Benefits	$42,030	$47,950

[a] *Due to waste heat*
[b] *Due to direct burning of biogas*

fish. And that opens up the prospects for another business for Northglenn in the future.

All of this, it must be emphasized, is speculative, but McNelly's ideas have been intriguing enough for him to produce a study of what he calls a "Wormglenn," or earthworm egg factory.

Northglenn Documents

Contracting a Rural — Urban Link
— Water for People and Crops —

AGREEMENT

THIS AGREEMENT, made and entered into this 2nd day of
September, 1976, by and between The Farmers Reservoir and Irrigation
Company, hereinafter referred to as FRICO, and the City of Northglenn,
a municipal corporation existing under the laws of the State of
Colorado, hereinafter referred to as Northglenn, Witnesseth:

WHEREAS the parties recognize that maintenance of existing
rural-urban linkages is essential to sustaining a desirable
quality of life in both the rural and urban sectors; and

WHEREAS the parties seek to work cooperatively in an effort
to strengthen and enhance these rural-urban linkages for their
mutual benefit; and

WHEREAS a majority of the shareholders of The Farmers Reservoir
and Irrigation Company authorized and approved the concept of a
water exchange as set forth in this Agreement by their vote at a
special shareholders meeting held on August 24, 1976;

NOW THEREFORE FRICO for and in consideration of the delivery to FRICO by Northglenn of that additional amount of water which totals not less than ten percent (10%) of the water delivered by FRICO to Northglenn as provided herein but not less than 500 acre-feet of water and 1500 acre-feet of storage space furnished FRICO by Northglenn during each of the years in which this Agreement is operative, FRICO, on an exchange of water basis, agrees to supply Northglenn (from Standley Lake operated and controlled by FRICO) sufficient water on an annual basis for the use of Northglenn as hereinafter provided, but, subject however, to all of the terms and provisions set forth herein below:

1.   The amount of water to be exchanged annually pursuant to this Agreement shall be based upon Northglenn's dry year demand for water in light of existing and projected population figures for the City. For the purpose of illustration, the dry year demand for the present population of approximately 35,000 would require the annual diversion of 6125 acre-feet; a population of 40,000 would require 7148 acre-feet; and the maximum population projected for Northglenn of 48,000 would require the annual diversion of 7785 acre-feet. It is expressly covenanted and agreed, however, that FRICO incurs no obligation to provide water to Northglenn beyond its own physical capacity to do so. Notwithstanding any provision in this paragraph to the contrary, FRICO shall not be obligated to retain any water in Standley Lake for Northglenn beyond that amount of water which Northglenn can immediately replace for use by FRICO stockholders.

2.   Northglenn at its sole expense will obtain Water Court approval of its plan which is that following beneficial application of the water delivered to Northglenn by FRICO pursuant to this agreement, Northglenn at its sole expense will collect the water, treat it in accordance with FRICO's specifications, store it and transmit it back to the FRICO irrigation network for delivery to FRICO stockholders.

3.   Northglenn, pursuant to directions from FRICO, will return all water exchanged pursuant to this agreement acre-foot per acre-foot to the FRICO system, via transmission facilities to be constructed by Northglenn. Net loss to the water supply occasioned by in-city consumption will be made up by Northglenn from direct flow and underground rights which Northglenn pres-

ently owns or will acquire for that express purpose. Northglenn may place water into storage in the Bull Canal storage facility or Northglenn Reservoir during times of a free river to supplement FRICO's supply, but only as approved by FRICO. The Bull Canal storage facility referred to in this paragraph shall be constructed at the sole expense of Northglenn and shall be in operating condition prior to the time when FRICO is required to exchange any water with Northglenn.

4. If, as a result of the multiple use of water which is contemplated by this Agreement, FRICO's priority rights to the use of water are threatened with imminent curtailment by a court or other competent authority, then FRICO shall be released from any obligation to exchange water with Northglenn. At such time as Northglenn has resolved any such problems to the satisfaction of FRICO, the water exchange contemplated herein shall be resumed, and the obligations of the parties under the contract shall be continued.

5. FRICO shall remain free from any obligation to divert water to Northglenn until such time as Northglenn has completed the construction of all necessary and related collection, storage, treatment, and transmission facilities, and has secured a decree from a court of competent jurisdiction for sufficient direct flow, underground, and storage rights to satisfy the obligations which it incurs under this Agreement, and further has secured from the Water Court, Water Division No. 1, approval of this water exchange Agreement. Furthermore, FRICO remains free from any obligation to deliver to Northglenn any water from Standley Lake at any time that Northglenn does not have in storage and available for immediate delivery to FRICO stockholders 500 acre-feet of water.

6. FRICO shall retain operational control over the release of water from Standley Lake. Before making any diversion to Northglenn, Frico may require that a minimum of 500 acre-feet of water in excess of the amount then being diverted to Northglenn be present storage, it being the intent of this provision to insure to FRICO that at no time will there be a deficit of water in storage.

7. As part of the consideration for this Agreement, any decrees for direct flow, underground, or storage rights presently

held by Northglenn or acquired by it in the future, in satisfaction of its obligations under this Agreement, may be utilized by FRICO for its own needs consistent with the terms of this Agreement.

8.   FRICO shall remain free from any obligation to divert water to Northglenn until such time as the total consideration to which FRICO is entitled under this Agreement is existing and capable of immediate implementation by FRICO. Furthermore, FRICO retains the right to discontinue the diversion of water to Northglenn in the event that Northglenn should fail to satisfy its obligations under this Agreement.

9.   It is expressly recognized and understood that the Cities of Thornton and Westminster have commenced condemnation actions against FRICO and its stockholders, describing Standley Lake and the water rights which are referred to in this Agreement, which actions are now pending in the District Court in and for Jefferson County, Colorado. Northglenn acknowledges that it makes this Agreement with full knowledge of the limitations and restrictions imposed upon FRICO by such pending condemnation actions.

10.   All administrative and legal expenses incurred pursuant to satisfying the terms and conditions of this Agreement shall be borne by Northglenn and in addition, Northglenn agrees to pay within thirty (30) days after billing from FRICO all administrative and legal expenses up to a maximum of $2,000 incurred by FRICO in the negotiation and preparation of this Agreement and related agreements. Northglenn further agrees, if requested in writing by FRICO to do so, to assume the defense of any litigation against FRICO as a consequence of its entering into this Agreement and to bear all costs directly associated with any such litigation holding FRICO harmless for the same. However, in any litigation commenced against FRICO as a consequence of its entering into this Agreement, counsel representing both FRICO and Northglenn shall have the right to participate.

11.   At no time, as a result of this Agreement, does Northglenn acquire any appropriative rights to the water provided by FRICO pursuant to this Agreement. It is expressly recognized and understood, however, that in order to effectuate the intent of the parties to this Agreement, the shareholders of the Standley Lake division of FRICO may desire to cause the creation of an

interest in their water rights in favor of the City of Northglenn.
Any agreement which may be entered into between the shareholders
and the City of Northglenn shall be consistent with the terms and
conditions of this Agreement and subsequent addendum thereto.

12.   It is expressly recognized and understood that this
Agreement shall in no way operate or be construed as a conveyance
or assignment of any water rights to Northglenn; rather Northglenn
agrees to contract with individual FRICO shareholders for the
purpose of securing the right to divert and use the water which
is contemplated to be exchanged pursuant to this Agreement.
During the period in which Northglenn is seeking to obtain the
contractual rights to the quantity of water required to satisfy
its needs as described in this Agreement, as well as after such
contractual rights have been secured, FRICO agrees that it will
take all steps necessary to insure the successful implementation
of the water exchange system contemplated and described in this
Agreement.

13.   If by March 2, 1977, Northglenn fails to provide FRICO
written evidence of its financial capability to construct or
acquire the water supply and all structures necessary to implement
this Agreement and the exchange of water contemplated, this
Agreement shall automatically terminate and be of no force and
effect excepting only as to those obligations of the parties incurred under the terms hereof prior to March 2, 1977, which prior
obligations shall remain binding upon the respective parties.

14.   Northglenn agrees to commence acquisition and construction of the facilities required to satisfy the terms and provisions
hereof by September 2, 1977 and the failure of Northglenn to
commence construction of facilities as herein provided shall
automatically terminate all of Northglenn's rights and privileges
hereunder.

15.   The term of this Agreement shall commence on September
2, 1976, and shall be in effect and binding upon the parties for
so long as Northglenn shall be in compliance with each of the
terms and conditions hereof.

16.   If Northglenn requests and agrees to bear all expenses
incident thereto, the parties shall immediately begin preparing an

addendum to this Agreement setting forth in all necessary detail the structural and operational principles of the proposed water exchange Agreement.

17. If, as a result of FRICO making and entering into this Agreement, any change in FRICO's tax status pursuant to Article X, Section 3, of the Colorado Constitution occurs to FRICO's disadvantage, then Northglenn agrees to assume all FRICO obligations arising directly from the change in its tax status. Provided, however, that should this provision be found to be void as contrary to law or as outside the scope of Northglenn's Home-Rule Authority, the illegality thereof shall not affect any other provision of this Agreement. Provided further that FRICO shall be released from any obligation under this Agreement in the event that Northglenn is prohibited by law from assuming FRICO's tax obligations as contemplated by this provision.

18. The parties will work in cooperation with one another and their respective supportive staffs to insure the design, construction, and operation of a system that will be mutually accommodating and will preserve the intent of the parties as evidenced by this Agreement.

IN WITNESS WHEREOF, the parties have executed the foregoing Agreement in duplicate original counterparts on the day first above written.

Financial Considerations of
Northglenn Water Management Program

After completion of a pre-design study, the citizens of Northglenn will be asked to authorize the issuance of bonds to finance the proposed project. The total cost of constructing the proposed water supply and sewage disposal system has been estimated at thirty-one million dollars. The cost to pay off the bonds and the annual operation and maintenance costs have been included in the estimated annual cost of the system.

The Northglenn Water Management Program has been designed to provide adequate water and sewer service to the ultimate City population of 42,500 people. Some money could be saved by phasing construction, but with the high inflation rates in the country it is in the best interest of the City to build the facilities needed for future conditions in the initial construction phase. Also, because it takes a minimum of three years to plan, design and build a utility system, the City would be starting the expansion design within a year after starting operation.

1. Cost per household under the Northglenn Program. The total cost to implement the Northglenn Water Management Program in $31,000,000 and the system will be fully operational by November, 1980. The project will be financed by General Obligation Bonds backed by the revenues of the utility system. Debt service will be $2,660,000 per year based on 25-year bonds and a 7 per cent annual interest rate. The water facilities annual operation and maintenance costs will be $874,000 and the wastewater facilities operation and maintenance costs will be $216,000 per year.

The total annual cost for the Northglenn Water Management Program will be $3,750,000. Based on the current number of taps, the total cost per household per year will be $375. As more taps are sold, the cost per household will drop because of connection fee revenues (tap fees), and because there are more taps to absorb the debt service cost and the fixed operation and maintenance costs.

2. Cost per household under the Thornton system. The total water and sewer cost for the average Northglenn household under the Thornton system is presently $220 per year. However, because of Thornton's offer of $21,000,000 for water rights of the three agricultural ditch companies they have filed condemnation actions against and because of the increased sewerage treatment costs to be expected when Northglenn sewerage is pumped over to the Westminster Big Dry Creek plant, the estimated average cost for water and sewer service will be $387 per household per year.

In addition to the above costs under the Thornton system, the treatment of urban runoff as required by Federal law will cost

Northglenn residents between 15 and 40 dollars per person per year. This means that the total cost for water and sewer service plus treatment of urban runoff under the Thornton system will range between $444 and $539 per household per year.

It is clear that it is in the best interest of the Citizens of Northglenn to implement the Northglenn Water Management Program which will provide fully adequate water and sewer service plus meet the requirements of Federal law with respect to treatment of urban runoff at a total annual cost of $375 per household per year. When the bonds are paid off, because this system will be adequate for all future needs, the annual charge for debt service of $2,660,000 can be dropped resulting in a savings of $181 per household per year.

4

Hartford

Food Policy Brings New Solutions

Urban Food Production

Community Energy Corporation

Job Creation

Energy Use Index

The City of Hartford, Connecticut (pop. 153,000) is squeezed into a 17-square-mile stretch along the Connecticut River, equidistant from New York and Boston.

The city was founded as a trading post by the Dutch in 1623; became a port and commercial center for the English, and in the 19th century emerged as the capital of the insurance industry and a major center for manufacture of machined metal products. It is the capital of the state.

Hartford currently enjoys an ambivalent status. It is a city of high unemployment and lingering recession, still sheltering the manufacturing workers whose factories moved South in search of cheaper labor and reduced taxes; but at the same time Hartford remains the center of a bustling insurance and service industry, most of whose employees commute to work from the suburbs. It contains within it both the seeds of the archetypal depressed New England city (Fall River) and the stirrings of a vigorous service center (Atlanta).

The costs of energy in the Northeast are high compared to what is spent in other parts of the nation. The price of energy becomes very much a part of the strained economy. In Hartford, energy is thus perceived as an important and related part of the political economy.

When Hartford first developed as a major manufacturing center in the middle of the last century, the nation's population, industrial markets, and sources of investment capital all were clustered around the Eastern seaboard. Now, of course, all that is changed. The South and West which a century ago were terminals for an inefficient transportation system with no markets, now offer important cost incentives as manufacturing centers. Energy is less expensive in the oil- and gas-rich Southwest.

Labor is less expensive in the South.

Hartford's own regional problems are compounded because the city also is at a competitive disadvantage with its own suburbs as a manufacturing location. Suburban industrial sites tend to be cheaper, larger and better connected to transport systems.

For Hartford, future growth lies in the non-manufacturing sector, especially insurance, which helped to build it as a commercial and industrial center a hundred years ago.

(The insurance industry currently employs 30,500 employees, some 23 percent of the workforce. Smaller service industries, including the health industry, account for 24 percent. Sixteen percent work for government. Fifteen percent are employed in wholesale or retail trade, and 10 percent in manufacturing.)

The insurance industry serves both national and international markets. Since it is not especially energy consumptive, it is not sensitive to regional energy costs. Its white collar work force of underwriters, data processors, and secretaries do not differ greatly in labor cost from region to region. Since non-manufacturing industries such as insurance can be housed in compact, high-rise buildings, land cost is minimized. In addition the close physical proximity of the different insurance firms and affiliates tends to be an attractive factor. That enables them to do business together, to jointly train personnel, jointly support specialized legal, accounting and advertising services.

But there are serious structural problems with all of this. Non-manufacturing industry tends to create job stratification: Growth in well-paying jobs of a technical or professional nature (computer programmer and underwriter, for example), most of which require a college degree. At the same time, it tends to create low-paying jobs (cleaning, food service, clerical, etc.).

The overall result is that large numbers of people in Hartford are under-employed or unemployed. Official unemployment figures for the city suggest that in mid-1978 6.7 percent of the labor force was out of work. Unofficial figures set the level at over 15 percent. Many of these people are black or Spanish-speaking. A good number came to the Hartford area to work tobacco fields, but that business is in decline, which throws them onto the highly stratified job market described above.

The problems of the region's under-employed are automatically the problems of the city of Hartford. Because of its low-priced housing and public housing facilities, unemployed or underemployed people come to live there.

Concentrations of underemployed people erode the tax base. Most of the city's multi-family dwellings which house Hartford's low income residents were not designed for low rent housing. When rental income falls short of operating expenses, one of the first items to be cut is property tax payments. Some landlords simply abandon the buildings rather than pay taxes.

This problem is compounded by the fact that much of Hartford's industrial tax base is being replaced by government, health and other tax-exempt institutions.

The effects reach into the city neighborhoods. A city study in 1978 said:

"The concentration of the region's underemployed in Hartford, and the ensuing municipal fiscal crisis, in turn, create a crisis for Hartford's neighborhoods. Neighborhood stability depends in part on income—income for residents who build its homes and support its stores, and income for the City which provides its schools, its police and fire protection, its parks and streets and social services. An income gap for Hartford residents and a fiscal crisis for the City of Hartford means abandoned housing and empty store fronts, unswept and unrepaired streets, crowded schools, and under-manned police and fire departments. Poverty, physical blight and inadequate municipal services demoralize neighborhood residents, and in doing so, sap the energies of the organizations which are the key to neighborhood health—political clubs, civic associations, community economic and housing development corporations, merchant associations, and parent/teacher organizations."

The only solutions to this crisis are to raise taxes and reduce services. The city has done both. Still, inflation reduces the purchasing power so that each year property taxes buy less services. As a result the city has to cut its labor force. That means reduction in police, fire protection and other essential services, fueling the cycle of neighborhood decay.

The long run solution is to change the stratified, job-short economy. The energy situation is viewed within Hartford as a major part of the solution, and a problem which must be attacked structurally at its roots.

There is no single political forum for debate over energy in Hartford. It is more nearly a stop and go political debate in the city, with efforts centered in the office of deputy mayor Nicholas Carbone.

A basic goal in energy is to reduce the cost of oil, gas and electricity, and in the process to find a way to employ the city's residents in a stable industry. This has led Hartford down several different roads.

What looks to be the most successful venture to date is the creation of an urban food plan which would put to work unemployed youngsters in growing food for the city's low income population. Since a great deal of energy is consumed in the production, processing and transportation of food this is an attack on energy costs, and at the same time, an effort to provide decent food at much less expensive prices.

In addition to the food program, the city has taken several other tacks.

Through the Community Services Administration, Hartford employs out-of-work youngsters in a winterization program. They are trained to help residents of the depressed parts of the city insulate homes.

Not long ago, the city created an organization called the Community Energy Corporation to train other out-of-work citizens so that they could be employed insulating homes of the middle class.

At the same time, the city sought to aid a neighborhood group in the evaluation and marketing of solar devices the

Beginning in the summer of 1977, representatives of a number of neighborhood, city and statewide organizations met to discuss how to meet the food-related needs of Hartford residents, especially low and moderate income people who comprise more than two-thirds of the city's population. Some of these organizations had experience in one or more aspects of the food delivery process; some had only an expressed interest in becoming more involved.

The City of Hartford, for its part, commissioned a major study intended to document effective self-help food programs operating in other cities and to outline the components of a comprehensive food system for Hartford. This report laid the groundwork for the cooperative effort which has become known as the Hartford Food System.

The Food System has received funding from city and federal agencies, area corporations and foundations and churches, in addition to generating some funds from its own programs.

The Hartford Food System, Inc., is an evolving network of self-help food programs designed to provide an opportunity for Hartford residents to participate directly in the production, distribution, and consumption of high quality, lower cost food. In its first year of existence, the Food System included a downtown farmers' market, community gardens, youth garden programs, and an urban agriculture school.

group wanted to produce.

The city also developed a computer program for conducting energy audits within the city government, and is now in the process of marketing this computer system to other cities and towns in the nation.

Finally, through the Metropolitan District Commission, the sanitation organization, there has been a move in the state legislature to permit the commission to undertake energy conservation programs, and to charge the cost of such programs to its customers.

Food

Hartford, like other communities in New England, imports 85 percent of its food, much of it by truck, which is especially expensive. As a result, food costs are six to 10 percent higher than the national average. Energy is a major component in food costs.

David Pimentel of Cornell has written:

"Energy use is essential to United States food production because of the food-land-population equation. The current high protein-calorie diet of the United States requires about 1.3 acres of cropland and three acres of pastureland per person. From our agricultural land, we must produce 4,800 kg of grain, 114 kg of meat, 129 kg of milk, 285 eggs, and a quantity of fruits and vegetables per person per year. Energy inputs in the form of fertilizers, pesticides, etc., are essential if this much food is to be produced from the available crop and pastureland in the United States.

"In the United States today with our high energy technology, about 350 hours of labor are devoted to producing, processing, and distributing food (assuming 17 percent of one's income is for food). The use of fossil energy in the United States high-energy intensive food system substitutes for the work of more than 79,000 man-hours or more than 30-times our current labor-input. (Note, about 330 gallons of fuel equivalents is employed to produce per capita food. As-

sume 20 percent efficiency of converting this fossil energy into work—hence 79,000 man-hours.)"

Rising food costs, of course, hit everyone. But in Hartford, where a disproportionate part of the population consists of lower-income people, food costs are a major problem. (A low income family in the city spends 30 percent of its money on food, compared to 21 percent for an upper income family.)

Not only are food costs going up, but availability of food for residents of inner city areas is a difficulty. Unlike upper-middle class people, inhabitants of the inner city cannot shop around for bargains simply because the food chains, which now control 57 percent of the food at retail, are pulling out of the inner city. They cite dilapidated stores, high insurance costs and security risks as reasons for the pullout.

In a report for the city, Catherine Lerza of Washington, D.C., urged establishment of an urban food system whereby unemployed youngsters could be employed growing food for the city's lower income population. She argued that a combination of increased community gardens, canning centers, farmers' markets, rooftop greenhouses and buying clubs, can substantially reduce the cost of food for the city's inhabitants, and at the same time, involve a relatively small capital cost. The summary points of her report follow:

Community Gardens

There now are 16 different community gardens within the city of Hartford with a combined total of 500 plots. The proposal would sharply increase the number of gardens by utilizing available public lands in towns adjacent to Hartford. To fertilize the plots, Hartford's wastes could be turned into compost.

Further, the city should seriously look into raising rabbits and poultry on sites adjacent to Hartford.

Unemployed youth could be hired with Labor Department funds to grow food for their own families and for those who need emergency food relief.

Lerza believes that it may well be possible to extend the growing season in a city such as Hartford through introduction of solar greenhouses, with cold frames as complements. Greenhouses last for 20 years and are not expensive: $5 per square foot when free-standing; $2.50 when attached to an existing building.

Food Distribution

Here the proposal urges a widescale adoption of buying clubs, coop stores, and coop warehouses. A key to the plan is to develop anew a relationship with the small farmers in the Hartford area,

luring them away from the big regional produce terminals outside the city, and getting them back into the city where they can sell through farmers' markets. Market days should be planned around arrival of welfare checks, and the markets should be certified to take food stamps.

Cost reductions achieved through the foregoing distribution setup can be enhanced through introduction of small community canneries. Estimates are that canning can result in food cost savings from $25 to $75 per household each year.

Lerza writes that the proposed food system "is based on maximizing household self-sufficiency in food production, processing and distribution. The system substitutes the labor of Hartford residents for the labor of Western farmworkers, cross-country truckers and local warehousers and supermarket checkers. The proposed food system is not a job-creation strategy. It is, in fact, exactly the opposite, a proposal to channel some of the surplus labor of underemployed Hartford residents into the provision of certain services to themselves.

"Viewed from a national perspective, the effort of the proposed food system is to take dollars and jobs out of the economy. Viewed from a local perspective, however, the proposed food system should increase the demand for regional produce. Three elements of the proposed food system—the buying clubs, the farmers' market and the food-processing center—could have a significant impact on local commercial agriculture, if large numbers of Hartford residents eventually participate in these programs."

All of this means preserving farmland. A bill before the Connecticut state legislature would subsidize farmers to hold prime agricultural land away from real estate development, while pledging its continued use to farming. The Hartford Board of Education, for its part, plans to establish a vocational agricultural high school, initially serving ninth to 12th grades. Eventually, the new school will accept students from the adult population, and attempt to recruit out-of-school teenage youth.

Education aside, one of the most difficult problems in agriculture is the large amount of money needed by new farmers to start up operations. The Hartford report makes this proposal:

"Truck farming, as most forms of small business operations, requires a large initial capital investment. There are several debt financing programs under the Federal Farm Credit System which make mortgages to farmers to purchase land and farm equipment. However, all of their programs require 10 to 20 percent equity participation by the farmer. Increasingly, the total amount of equity required prohibits new and young farmers from entering the market. A way needs to be devised to enable young and new farmers to generate equity through their own work. One possible public resource for this purpose is the Federal Public Service Employment Program, funded under Title VI of the Comprehensive Employment Training Act of 1974. The Public Service Employment program is administered locally by the Hartford Comprehensive Manpower Program. Public Service Employment funds, for example, could be used to pay the wages of new and young farmers working on a public "incubator" farm. The revenue generated by the sale of farm produce could be used to make capital grants to 'graduates' of the farm."

Summary of Costs and Benefits of Five Approaches to Food Cost Reduction (Per Household)

	Community Gardens	Solar Greenhouses	Buying Clubs	Canning Center	Farmers' Market
Annual Savings	$195	$195	$265	$25	$150
Annual Subsidy	20	15	15	25	5
Capital Requirements	minimal	1000	40	70	minimal

Stable markets are essential. Lerza suggests the basis for such a market may be found in the Board of Education, which now purchases $1.8 million of food annually for its school lunch program. In addition, the Community Renewal Team of Greater Hartford spends $360,000 each year for nutrition programs that serve the elderly and youngsters. Both these programs might divert some of the funds used for food purchases from contractors to buying from the new network of city-sponsored coops, community gardens, canneries, and from nearby small farmers.

Paying for Energy Conservation

In a city where many residents are poor the cost of energy conservation is exorbitant. In an effort to meet this problem, the Metropolitan District Commission, an organization which provides water and sewerage for several different communities, undertook to persuade the state legislature to broaden its charter so as to permit financing energy conservation programs. That would mean the Commission, which is dominated politically by the city of Hartford, would contract to perform the work, and then bill residents over a lengthy period of time via their water bills.

The legislation was favorably reported out of committee, but did not pass the legislature. (See Document entitled "Amendment to Metropolitan District Commission Charter").

The Energy Unit Index

Among the most important, and by all accounts successful, programs in the city is a scheme for rationalizing and making more efficient energy use in the city buildings.

In the past each municipal building was billed by the utilities or oil dealers on a separate account. In certain cases, buildings would receive two billings for electricity, two for oil. The process involved a great deal of time and immense amounts of paper work. Moreover, the billing procedures did not yield useful information to the city in terms of enabling Hartford to embark on energy conservation within its own structures.

Through the work of Fran Daniher, the city's energy conservation coordinator, a new system has gradually emerged. Based on energy conservation measures undertaken by two of the big Hartford insurance firms, Daniher persuaded the utilities and oil dealers to provide the city with a tape from their computers for each of the 180 different buildings. The computer tape, unlike the bill, included detailed analysis of energy used by each building. The information allowed the city to develop a basic measurement for comparison, the energy unit index. The index is the total BTUs per square feet per degree-day.

With the utility tapes in hand, the city worked on a computer program for comparisons. Major computer firms provide such programs, but they are difficult to use in a city such as Hartford where buildings are old and difficult to compare. With its own tapes, the city can instantaneously call up energy information on any of its buildings, compare the energy use against past use or with other buildings.

Hartford now wants to provide this sort of energy audit information for other institutions or municipalities who might need it, for example, schools, colleges, hospitals, etc. And the state of Connecticut has discussed the possibility of sub-contracting with the city to provide energy audit information for all non-profit institutions in the state.

Thus, the Hartford system could become a valuable source of income for the city, as well as a useful tool for other communities and institutions. For the provisioners of energy, it means bills get paid more quickly.

Solar Equipment Manufacturing

As part of its desire to create new jobs in a new, hopefully burgeoning industry, the city of Hartford contracted with the Upper Albany Community Organization, a neighborhood group, to conduct a study of the possibilities for manufacture of different sorts of solar appliances.

The resulting study proposed four different products: a science kit for schools incorporating a collector; a concentrator; a special sort of fluid; and a flat bed collector. It proposed a detailed scheme for a new organization, incorporating private and public sector interests in a new institution. A market analysis for the different products also was provided.

Subsequently the City of Hartford asked the Technical Development

Corporation in Boston to assess the UACO report, with its four products. Technical Development narrowed the product mix down to two major entries—the solar science kit and the concentrator. Both had good possibilities for securing fair share of a widening market.

A significant aspect of the report was its proposal for a new organization to engage in solar manufacture within the city. This organization would involve private and public sectors, with representation from the neighborhood group, the city, and private industry. The organization would be financed by public funds. The inventions themselves were mostly the work of a Hartford citizen.

The Community Energy Corporation

The idea behind the Community Energy Corporation was for the city to help create a private corporation which could bring together the interests of

both the city and private enterprise in the creation of new jobs in a new industry.

Essentially the idea was this: Unemployed youngsters who were taken up and trained through the Community Service Administration's weatherization programs could move along to further employment with the new Community Energy Corporation. This corporation would contract with the owners of various family units which predominate the Hartford housing market, for energy conservation services, i.e., audits, insulation, refurbishment, etc.

The objectives of the new corporation were set forth in a planning paper as follows:

"—to create good jobs for Hartford residents, paid for by the energy savings it achieves;
"—to reduce the burden of energy cost on those who can least afford it;

"—and similarly to reduce the burden of energy waste on the taxpayers."

Specific plans for the energy corporation are described in the Document entitled "Community Energy Corporation."

To date the Community Energy Corporation has not really taken off. In part that is because there is no clear market among the owners of the multi-family dwellings originally perceived to be wanting energy conservation. Probably this is due to the high cost and unknown results with certain types of insulation. Secondly, the corporation has not received federal funds because the government has balked at financing what appears to be a private corporation with funds meant to be spent for municipal purposes.

Hartford Documents

"Amendment to Metropolitan District Commission Charter"

State of Connecticut

Raised Committee Bill No. 574

Referred to Committee on REGULATED ACTIVITIES AND ENERGY

AN ACT AMENDING THE CHARTER OF THE METROPOLITAN DISTRICT COMMISSION.

Be it enacted by the Senate and House of Representatives in General Assembly Convened:

Section 1. Section 2 of number 511 of the special acts of 1929, as amended by number 327 of the special acts of 1931, is amended to read as follows:

Said district shall have within its territorial limits, except as hereinafter provided, the following powers and duties: (a) The layout, construction, maintenance, paving, repair, improvement, widening extension, alteration and discontinuance of public highways, streets, walks, bridges, viaducts and ways, street lighting and sprinkling, the removal of snow and ice and the establishment of street, building and veranda lines, provided the authority of said district shall include only such streets and highways as enter more than one of the towns of said district or shall form a boundary or part of a boundary between two or more of such towns, and have, from time to time, been designated and described or laid out by vote of the district board, or streets or highways existing or proposed, which are voluntarily turned over to said district by any town or city within said district acting through the duly constituted authority of any such town or city having authority to lay out highways and have been accepted by said district; (b) the layout, building, creation, maintenance, improvement, alteration, repair and discontinuance of sewers and sanitary systems and plants for the disposal of sewage, the collection and disposal of garbage and refuse, the construction of drains for water or sewage and the control and maintenance of all the foregoing in the public highways and elsewhere throughout the district, together with such control of the streams and water courses of said district as is necessary or convenient for the foregoing as hereinafter more particularly stated; (c) the creation, maintenance, extension, improvement, alteration, repair and operation of a water system including the impounding of water both within and without the territorial limits of said district, and the transmission and transportation of the same and the sale and delivery at retail or otherwise by means of a pipe system or otherwise; (d) THE CREATION AND OPERATION OF A COMPREHENSIVE ENERGY CONSERVATION SERVICE FOR PROPERTY OWNERS INCLUDING, BUT NOT LIMITED TO, THE MARKETING, INITIAL INSPECTION, MAKING OF RECOMMENDATIONS, CONSTRUCTION, INSTALLATION AND FINAL INSPECTION OF ENERGY CONSERVATION SERVICES, TECHNIQUES, MATERIAL AND EQUIPMENT WITHIN THE TERRITORIAL LIMITS OF SAID DISTRICT, THE CONTRACTING WITH OTHERS TO INSTALL SUCH MATERIAL AND EQUIPMENT AND THE SUPERVISION OF SUCH INSTALLATION TO MAKE BUILDINGS, DWELLINGS AND OTHER STRUCTURES MORE ENERGY EFFICIENT; (e) in connection with any of the foregoing functions, so far as may be necessary for the convenient carrying out of the same, said district shall have exclusive charge of regional planning and, so far as may be necessary for the convenient carrying out of all or any of the foregoing functions, engineering, control of finance, the right to lay and collect taxes, the right to borrow money and to pledge the credit of the district, as security therefore, the right to issue evidences of indebtedness for and in behalf of said district and such other necessary or convenient auxiliary and collateral functions as are hereinafter indicated, including the right to take property by right of eminent domain, the right to assess benefits and damages in the layout of any public improvement included within the scope of the powers herein granted and generally the powers granted to municipal corporations by the general statutes so far as may relate to functions hereby transferred.

Section 2.   Section 18 of number 511 of the special acts of 1929, as amended by number 285 of the special acts of 1949, is amended to read as follows:

The purposes for which such bonds, notes, or other certificates of debt may be issued and for which the avails thereof shall be used are: To meet the cost of public improvements AND SUCH OTHER IMPROVEMENTS authorized by the charter of the district; to raise funds in anticipation of a bond issue for the purpose of financing such improvements for a temporary period previous to the issue of such bonds; to raise funds in anticipation of taxes or in anticipation of water revenues estimated to be received by the issue of notes maturing in six months or less from date of issue; to redeem or refund outstanding bonds or other obligations of the district, not intending to include bonds or other obligations of the component towns not assumed under the provisions of this act; to meet the cost in whole or in part, including damages awarded, which the district is required to defray temporarily in connection with public improvements duly authorized where benefits assessed cannot be immediately collected, provided this authority shall be an alternative to and not a limitation of the power of the district board to provide for the issue of assessment certificates.

Section 3.   The Metropolitan District, in the performance of its duties to create and operate a comprehensive energy conservation service for property owners within the territorial limits of said district may implement a marketing plan, make inspections and recommendations to property owners concerning energy conservation services, techniques, material and equipment, construct and install, either directly or by contract, energy conservation material and equipment, supervise the provision of such services and the construction and installation of such material and equipment, receive and make payments for such energy conservation services and in general do any other act necessary or convenient for accomplishing the purpose of providing property owners within said district with energy conservation services.

Section 4.   The district may enter into contracts with property owners to provide energy conservation services and may file a copy of such contract or notice thereof with the town clerks of the town wherein such property is located. The cost of services provided, including inspection, consultation, recommendations and construction and installation of energy conservation material and equipment shall be secured by a lien upon the land and improvements benefitted thereby. A certificate of such lien describing the property on which such lien exists and the amount thereof shall be filed with the town clerk of the town within which such land is located. Such lien shall attach from the time such certificate is filed or from the time the provision of such services begins, whichever occurs first, but such lien shall not attach unless such certificate is filed within sixty days after completion of the provision of such service. Such lien shall be enforced in the manner provided by chapter 205 of the general statutes for the enforcement of municipal tax liens.

Section 5. The district board shall adopt ordinances and regulations concerning the provision of such services.

STATEMENT OF PURPOSE: To enable the metropolitan district commission to provide energy conservation services.

"The Community Energy Corporation"

The Community Energy Corporation is a non-profit Connecticut corporation, formed on behalf of and controlled with respect to broad policy by the City of Hartford, but professionally managed as a private enterprise. It will be accountable both to the conventional business criteria and balance sheet, as well as to the public-policy decisions of its City-appointed Board. Its objectives are to create good jobs for Hartford residents, paid for by the energy savings it achieves; to reduce the burden of energy cost on those who can least afford it; and similarly to reduce the burden of energy waste on the taxpayers. Its plans are summarized in the following paragraphs.

1. Three "markets" must be served:

    (a) Private homeowners who can afford to pay for conservation
         services but whose investment has been inhibited by a
         lack of trusted, comprehensive contractors and lack of
         access to financing arrangements that allow recovery of
         the investment out of future dollar savings. For these
         customers as well as the others, a high quality inte-
         grated service is planned, and final inspection to en-
         sure optimum savings for each home -- and a financing
         plan intended to keep monthly payments below monthly
         savings. The careful linking of responsible retrofit
         design and financing keyed to savings is essential if
         the homeowner is to be encouraged to optimize rather
         than limit his investment to simple insulation.

    (b) Public buildings -- schools, hospitals, municipal and
         State facilities, and others -- where the taxpayers'
         funds are daily wasted by inefficient and poorly-managed
         facilities and equipment. For these buildings, a more
         rationale investment of public funds is planned, in the
         scientific identification and correction of major sources
         of waste.

    (c) The poor in rented dwellings and their own homes who
         cannot afford either the cruel escalation of energy
         prices or the cost of conservation services. For these
         consumers, a fully subsidized program is planned, using
         City, State, and Federal resources.

2. The integrity and quality of CEC's work will be established
    at the beginning and maintained without compromise, as befits
    a public trust. The corporation has sought and received ex-
    pressions of support from all relevant City and State agencies,
    private industry, organized labor, and community advocates.
    It must, however, maintain its management independence within the
    confines of legitimate public policy.

    An important part of that policy is to seek the maximum
    energy saving (and job creation) potential consistent with
    the economic interests of the customers. Already the field
    is flooded with marginal producers offering fast savings and

doing work that is, at best, not properly tailored to the needs of each particular case and, at worst, misleading, destructive, or harmful to health and safety. In this time before standards are widely adopted and the costs and benefits of competing techniques fully understood, the existence of a publicly responsible comprehensive service stands as an essential public initiative. Each home or facility must be examined as a special case to determine the best mix and appropriate depth of conservation techniques. Even with high-quality work, conservation services and products are often ineffectively matched to the peculiar needs and potential of each individual building resulting in missed economic opportunities for the nation. Techniques for optimizing this match exist, however, and have been well documented in Federal and private work over several years. CEC's audit design is based on the best of this work and careful adaptations of its general principles to the Greater Hartford housing stock.

3. The employment generated by CEC activities will constitute a net economic gain and an advantage for all classes of workers. The corporation will employ skilled workers, CETA trainees, and professional subcontractors in its work. Initial employees will be recruited from experienced but presently unemployed workers with the skills necessary for successful installation and inspection work. At the same time, it will assign some of its CETA workers (88 have been requested) to on-the-job training with experienced community organization(s) operating under Federal subsidies to serve low-income markets. Conventional subcontractors will also be engaged, to bring in skills not practical for the company to hire full-time at the start and to absorb normal fluctuations in demand. A substantial amount of subcontracting is planned indefinitely, for these reasons and for the purpose of sharing the expanding market with private employers.

As the CETA workers demonstrate competitive productivity, they will become the major source of new employees for the corporation. They will have access to the most efficient and realistic training, in the form of closely-supervised work in the subsidized market funded by CSA, FEA, NERCOM, and the CETA wages. Their initial assignment (to community organizations experienced in "winterization" projects) thus

allows them to enter the primary labor market at the point
of competitive productivity, while insuring them the opportunity to contribute to their own communities. Their ad-
vancement, and the quality of the community organization's
work, will be monitored by the CEC inspectors, who, in all
cases, will be responsible for initial energy audits, speci-
fication of work to be done, and final inspection.

4. The CEC will be able to reach the intended three markets
    by virtue of these specialized arrangements and its public
    commitment to optimized service.

    (a) Through contract with the officially-designated
         grantee(s)of Federal subsidies, materials and
         supervisory costs will be covered for low-income
         residents. To these subsidies the City will add
         the number of CETA job slots necessary to maximize
         the impact of Federal expenditures, using CEC as
         the employer. The cost of energy audits and inspec-
         tion, performed by CEC, will be covered by the 10%
         non-labor costs allowed under CETA, the employment
         of some skilled but unemployed inspectors qualifying
         for CETA wages, and the availability (if needed)
         of Federal energy funds, through the State or directly
         granted. The number of low-income homes reached will
         be expanded by this relationship, through leveraging
         CEC's access to technical skills, additional Federal
         Aid, and working capital. In return, the subsidized
         operations provide a natural training experience for
         the new workers needed by the expanding CEC. This
         contract will also provide for worker recruitment,
         consumer education (vital to lasting energy conser-
         vation), and determination of consumer eligibility
         for subsidized work.

    (b) Public housing, State and City buildings, schools and
         other public facilities will be expected to contract
         with the CEC at competitive prices, for the comprehen-
         sive range of services it offers. The substantial
         public commitment to energy conservation -- exemplified
         in part by the formation of CEC -- suggests that this

market will be quite large although precise figures
are as yet unavailable. Since about half the work will
be subcontracted (but with initial and final inspection
work retained in the hands of CEC's skilled professionals),
private-sector contractors will share in the benefits of
this expanded market.

(c)   The private homeowner market is expected to respond
strongly to the combination of a publicly-endorsed
comprehensive service with favorable financing terms.
The President's tax credit proposal offers an additional
potential inducement.

The above plans have been developed in response to the dual
needs of energy conservation and new jobs. Their joint pursuit
by The Community Energy Corporation, publicly formed and guided
but professionally managed, is possible because of the combination
of dollar savings and Federal subsidies accessible only to such
a partnership. The resulting economic expansion is non-inflationary
because of the added economic value of saving energy that would
otherwise be wasted. It does not displace other workers or
compete with existing firms because it serves a new market;
indeed the introduction of public capital should stimulate a
general expansion of the industry, benefiting present employers
as well as making possible new ones. We believe a successful
enterprise of this design to constitute a prototype of national
significance.

5

Community Innovations

Using and Financing Renewable Energy Resources

Wind Power—Clayton, New Mexico

Wood Power—Burlington, Vermont

Energy Audits—Greensboro, North Carolina

Energy From Wastes—Ames, Iowa

Source Separation—Seattle, Washington

Finances—Small Businesses and Community Energy Corporations

Cities and towns across the nation are trying out different approaches for making use of renewable energy resources. In this section, we take a look at some of these various applications: Producing substantial amounts of electricity from wind in Clayton, New Mexico and from wood in Burlington, Vermont; Ames, Iowa has pioneered a system for making energy from garbage; and Greensboro, North Carolina set up an energy audit to involve citizens in energy planning.

At the same time, however, one of the major problems in the implementation of alternative energy systems is the cost involved. Also presented in this

section are several different approaches towards creating a financial system to facilitate change from fossil fuels to alternative energy: Seattle Trust & Savings initiated an energy conservation loan program at rates below the market; San Diego Federal Savings & Loan developed a method for extending home mortgages so as to facilitate solar retrofit installations; and a South Dakota community development corporation set up Weatherization Contractors, Inc.—specializing in providing insulation for homes—an example of public/private financing mechanisms in action.

Wind Power

CLAYTON, NEW MEXICO

In the flat, sleepy, cattle-country of northeast New Mexico stands a "space-age" style windmill, called a "wind turbine generator." The 100-foot-high tower with its 125-foot-diameter rotating twin blades abruptly breaks the homogeneity of the area's low, natural landscape.

The windmill, located in Clayton, New Mexico (pop. 4,200) was funded by the U.S. Department of Energy (DOE). It was designed, built and installed by NASA's Lewis Research Center in Cleveland, Ohio. Clayton was chosen as the first of three test-sites for experimental wind generators in the United States and Puerto Rico. At the time of completion in January, 1978, Clayton's was the only windmill in the world being utilized by a public utility company to generate electric power for a community.

Clayton was one of three towns with small, municipal utilities in competition for a windmill, and was chosen out of a field of 65 prospective sites. The wind turbine generates up to 200 kilowatts of electric power for the town, enough to power 60 homes, or provide on the average, 15 percent of the town's electric power. Clayton will continue to rely on oil and natural gas for about 86 percent of its power.

Clayton's windmill was built through the Federal Wind Energy Program, initiated in 1973 under the auspices of the National Science Foundation (NSF). The program was moved to the Energy Research and Development Administration (ERDA) in 1975, and then incorporated into the newly-formed DOE in 1977.

The purpose of this particular phase of the federal wind program is to assess the technical and economic feasibility of large wind energy systems interconnected with a conventional power plant, and used to provide electric power through existing utility lines. The three test sites chosen, (Clayton, Culebra Island, Puerto Rico, and Block Island, R.I.) give data from a variety of climates, topographies and energy use factors.

Though windpower is not yet economically competitive with conventional energy resources, such experiments are important steps towards making windpower—a clean, inexhaustible resource—viable on a community scale.

The cost to DOE for the wind turbine was about one million dollars, including the cost of research and monitoring equipment. Though no one, even in Clayton, is saying it is yet worth the money, "as far as most citizens are concerned the wind turbine is one of the most exciting things to happen in Clayton since outlaw Black Jack Ketchum was hanged in 1901," according to D. Ray Blakely, reporter for the *Union-County Leader* in Clayton.

The city's enthusiasm for the windmill was a major reason why Clayton was chosen over other communities, according to Lewis Research Center. Other factors include the high wind speeds there, and similarity of wind force to other areas of the Central United States. Also, Clayton's office of the National Weather Service is one of the few in the nation that has consistent wind records going back 40 years.

Clayton is located in the heart of New Mexico's ranching and farming country. It is a commercial center for the surrounding ranches and towns. But there is little industry to provide job opportunities for the townspeople. Clayton is no longer the prosperous shipping point for the Colorado and Southern Railroad it once was in the late 1800's. Today, that railroad rarely stops in Clayton.

Now, Clayton's windmill is having a tremendous effect on the isolated town. The huge windtower with its spinning blades can be seen for miles around. Thus, besides conserving energy, Claytonians are benefiting from increased tourism and commercial activity due to the wind machine in their midst.

Though the new wind turbine is a cause of great excitement in Clayton, New Mexico, wind generators are nothing new in the rural west. Many residents of Clayton grew up on farms equipped with small generators for family farming and household electric power. By the turn of the century, a significant windmill industry existed in the United States making wind a cheap source of electric power in rural areas. Until the establishment of the Rural Electrical Administration in 1930 which made federally subsidized, centrally generated electrical power available to farms, isolated premises could not be linked economically to the public supply networks.

Though one can still see old, broken windmills in the area around Clayton, and quite a few still operating to pump water for livestock, until recently, wind-generated power was considered a thing of the past.

Now that the price of fossil fuels has risen sharply, wind power is again being looked upon with great interest throughout the country. In Clayton, energy costs have risen fivefold since 1973. During much of 1977's harsh winter, the gas company was forced to curtail supplies to Clayton's power plant, forcing the town to truck diesel fuel from Amarillo, Texas at 47 cents per gallon.

Though the DOE-sponsored wind-turbine has not yet had a noticeable impact on consumer utility bills, the lure of greater energy self-sufficiency induced the town to apply for the program. In early 1976, then Clayton city attorney Alvin F. Jones heard of the ERDA-sponsored test program and urged the town leaders to develop a proposal. The suggestion was immediately met with great enthusiasm by the town's four-member city council, though no one entertained great optimism that Clayton would be successful.

Jones contacted the Southwest Research Institute in Santa Fe to conduct a preliminary feasibility study of

Clayton, New Mexico: 200kW Experimental Wind Turbine

Clayton's wind potential. The Institute's testing procedures found that Clayton receives winds of at least 8 miles per hour 90 percent of the time, while winds in excess of 28 mph blow 20 percent of the time. On the average, winds of 16 mph occur in the area. There is no wind in Clayton less than one percent of time. Thus, Clayton has the wind potential to make wind generation worthwhile.

In order to be eligible for the government-funded wind system, the city of Clayton was responsible for providing $500,000 in insurance, along with donating city-owned property for the site and an extension of the existing power lines to connect the wind generator with the Clayton power plant. Financial responsibility of the city includes general maintenance and operating costs.

Clayton's windmill began operating on January 28, 1978. During the initial two-year period, DOE will be carefully monitoring the equipment "during a typical operating situation." At the end of the two-year testing period, ownership of the generator will be assumed by the town. To prepare for that takeover, Clayton sent three staff members from the city's power plant to the Lewis Research Center in the fall of 1977 to learn how to operate the generator. At the end of May, 1978, after six months of operation, the windmill had successfully supplied more than 100,000 kilowatts of electric power to Clayton's city-owned utility.

The power output of a wind machine depends primarily on wind speed and the diameter of its blades. Clayton's windmill has two aluminum rotor blades that resemble airplane wings. From tip to tip, they span 125 feet.

Windpower generators operate at their rated capacity only when the wind is blowing at or above some minimum speed. The Clayton turbine produces 200 kilowatts of power at wind speeds between 18 and 34 mph, measured at 30 feet above ground level. The propeller like rotor that turns the blades responds automatically to changes in wind speed and direction. It starts to turn when the wind reaches 8 mph, and shuts off automatically when wind exceeds 34 mph. Within this range, a constant speed of 40 rpms is maintained by the control system which varies the pitch of the blades. This process is called "yawing."

Power produced by the machine feeds directly into Clayton's power grid. When it is operating, the generators at the power plant "sense" a decreased demand for conventional power and so burn less fuel. Typically, a wind generator operates at an overall load factor of 15 to 25 percent, thus producing only one-fourth the energy of a conventional plant with similar capacity. When operating at its "rated wind speed" of 19 mph, the windmill supplies 60 homes with full electric power.

DOE has equipped the Clayton test unit with a range of scientific instruments which monitor stress in the blades, the amount of "shaft bending," and the temperature of the bearings in the yaw system, along with other potential technical problems. Additionally, Clayton's weather service measures wind speed, direction and temperature.

During the first several months of operation, several minor problems developed. Small cracks appeared in the blades, which resulted in loud groaning noises. The blades were removed and sent back to Lewis Research Center for analysis of the problem and repairs. To keep it operating during that time, the blades designed for Clayton were replaced temporarily with those of another system. The original blades have since been returned to Clayton. Aside from that problem, the townspeople of Clayton are satisfied with operations of the machine, and consider it "pleasing to look at" as well.

At present, it is unlikely that individual communities can undertake to build sizeable wind energy systems without federal assistance. However, current scientific views on the future economic feasibility of windpower are optimistic. As early as 1973, a NSF/NASA study estimated that an annual output of 5.1×10^{15} BTUs of wind energy would be possible by the year 2000. That amount approaches total electrical demand in the United States in 1970, and represents an estimated 5 to 10 percent of our total energy needs in the year 2000.

Lockheed Corp. believes that by 1995, United States utilities could supply "up to 18 percent of the national demand for electricity through wind energy systems."

Generally, however, wind systems

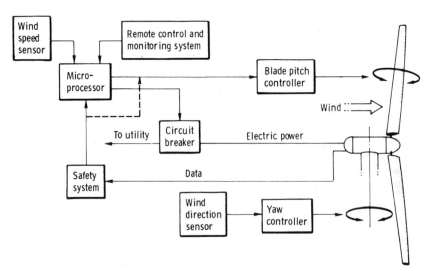

Simplified wind turbine control schematic.

are not yet competitive with conventional power systems outside of limited high-wind region applications. The most significant remaining barrier is the currently prohibitive cost of energy storage systems. Storage capacity is necessary to preclude the need for conventional back-up systems for use when the wind is not blowing. Some wind advocates argue that the solution may be giant windmill grids

that cover an area large enough to ensure that some wind power will always be available. However, this would have aesthetic and land-use drawbacks. A single machine might not occupy much space, but a string of large windmills would. If these problems can be overcome, energy from the wind will no doubt be looked upon with growing interest in future years.

Wood Power
BURLINGTON, VERMONT

Vermont, like most of New England, is far from the main sources of fuel. Oil and natural gas are in the South and Southwest. The nearest coal is in Appalachia. Transportation systems to facilitate import of fuels are deteriorating; railroads are run down, electric transmission lines lack interconnections; port facilities are non-existent for hauling fuels from abroad. Hence, costs—excluding environmental considerations—for importing fuel, whether from other parts of the United States or abroad, are high.

As for indigenous sources of energy, hydroelectric sites are limited. There has been ongoing discussion about harnessing tidal flows in the Bay of Fundy off the coast of Maine. Electricity produced by tides might ease the situation throughout New England, but the project is blocked for myriad political, technical and economic reasons.

But Vermont does possess large quantities of wood. Wood stoves always

have been common in the state. And, since the energy crisis, Vermont has become the center for a mushrooming wood stove industry, with small factories springing up everywhere. Energy-efficient stoves have been developed to produce heat and work has been done to rejuvenate the wood furnace.

Amidst all the excitement over rediscovering wood as an important source of fuel, the City of Burlington (pop. 40,000) which lies in the northeastern part of the state, has initiated an experiment in burning wood to generate electricity.

Burlington has a municipally owned electric utility. The Burlington Electric Department serves 15,000 customers a year with a peak load capacity of 60 megawatts. Right now Burlington's electric system imports most of its power. One-third of the electricity comes from the Power Authority of the State of New York, and from power projects along the St. Lawrence River and at Niagara Falls. Another one-third comes from the Vermont Yankee Nuclear Power plant. The remainder comes from the Department's three coal or oilburning plants, their gas turbine, and a coal-burning power plant in New Hampshire.

In October, 1977, the municipal utility company in Burlington succeeded in converting one of its three standard, 10-megawatt power plants from coal to wood. The plant is equipped with a normal coal-fired boiler unit, identical to hundreds of other coal-burning facilities around the United States. It could already burn three fuels: coal, oil, or natural gas. But power plant supervisor and mastermind of the system, Tom L. Carr, was convinced after visiting a wood-burning facility in Eugene, Oregon, that his plant could also be made to burn wood. He obtained authorization for $50,000 from the commissioners of the publically-owned electric department to test his idea.

Carr and his crew designed, constructed, and installed all the necessary equipment themselves. They managed to put the project on line for only half the budget, and within two weeks it was declared "commercially acceptable," making it possible to deliver the wood-power to residents' homes on an intermediate-load basis.

The plant burns 1,000 tons per week of commercially unmarketable waste wood. The wood, "culled" from dead, diseased, and dying trees is purchased from an experimental wood-harvesting site in nearby South Duxbury, Vermont.

Vermont is currently 76 percent forested and the State Department of Forests argues that waste wood is sufficiently abundant in the area to use for power generation without damaging the forests. In fact, many Vermonters argue that the project is an effective "forest management tool" since weeding the dead wood will increase the growth of high quality timber.

(Critics, it should be noted, argue that the utility will devastate the forests with their clear-cutting practices. Others insist that estimates of timber surplus are far too optimistic, and that we cannot afford to use wood to create electricity.)

The harvested wood is chopped up into matchbook-size pieces for burning. There are several advantages to burning chipped wood. Because of their similar size, it is easier to convert from coal to wood chips. Also, scrub wood, brushy undergrowth, trash wood, and even rotten wood can be chipped and used for fuel, along with low quality standing timber. In addition, the use of chips means the utility will not have to compete with wood stove and fireplace owners for high quality hardwood.

At the harvesting site, the trees are run through a large "chipharvester" machine which has high-speed rotating blades that chop trunk, limbs, and leaves into chips. An entire tree can go through the chipper in 25 seconds. The chips shoot directly from the machine into tractor-trailers which transport the 20-ton loads to the Burlington generating facility.

There, the chips are shoveled out of the trailers and bulldozed onto a conveyor belt which carries them up to the plant's top floor. Then the chips are gravity-fed through four chutes to the boiler. An automatic stoker feeds an even flow of the chips into the burner at a rate of 10 tons per hour. The fuel heats 6,000 gallons of water into steam inside the boiler. Up to 100,000 pounds of the steam is fed into a turbo generator to produce as much as 10-megawatts of electricity.

The chips contain 40 to 50 percent moisture so they must be burned at a mixture of 75 percent wood chips to 25 percent No. 2 fuel oil in order to obtain the full rating of 10 megawatts. The oil is introduced with an existing overfire system only when full capacity is desired. But even when the small plant is run at 70 percent capacity, it can produce up to 10 percent of Burlington's power needs.

Though it takes about three tons of wood chips to produce the equivalent heat of one ton of coal, the cost of the wood chips is only $12 to $13 per ton, while Burlington has purchased coal for as much as $50 per ton. The wood chips produce electric power for 2.1¢ per kilowatt hour—one third less than the cost of burning coal at the same facility. State pollution standards required that a costly mixture of 45 percent coal to 55 percent oil be burned in the past. Wood is currently the cheapest fuel Burlington can buy, and the town expects the relative cost of burning wood to be further reduced as the price of other fuels climbs.

Burlington Electric was quite pleased with the success of the wood-burning experiment and community reaction to the project was also highly favorable. As a result, the Department

proposed a bond issue for construction of a new $80 million dollar, 50 megawatt, wood-fired generating plant to be built. This will be the nation's largest wood-burning facility for the commercial production of electric power. Along with the wood plant, the town also proposed to build a 10 megawatt hydroelectric generator, and a municipal refuse incineration plant to replace landfilling for trash and to provide steam heat for the town.

On March 7, 1978, voters in Burlington approved the three energy-related bond proposals of which the wood-burning facility was the centerpiece.

"The vote certainly shows that our citizens are overwhelmingly in favor of the development of alternative, renewable energy sources," said Joseph C. McNeil, Chairman of the Burlington Board of Electric Commissioners, after the vote. Soaring prices for fossil fuels, the long, winter coal strike, and the resourcefulness of Burlington Electric's wood power experiment all contributed to the strong vote of confidence the plan received.

The new plant will be funded in part through the sale of $40 million in revenue bonds and also by selling portions of the plant's capacity to a consortium of nearby municipal utilities. The Vermont Public Power Supply System is a group of 13 municipally-owned utilities formed to explore ways of becoming independent of Vermont's large, investor-owned utilities. Though the expected purchase will provide the group with 50 percent of the plant's power, Burlington will retain control over day-to-day operations and decision-making for the plant.

The proposed 50 megawatt unit will use 1,500 tons of wood daily, but this is more than is available from the state-owned forest-thinning projects which are supplying wood for the smaller, test-unit. One survey done by a Washington, D.C. firm indicates that there is enough annual wood growth within 75 miles of Burlington to feed the proposed 50 megawatt generator its estimated annual consumption of 470,000 tons of wood indefinitely. Any waste-wood harvesting would be strictly monitored by state-registered professional foresters. But, the town of Burlington is exploring several innovative ways to avoid having to rely on whole-tree chips in order to prevent any damage to the heavily-forested area.

One proposal would use old railroad ties for fuel. Two and a half to three million deteriorated ties are discarded annually by the railroads. Each tie weighs 150 to 200 lbs., and they could be purchased for the cost of transportation. It is uncertain, however, how well the ties will burn since they are coated with creosote to impede rotting. Tests are being done to determine if this chemical will inhibit burning or pollute the air.

Another alternative being studied is the use of sawmill residues. The town is also negotiating with private loggers to purchase more waste wood than is currently available to them. It is likely that the proposed plant will burn wood gleaned from a combination of all the above sources.

It is impossible at this stage to predict the impact of the proposed plant on the Burlington community, or on the energy future of New England—the end of the "energy line." But Burlington and the surrounding towns that are eager to participate in the wood-power project are assured of sufficient energy for the foreseeable future. For rural Vermont and other heavily forested areas with low-population density, the use of trees instead of fossil fuels for fuel is a simple, old-fashioned, yet innovative way to beat the current energy crunch.

Energy Audits
GREENSBORO, NORTH CAROLINA

Greensboro, a city of approximately 155,000, has developed the first door-to-door energy audit program with the ambitious goal of contacting every homeowner in the city. Developed under the auspices of their two-year-old Energy Conservation Commission, the program is jointly administered by the city government and Duke Power Company, the utility which provides electricity to Greensboro. The audits, which are conducted by the city's fire department, provide residents with an array of useful information about the present energy efficiency level of their homes and the various insulation techniques which can lower their monthly energy bill by reducing energy consumption.

North Carolina imports 99 percent of its energy. This problem has recently stimulated a high level of energy consciousness in Greensboro, as it has in so many other cities located in non-energy producing states. Greensboro's residential energy audit program is but one component in a full range of energy conservation programs developed there since the 1973 Arab oil embargo. Starting in 1974, the city government initiated an energy audit/conservation program for all municipal buildings, a carpooling program for city employees, and a maintenance and life-cycle costing program for the city's vehicle fleet. These and other programs were implemented "in-house" by the City Council. Later, they were expanded to the community at-large in order to "let people know that we (the city) were willing to do it (conserve energy) ourselves too," according to Don Weaver, Assistant City Manager and member of the Energy Conservation Commission. This conscientious attitude displayed by Greensboro city employees has been a major force behind the success of the home audit program.

The program has several goals. The town was looking for a way to more productively utilize fire department personnel. Through the program, firemen can learn more about the area's housing stock and become personally acquainted with the residents they serve. To Duke Power, the program is a way to boost its image as a service provider in Greensboro. Finally, the city managers believe the program will raise the level of energy-awareness among the people

of Greensboro and thus promote other conservation measures as well. Income dollars saved through conservation can be channeled into local business to ensure greater financial stability for Greensboro's economy as a whole.

Firefighters canvas the city's neighborhoods in teams of three making about 500 calls each week. One member of the team remains in the truck to monitor fire calls while two visit each house. If no one is home they leave a door hanger which briefly describes the program and lists the number to call to request an audit. If the resident is home, he or she can allow the audit to be conducted on the spot or set an appointment for a later date. The audit itself takes about 45 minutes, and the firemen are trained not only to measure the heat loss in the home through walls, ceiling areas, doors and windows—but also to answer questions about the pros and cons of different insulation methods. The homeowner is given a comprehensive brochure on the program and the benefits of energy conservation, along with a copy of the audit. The fire department sends the completed energy evaluation to Duke Power for analysis. Within two to three weeks of the initial visit, the firemen return to the home with the results of the audit. The utility will have provided the following information:

• An estimate of current energy costs based on usage estimates, current energy prices, type of house, weather conditions and other factors;

• A prioritized list of recommended insulation improvements;

• A rough cost breakdown on the recommended improvements;

• An estimate of the amount of money the homeowner can expect to save once the home is made energy-efficient;

• The length of time required to bring a return on the investment;

• A list of approved contractors;

• An offer for free technical assistance from Duke Power if desired.

Figures for current efficiency and recommended improvements are given in terms of "R-Values." R-Value is a way to express how readily heat will transfer through material, such as a wall. Building materials plus the existing insulation are combined to determine R-value. The higher the value, the better protected the area is from heat and cold, e.g. an area of R-30 reduces heat flow more than R-11. Homeowners are provided an explanation of the R-value system to get the best value they can when purchasing insulation.

Initially, the city of Greensboro embarked on the audit program without a clear conception of long-range goals. Having no prior models to draw from, it was an experiment that has required continual evaluation, modification, and improvement.

Results compiled from the first year of the program indicate that, although not an unqualified success, the program has enjoyed a response rate as high or higher than other energy audit programs elsewhere. Out of 24,223 calls, 14 percent resulted in audits. Of the remainder, 18 percent declined the offer to audit, in most instances because the home was rented (and therefore presently ineligible) or because the resident felt his or her home was already sufficiently energy-efficient.

Most significantly, 56 percent of the residents were not home at the time of the visit.

The commission believes this problem has reduced considerably the response rate. During the first six months, all visits were made during working hours diminishing the likelihood that someone would be home. The door hanger is far less effective in generating an audit request than a face-to-face meeting. Now, some visits are made between five and seven p.m., and telephone calls for audit appointments are now made during these hours as well. It is hoped this adjustment will cause the response rate to rise. Moreover, the Commission has endeavored to publicize the program more extensively through the media to spur greater interest.

Statistics on the number of homeowners who have made improvements to their home subsequent to the energy audit are available at present, only for the first six months of the program. In December of 1977, the city conducted a follow-up survey on those 2,431 households that had been audited. The firefighters attempted to personally re-visit these homes with a questionnaire and recorded comments on the program. It was learned that slightly less than half of the homes had made some of the recommended changes. Others indicated that improvements were planned for the future. It is apparent from the comments that opinion about the program was mixed.

Several interesting problems had developed. The utility's estimates of current energy costs were often quite different from the actual experience of the homeowner. For some, this seemed to have resulted in a level of distrust towards Duke Power, as well as the audit as a whole. The problem according to the Energy Commission, was that the estimates were based not on the actual monthly energy bills of the individual homeowner, but rather on general factors common to all similar dwellings and households.

Another factor was that in the winter of 1977, an insulation shortage had developed in the Greensboro area, resulting in some homeowners being unable to make the desired improvements. Despite these problems, the Greensboro Energy Conservation Commission is pleased with the results.

In undertaking a program which asks members of the community to conserve energy in their own homes, Greensboro is fighting a high level of public apathy that has plagued conservation advocates from the White House on down. People question the efficacy of individual efforts to conserve energy if "no one else is doing it." Thus, it is important to be able to show the concrete results of that individual effort. To that end, plans are underway in Greensboro for a full-scale evaluation of the total energy savings to the city from the home audit program. In Greensboro, as in other cities, energy awareness has been slow to come. But the Greensboro model—a thorough, personalized

approach—is likely to prove that the most valuable solutions to the energy crisis are to be found on the local level.

Greensboro was one of the first cities to adopt municipal initiatives to help residents discover ways of conserving energy in their homes. Now, under the 1978 National Energy Act's residential energy conservation program, states must submit plans requiring their major electric and gas utilities to help home owners select and install energy saving measures. The program design is the responsibility of each state, but it must conform to federal Department of Energy regulations if the state is to receive federal energy funds. Utilities will perform free home energy audits upon request to determine which conservation measures would be most useful and cost-effective for the individual household. The act also requires that utilities help arrange financing and installation by supplying lists of lenders, suppliers and contractors in the area. In most cases, the utilities are prohibited from doing the installation work themselves in order to protect against them recommending unnecessary work. The Department of Energy has estimated that this program could save residential consumers $30 billion now being spent each year on home energy consumption.

Energy from Wastes
AMES, IOWA

There is one problem that every community has in common—how to

dispose of the garbage. Most towns in the United States still "solve" their garbage disposal problem in the timeless, conventional fashion—the "city dump."

Beginning in the 1920s, many towns took to burning their trash before dumping it to reduce the volume. A more recent invention is the "sanitary landfill" in which refuse is buried on a bed of clay or plastic between layers of dirt.

But whether it is heaped into an open-air dump, buried in a sanitary landfill, or incincrated and then buried, garbage, or "municipal solid waste," may be out of sight, but it never disappears. Sooner or later, as hundreds of millions of tons of non-biodegradable material is discarded each year, every community will run out of landfill space. Obviously then, in the long run, the dumping of municipal solid wastes is an unsatisfactory solution to the garbage dilemma.

One town that found itself running out of landfill space and chose a more adventurous solution to the problem than yet another landfill, is Ames, Iowa, a town of 46,000 in north-central Iowa. Ames was the first community to build a full-scale solid waste recovery system (SWRS) for the processing and separation of recoverables, and for the burning of "Refuse Derived Fuel" (RDF) for electric power generation.

When the Ames City Council learned in 1971 that the town's landfill would be full within five years, it appointed a task force to explore alternatives to landfilling for the town's solid wastes. The task force, composed of three members of the city staff, and three technicians from the Iowa State University of Science and Technology lo-

cated in the town, reported that the Ames municipal utility could, with some modification, burn shredded garbage as a supplemental fuel along with coal. Spurred by the task force's findings, the City Council hired an independent consulting firm to conduct a thorough feasibility study. The consultants considered a range of questions such as: What kind of refuse does Ames generate? How great a quantity will there be on a continual basis? How well will it burn? How hot will it get when it burns? Are there ready markets for recoverables? Conditions for the implementation of a SWRS were found to be ideal.

The electric utility and the disposal of solid waste are both under municipal control, though refuse is handled for the city by private haulers. Thus, the city of Ames could control both ends of the system. Expert technical knowledge was available locally, due to the presence of the university. And, the progressive, science-oriented institution in the Ames community meant that people were unusually well-informed and enthusiastic about recycling, energy conservation, and alternative energy systems.

But, expectations for the system proved to be unrealistically high. Despite this beneficent situation, the system encountered a plethora of problems including large cost-overruns, excessive downtime, inadequate markets for recoverables, and under-utilization of machinery. The system is highly capital-intensive; even at full capacity, it may not be self-supporting. Thus, at present, it is not competitive with landfilling though

Ames expects that it will be in several years as land costs rise and initial problems dissipate with experience. These snags now generate a mixed reaction to the system in Ames.

The decision to construct the Ames SWRS was made by the city council. It was financed through the issuance of $5.3 million in general obligation bonds. A special act of the Iowa state legislature was needed to allow bonds for the plant to be sold at an interest rate higher than previously allowed by law. This made the bonds more attractive to prospective buyers.

To ensure a sufficient flow of refuse, Ames contracted with the 12 smaller communities in Story County. Each town shares the processing costs with Ames on a per capita basis and in return, Ames has guaranteed to handle their garbage for 25 years. The total number of persons served by the Ames system is 65,000 including the 13 communities, Iowa State University, the State Department of Transportation, and the National Animal Disease Laboratory.

According to Terry V. Sprenkel, Ames City Manager, "Only very large municipalities generate sufficient solid waste to preclude the involvement of other surrounding local or regional governmental entities." The capital intensive nature of SWRS makes this inevitable. "There are significant ongoing costs that cannot be reduced. These include principal, interest, depreciation, and utility costs," says Sprenkel.

It is unlikely that Ames alone could have supported a full-scale solid waste recovery system. But outside contracts were readily obtained since these towns too were faced with dwindling landfill space.

Now that operational costs have proven higher than anticipated, however, this inter-governmental arrangement has created some opposition among towns in the system. Some communities have unsuccessfully attempted to break their contract, but Ames is sanguine that costs can be eventually reduced to their satisfaction. In Ames itself, no appreciable increase in municipal tax rates can be attributed to the system.

The electric utility generally burns a mixture of 80 percent coal, 20 percent RDF to supply the town of Ames with its own power. Emergency power is purchased from the State of Iowa System, more rarely from Iowa State University. Only the town of Ames itself receives power from the Refuse-Derived-Fuel. The other 20,000 persons in the county are served by the SWRS only in that Ames buys their garbage. Fuel costs for consumers with RDF per BTU are currently on par with costs for those using only coal.

The solid waste recovery plant processes 150 tons of refuse per day. The system incorporates an intricate series of grinding and separating processes out of which recoverables such as aluminum, glass, and ferrous material are separated for sale from the "light fraction" that can be burned as RDF. There are sub-systems for recycling oil, a wood-chipper, and a paper-baler. On the average, the system recovers 93 percent of the solid wastes that enter the plant, sending only seven percent to a small landfill area.

The system can accept all types of garbage except dead animals and liquid, or hazardous wastes. The garbage is delivered to the plant by private citizens and commercial haulers. No source separation by consumers is required. Demolition materials go directly to the landfill; large appliances are accepted at the plant, but are processed separately from other materials.

The solid waste recovery process begins when the refuse truck rolls into the plant and onto a scale which records the weight of its load. The load is then dumped onto the floor of the "tipping room" where preliminary separation of large appliances and other bulky items occurs. Next, the refuse is loaded onto a conveyor from which it drops into the first, or "primary" shredder. The shredder's spinning hammers mill the raw refuse into six-inch chunks that are small enough to fall through grates at the bottom of the machine. From there the material passes through a "degritter" recently installed to reduce wear and damage to the machinery which had been caused by glass and grit. The grit is rejected and sent to a bin destined for the landfill. The potentially combustible fraction is then sent on to the first electromagnet which separates out 90 percent of the ferrous materials for resale. There are two additional magnets in the system which recover 97 percent of all ferrous materials that enter the unit.

Ferrous material is a major source of revenue for the Ames system though it has also been the site of major equipment breakdowns, resulting in far less income from the system than anticipated. The material is shipped to Vulcan Materials Co. in Gary, Indiana. A buyer could not be located closer to Ames, so about one-half the profits for recovering ferrous materials goes for transport costs.

Next the garbage is sent to the secondary, smaller shredder where it is reduced to two-inch pieces. From there it moves into the "air classification system" in which the light, burnable pieces of refuse are billowed into the air and the heavier, nonburnables fall through a chute to a conveyor below. When the lighter fraction is blown up through the air classification unit, it becomes known as refuse-derived fuel. Approximately 84 percent of the total mass flow of refuse results in RDF. The fuel is conveyed through a pneumatic tube to a storage bin from which it will be drawn into the boiler and burned along with coal to produce electric power. The original machinery is expected to operate for a period of 20 years.

It is apparent even from this brief description that the solid waste recovery process involves a complex interaction of machinery. Prior to the Ames project, the equipment needed for a full-scale system had not operated in concert anywhere. Madison had been using a small shredder to grind its refuse into pieces that would reduce the volume of their landfill. St. Louis and the Environmental Protection Agency were jointly experimenting with using the burnable material. But some parts of the equipment used in Ames are being used in ways for which it was not originally designed. For example, the storage bin was designed to store lumber material. Ames was the first community to put it all together into one complete system.

Thus, the city of Ames undertook a great risk both financially and politically by building a SWRS in 1971. But, Ames' initiative has considerably advanced the pool of knowledge regarding resource recovery. In a study prepared by the Ames City Manager, he candidly acknowledges Ames' mistakes in an effort to save other communities from duplicating them. There are several "golden rules" which have emerged from the Ames experience:

1) **Know your refuse.** The feasibility study conducted for Ames was thorough, but in retrospect, it was not thorough enough. Initial enthusiasm may have impeded rational evaluation. Estimates of refuse volume have been consistently inaccurate and this has greatly hurt the plant's financial standing. During the first year of operation, total volume was only 75 percent of the estimate. "Without an accurate volume measurement, there is no way to predict cost, revenues, or equipment requirements. Capital costs remain the same, but a loss in volume means a loss in revenue to the system," says Sprenkel. There are several variables such as the weather and the economy which can affect the quality and the quantity of the solid waste flow and these must be taken into account.

2) **Choice of equipment should be determined based on available markets.** In Ames, too much equipment was purchased in an effort to acquire a total system. For example, Ames' woodchipper ran well, but the market was inadequate to warrant the system's costs. During a five-month period in 1976, 80 tons of wood chips were processed and sold, but costs for maintenance, labor and trailer rental to store the chips surpassed revenues by nearly $500. The "al-mag" ferrous recovery system has never worked properly. At the time of the Ames purchase, the technology was unproven. Its "downtime" has totaled over a year and a half in three years of operation. Very little revenue has accrued to Ames from this system, though it had been expected to produce the bulk of the profits. The paper-baler has also proven to be a deficit operation. The success of the "recycling movement" in Ames has meant that people now discard less newspaper with their trash than they used to. Supply has been greater than demand for baled paper, resulting in lowered prices.

3) **Always estimate revenues on the conservative side and costs liberally.** This is always good accounting policy. At time of construction in Ames, the estimate of processing costs was $5.68 per ton. The actual net cost was over twice that amount. Ames underestimated the amount of time that both components, and the entire system would be out of operation. Downtime has been up to seven percent per year. It must be expected that downtime will increase throughout the first year of operation, and then level off as the system smooths out and employees acquire expertise in operating the equipment.

Now that Ames has broken important ground in this area, more communities will be entering the business of resource recovery. This will undoubtedly improve performance and lower costs. Refuse-derived fuel will invariably be used increasingly in the future, particularly in non-energy producing areas.

Hempstead, New York, opened up a waste-into-energy facility in mid-1978. A $73-million, 2,000-ton-per-day facility, the design is a scaled-up version of the Black Clawson plant in Franklin, Ohio, where garbage is fed into "hydrapulpers" and material is salvaged. In Hempstead, the original forecast when the plant opened was that 15 percent of the community's residential electricity load would be produced.

In Massachusetts, 1,500 tons of garbage from Saugus and nearby towns enter a $45-million plant located on the grounds of the old landfill dump and are turned into steam for the General Electric plant in Lynn.

One financial analyst has estimated that within 10 years, resource recovery in such plants will evolve into a billion-dollar industry, with about 30 to 50 percent of the 150 million tons of garbage created annually being converted into fuel in more than 100 plants. The plants, he forecasts, would generate as much as five percent of the electricity for utilities and almost 20 percent of the gas requirements in certain metropolitan areas.

Others caution against such over-optimistic projections, calling the process "unproven," citing problems in such plants and the low costs of landfilling where cities are still able to do so, and warning that one explosion can be expected for every 20,000 tons of garbage shredded.

In a Worldwatch Institute study on recycling, "Moving Toward a Sustainable Society," author Denis Hayes records these objections from critics of resource-recovery plants:

"Proponents of source separation feel that centralized facilities are capital-intensive behemoths that produce little net energy and recover a comparatively small fraction of the material value of trash. Resource recovery centers are viewed by this group as marginally better than landfills as a destination for whatever is not successfully recovered through source separation. But there is a strong fear that economies of scale will dictate that huge units be built at high expense to handle the entire current volume of urban waste. Afterward, cities would have a strong vested interest in maintaining the same level of waste in order to maximize the return on their sunk investments. This could lead to official discouragement—or even forbidding—of community recycling schemes."

In a study of "Energy Production from Municipal Wastes," Donald L. Klass of the Institute of Gas Technology in Chicago has calculated that the heating value of municipal solid waste (MSW) is about 3,000 to 7,000 BTUs per pound received. (His "typical MSW" contains about 15 to 35 percent moisture by weight, 40 to 70 percent organic components, and 10 to 20 percent inorganic components.)

Concerning particle size reduction to prepare material for direct fuel use, Dr. Klass notes that the size of the material influences the rate at which the gasification process occurs. He also points out that co-combustion of RDF with coal has recently been started in full-scale systems, permitting RDF to be used in large existing electric power plants.

Source Separation
SEATTLE, WASHINGTON

Seattle has embarked on one of the most ambitious and energetic research programs ever undertaken by a local government to study the economic feasibility and practical application of source separation collection service. The Seattle Solid Waste Utility, under a contract to Seattle Recycling Inc. (SRI), has initiated Project SORT (Separate Our Recyclables from Trash) in an attempt to answer some of the questions which are facing many local governments today in the area of solid waste management. Specifically they are hoping to learn what the actual economics of collection service will be.

The idea for the SORT program originated more than two years ago after a group of citizens went to the Seattle City Council to protest the fact that residents with little or no garbage still had to pay the city $5.20 each month, the standard rate charged to households with four or less cans of garbage. The citizens' committee reasoned that people who had no garbage, or only one can, should not have to subsidize their waste-producing neighbors. What made this situation seem even more unfair was that the people with little or no garbage were taking the extra time and effort to separate their garbage, recycle some of it, and compost the rest. And yet they were being penalized for their efforts.

The city council of Seattle, faced with a potentially critical shortage of landfill space and ever increasing disposal costs, studied the situation and came up with the idea of a program to test the feasibility of variable garbage rates. At the same time, the pilot program was designed to look into other factors affecting the feasibility of recycling in the Washington city. Those are: the possibility of city-wide home collection of recyclables, what the city's role in this recycling process should be, how to encourage recycling in general, and the efficiencies of the collection and processing of recyclables.

The SORT program is a 16-month study involving 15,000 households in 30 neighborhoods, all corresponding with existing garbage routes and divided into three research groups. One group has the option of a variable can rate with free curbside or alley collection of recyclables; the second group has the opportunity for the collection of recyclables but without the variable can rate; and the third group can take advantage of the variable can rate but they do not receive recycling collection service.

(The following information on source separation of garbage in Seattle reflects an approach opposite to the centralized Refuse Derived Fuel system, yet obviously relates to energy conservation. The information is written by Kevin Mulligan and appeared originally in the January-February, 1979 issue of Compost Science/Land Utilization.)

The variable can rate study, which charges a uniform rate of $5.20 for two to four cans per week, a reduced rate of $4.00 for one can, and $1.00 for no cans, is attempting to measure the impact of monetary incentives on the waste generating habits of the participating households. The idea behind the $1.00 charge for no garbage service is that the city feels it is virtually impossible to eliminate trash; even if you recycle everything you will still have some plastics and other wastes which must be hauled to the transfer station for disposal, and though dumping at the transfer station is free to the public, it represents a significant cost to the municipality.

The variable can rate, being offered to 10,000 homes, has run into some problems in the determination of the economic motivation in waste reduction because many people, including project directors and staff, do not feel the difference between $5.20 and $4.00 is significant enough to convince people to reduce their waste generating habits. Another problem which has been encountered is that while the resident in the variable can rate area may be interested in recycling or reducing the number of cans each week, if he/she rents or leases the house or apartment, the variable rate produces no incentive for the resident household because the bill is paid by the homeowner who is unaware of the occupants willingness to support and participate in the program. However, this problem would be difficult to overcome in any municipal operation.

In the areas with recycling collection, people are being offered the op-portunity to recycle glass, newspaper, and steel cans and aluminum on a once-a-month basis. So far, participation has been less than the 50 percent hoped for by project sponsors, but is still encouraging, as participation is increasing each month and volume amounts have generally been higher than anticipated. In the 20 neighborhoods where curbside collection is offered, participation has been in the 30 percent range, with a high of 46 percent and a low of 10 percent, with only four areas being under 20 percent.

The neighborhoods in this study were selected to reflect a sampling of the socio-economic makeup and structure of the city, to measure the relationship between socio-economic conditions and the recycling participation rate. While the evidence from the first five months of the study is not complete, or represents the final conclusion of the research study, the preliminary evidence indicates that generally the interest in the program and the willingness to recycle is highest with middle and upper-middle income groups, with lower participation and interest being the rule in economically poorer nejghborhoods. However, the study has shown that most of the non-participating households cite that they "don't have enough materials," or "we were on vacation," or that they simply "didn't know about the program" as their reasons for not participating. Very few people expressed adamant opposition to the program as their reason for not participating.

An extensive campaign to educate

and inform the target neighborhoods was undertaken before the recycling program began and has been continued with a steady stream of reminders, public service announcements, and information booths at "Energy Day" and "Sun Day" activities as well as at other places where the public congregates in Seattle. Calendars were distributed listing the collection dates for each of the areas and every home was contacted personally to be a SORT representative. Additionally, the city has established a public access Recycling Hotline to handle inquiries and provide assistance to households who may be having any difficulties with the program.

The tonnage from the project to date has been about 5,300 pounds per daily route in the variable can rate areas and about 4,250 pounds per collection in the non-variable rate areas, for an average of about 47 pounds per month from each participating household. This has resulted in an average market value of $2,379 in recyclable materials collected each month. While these are not earth shaking statistics, no one, including the project directors, expects home sorting and collection of recyclables to break even or make money.

The program operators, Seattle Recycling Inc., have experienced very few problems with collections or the ability of participants to properly prepare their materials. One minor problem which has been encountered however is due to the lack of a city ordinance against scavenging. People are sometimes getting to the routes before the collection crews and making off with the newspaper, aluminum, and other valuable recyclables.

A flat bed truck with specially designed collection bins is being used for the route collections with a crew consisting of a driver and one swamper. Special separation and processing equipment has been installed at the SRI warehouse to remove the aluminum fraction from the other metals, and to reduce the volume of metals and glass. All other materials are being marketed by SRI, a private recycling company whose primary business has been in offering a public buy-back program. By marketing the small volumes of SORT collection tonnage with their other materials, SRI is able to receive a higher price for the materials than they would otherwise be worth.

The goal of SORT is to accurately assess the economics of source separation recycling collection. The program will run for 12 more months at which point the contractor, Seattle Recycling Inc., will present the city of Seattle with a report which outlines the suggested role of source separation in the city's overall approach to the solid waste problems. It is hoped this report, in conjunction with city work, can lead to a new, four-pronged approach to solid waste management in Seattle which may call for a city-wide recycling collection program, a yard waste composting project, a possible resource recovery program, and a more practical and efficient landfill management policy for the remaining fraction of the garbage.

Finance

SMALL BUSINESSES AND COMMUNITY ENERGY CORPORATIONS

One major roadblock to widespread adoption of alternative energy is cost. While it is unquestionably true that the "life-cycle" cost of alternative systems and conservation makes their installation attractive over the long run, few homeowners, businesses, institutions or communities can obtain financing for the change.

Within the last few years, however, there have been several different approaches towards creating a financial system to facilitate a change from fossil fuels to alternative energy. Seattle Trust & Savings initiated an energy conservation loan program at rates below the market. In San Diego, San Diego Federal Savings & Loan has developed a method for extending home mortgages so as to facilitate solar retrofit installation.

Still another financing mechanism is being developed in many United States cities and regions, as public agencies team up with private sector efforts to provide needed capital for energy creation and conservation. For example, in South Dakota, the State Office of Economic Opportunity, working with a community action program, recently established a Community Development Corporation (CDC) charged with providing financial and technical assistance to small-scale community-oriented businesses. The South Dakota CDC was inititally set up mostly with

funds from a federal emergency weatherization program. Hence, the first company invested in was Weatherization Contractors Inc., a home weatherization business. The company is projected to employ approximately nine people in the first year with total start-up capital requirements of about $30,000. As its name implies, Weatherization Contractors, Inc. specializes in providing insulation for homes.

According to Harold Storsve, Resource Mobilization Specialist for the South Dakota agency, the CDC is a good mechanism for small town and neighborhood business development for several reasons. First, because of its nonprofit status, it is eligible for resources normally unavailable to the private for-profit sector, yet it can shunt capital toward for-profit ventures. To illustrate, as a nonprofit, a CDC is qualified for a number of government grants, as well as private individual and private foundation tax exempt donations. Moreover, it can recruit the volunteer services of the community on behalf of a business. This activity of "pooling" people and money resources from diverse locations is an important advantage of a CDC.

Second, a CDC is not restrained by federal turfs. That is, it can pool financial resources from different federal agencies and build a business assistance program that offers all the necessary services for the entrepreneur. It could, for instance, garner investment grants from the Community Services Administration, obtain funds from the Department of Energy for energy-related businesses, finance some job positions through the Department of Labor programs, and offer technical assistance under Small Business Administration programs.

Finally, CDCs will take a risk on local ventures that conventional sources of capital will not touch or will touch only if some other investors will go first.

Storsve supplies these additional details on the South Dakota energy conservation project:

The goal was to develop a model project that would demonstrate how low-income home weatherization activities can be accomplished at the same time that permanent employment and business ownership opportunities are provided. Because the weatherization program was experiencing a shortage of CETA trainees assigned to it by the local manpower board, the reprogramming was thought to be a way to create an alternative labor supply. The CDC, incorporated as the Northeast South Dakota Energy Conservation Corporation (NESDECC), became the implementing mechanism for this effort.

NESDECC received approximately $133,300 from NESDCAP. Of this amount, about $30,000 was used for CDC board and staff development; $96,000 for contracts to weatherize low-income homes; and $7,300 for venture capital. (The latter amount was available in the "flexible" form of unregulated interest earned on one of NESDCAP's energy program accounts). With these resources at its disposal, NESDECC formed a board of directors composed of 15 community representatives, and hired a business management specialist. In addition, NESDCAP assigned one of its staff to the project to work as acting director.

Formal non-profit incorporating activities proceeded simultaneously to identification of an entrepreneur. Ultimately, an entrepreneur was recruited from the NEDSCAP weatherization program where he had been a crew supervisor. Working closely with him, the business management specialist designed a financial and operational plan for a new business called Weatherization Contractors, Inc. This business is projected to employ approximately nine people in the first year with total start-up capital requirements of about $30,000.

The financial goal of the CDC was to use its technical and financial resources to leverage additional capital and to build relationships with the financial institutions of the area in a way that would be useful to future projects, as well. Thus, the equity in the business, which was split 52 percent NESDECC, 48 percent Weatherization Contractors, Inc., and which totaled about $14,000, was used to leverage a $15,000 loan from a local bank. Since business startups represent high risk to bankers, NESDECC negotiated a Farmers Home Administration ninety-percent loan guarantee, reducing bank exposure to $1,500. Collateral for the loan was provided by the entrepreneur.

Once financing was secured and operations were ready to begin, $96,000 in weatherization contracts were assigned to the business. The contracts provide a sheltered research and development market during the start-up phase. They allow the business a secure income while it tests its market capture strategy in the private sector.

Weatherization Contractors, Inc., has begun performing on the low-income contracts with a crew of three. In addition to management responsibilities, the entrepreneur is lining up private sector business for the spring season. At that time, crew size will more than double.

Benefits to the CDC from the activities of Weatherization Contractors, Inc., are many. Through the device of an investment agreement, the business has agreed to employ at least fifty percent low-income people; develop a bonus system for employees; explore the feasibility of profit sharing; participate with NESDECC in a training program for prospective low-income managers and entrepreneurs; and weatherize a minimum of 60 low-income homes that might not have otherwise been weatherized.

On the other hand, the incentive to the entrepreneur is that he will have the opportunity to buy out NES-DECC's share of the business. This will be accomplished through a three to five year buy-out plan, with share prices based on the value of the business at the time of sale. The result will be full ownership by the entrepreneur

and a projected return of at least $21,000 to NESDECC, $14,000 of which represents profit. This total amount will be returned to a venture capital pool for reinvestment in other ventures.

But the benefits derived from the activities of Weatherization Contractors, Inc., are not the sole return on NESDCAP and the SEOO's efforts. While meeting the obligations accompanying weatherization funding, NESDCAP has also created an economic development institution which transcends the limitations of that funding. It is hoped that this institution, NESDECC, will remain in the community for years to come to provide a vehicle for residents to address other economic needs as well. As a beginning in that direction, two small grants have been received—one to provide a small business loan guarantee program and the other to facilitate citizen participation in rural economic development issues.

Robert Friedman, who organized a national conference on "Local Private-Public Enterprise" sees solar energy and energy conservation as "the frontier of job creation." Writes Friedman:

"Traditional modes of research, development and stimulation hold little promise for serving low-income people and the communities hurt the most by rising energy costs. Around the country, however, local private/public corporations are expanding this relatively non-displacing, labor intensive new industry to serve poor communities.

"For four years, the Westside Community Development Corporation of San Bernardino, California has been pioneering the solar industry—designing, manufacturing, and installing low-cost solar water heaters, and collectors in low and moderate income housing. Combined with weatherization efforts, these activities have often resulted in reducing energy costs by 60 to 80 percent. The corporation presently employs an administrative staff of 30 and over 200 minority and low-income trainees."

Jerry Yudelson, director of the state of California's SolarCal Office in Sacramento, also sees significant potential for state government assistance to local solar energy enterprises. A "Task Force of Financing the Solar Transition" was set up by the SolarCal Office to explore financial needs and possibilities for both 1979 legislative proposals and state administration action. California's official goal is 1.5 million residential solar applications by 1985, with a potential annual employment of over 50,000 people in solar applications. "Many of these applications are suitable for local public-private enterprises," says Yudelson.

Peter Sardagna, vice president of San Diego Federal Savings & Loan Association, has proposed a scheme for financing retrofit solar hot water systems in California. The plan involves extending the house mortgage. Sardagna believes this "Energy Saver" plan "is the financial key to large scale commercialization of solar energy in California."

"The importance of such a program is that it can be put into motion immediately," he explains. "It taps the expertise and resources of the existing financial institutions and does not rely on the creation of new, untried and probably inefficient and ultimately more expensive lending sources, such as utility companies or taxpayer subsidized 'state solar banks.' "

The scheme is new—Sardagna introduced it in mid-1978—and the bank has had little experience in administering it so far.

Sardagna's description of the plan is set forth below:

I.) *Home buyers*— This program can be used where the home buyer wishes to install energy-saving devices at the time of his purchase:

A. The buyer provides a cost breakdown and contract showing the improvements to bé made.

B. The appraisal will be completed utilizing this additional cost as value added to property and the loan to value will then be based on the total appraised value.

C. If the funds required for conservation devices are less than two percent of the purchase price, these funds will be released to the buyer at close of escrow.

D. If the funds required for conservation devices are in excess of two percent, but less than 10 percent, the funds will be placed in a non-interest bearing, Loans-in-Process account until the work is complete. Upon completion, the borrower will request in writing these monies and an inspection will be made before the funds are released.

E. A maximum of 10 percent of the sale price will be provided for the energy conservation devices.

F. Only 80 percent loans will be included in this program.

G. It is important for the loan officer to use discretion in determining the increased value to the home after considering the feasibility and workability of the system and materials chosen.

II.) *Home owners*— This program will help existing SDF borrowers convert to lower cost, alternative solar energy sources, mainly for hot-water heating.

A. Maximum loan amount of $4,000, or 10 percent of market value, whichever is less.

B. A flat $200 fee will be charged to cover the cost of title policy, appraisal, processing, credit reports, recording fees, etc. If additional costs are incurred, due to the subordination of junior liens, these fees will be added to the basic fee.

C. San Diego Federal must receive evidence that the solar system qualifies for the California 55 percent tax credit. This is necessary since the state requires the system to meet certain specifications and we want all systems financed by San Diego Federal to meet the state's minimum requirements.

D. Funds will be disbursed when installation has been completed and the system is operating properly. This fact will be verified by letter from the applicant.

E. The amount of the additional advance will be at current residential prime rate. The existing loan will not be raised. Therefore, the rate stated in the Modification Agreement will be a weighted average of the existing rate and the current rate. The new rate will be rounded up to the nearest .01 percent. The automatic document printer has the capacity of calculating the monthly payment and daily interest factor.

F. The mortgage will be recast up to 30 years, if necessary, in order to keep the payment as close to the original amount as possible.

G. If additional funds are required to pay off existing junior deeds of trust, the borrower will not qualify under the program. A standard refinance will be conducted utilizing San Diego Federal's current outstanding policies.

H. The maximum loan amount permitted will be 90 percent loan to value.

I. The customer should be urged to open a San Diego Federal savings account. It is hoped that the customer will place all savings from this alternative energy source in this account. By doing so, this program becomes self-perpetuating.

In 1976, the Seattle Trust & Savings Bank initiated a similar conservation loan program, which the bank says has been a considerable success.

Under the program, borrowers may take out an energy conservation 30-year mortgage with 20 percent down, at one quarter percent below the market rate, compared to a 30-year mortgage, requiring 25 percent down at the market rate. Home improvement, auto and boat loans all are offered at an annual percentage rate, three quarters of a percent below the normal market rate.

To qualify for the energy mortgage loan, the property must meet at least 20 or 25 points (depending on the value of the house) out of 48 on an energy conservation list developed by the bank. The list provides, for example, five points each for adequate ceiling, wall or floor insulation, five points for storm windows or double glazing or one point for plastic sheeting over windows, one point for fireplace damper integrity, and five points for solar heating.

No maximum or minimum amounts are set. Developers can pre-qualify entire subdivisions by adhering to the bank's energy conservation criteria.

The energy home improvement loans also depend on the home's qualifying for at least 25 points on the list, while the auto loans require that the car purchased have an Environmental Protection Agency rating of at least 25 miles a gallon on the highway. Boat loans qualify if the vessel is wind-powered or meets the bank's standards for engine efficiency.

Bank officials have said that in part they set up the energy loan program as a device which would allow them to loan funds to inner city residents while avoiding the appearance of "patronizing" them. J. C. Baillargeon, president, also said the bank chose to institute the program "because in a period of good bank liquidity, it would enable us to expand loans into the consumer sector at better rates than we were receiving on shorter term investments."

Housing

6

The Horizontal City

Architecture Designed to Natural Climate

Low-Rise, High-Density Settlements

Extensive Walkways

Compact Gardens

Perhaps the most important way to obtain the energy savings promised through solar power is not in the equippage of buildings with collectors, photo voltaic cells, etc., but in the more fundamental reorganization of urban architecture to take advantage of the natural climate.

With fewer and fewer people able to buy a house, and with much of the nation's housing stock in decay there may well be an opportunity at hand to make a fresh start on housing design.

The city of Davis, California, made a beginning in this direction with its building ordinance. The ordinance requires that new houses be carefully sited on lots and built to take utmost advantage of the climate. That means such things as emphasis on southfacing windows, reduction in setbacks, narrower streets, upgraded insulation, etc.

Peter Land, a British architect who recently designed an innovative housing project for the United Nations in Lima, argues that the energy crisis of-

fers an opportunity to reorganize much denser urban settlements away from alienating high rise slums to what he calls the "horizontal city." Land is well known for his extensive research into low-rise, high-density and expandable architecture. "In contrast to the neighborhood as a vertical concept, the problem of the individual house on its own lot and its multiplication into urban form received insufficient attention during the pioneering period of modern architecture," Land writes. "The low rise concept is a very viable and attractive alternative, if high densities can be achieved."

In his work Land has shown that densities of up to 200 persons per acre could be achieved in urban situations using only two-story patio houses with individual gardens that are pleasant for families with or without children. (Two hundred persons is the top limit in London for density, although some of the hideous housing projects in New York City have obtained densities of 500 people per acre. Then again New

York City land is so ill-used that in many places there are densities of but 46 persons per acre.)

The centerpiece of Land's work is the patio or courtyard house. These houses are built in sections and can be added to as the owner desires. They tend to offer great potential for energy savings because of inherent design: zero lot lines (i.e., houses abut one another); front and back lawn space is eliminated and instead created in the form of an inner court yard. The houses can be clustered or nested together in a variety of different ways so as to take advantage of the climate (prevailing breezes, sun, etc.). Streets servicing the houses are narrow (that helps to save energy) and on the periphery. Gardening and walking are two basic, recurrent themes in Land's scheme for low-rise, high-density housing.

Land, of course, is not alone in arguing for high-density, low-rise housing. As he points out, there are many fine examples of this sort of housing in the United States: Beacon Hill in Boston, Georgetown in Washington, DC, parts of Philadelphia and San Francisco, etc. Indeed, the sort of housing Land and others espouse recalls Greek designs around the time of Christ: Having denuded their land of trees needed to build ships, the Greeks were left without fuel. To remedy this situation the Greeks designed and sited their houses for maximum use of the sun. They built courtyards with living rooms set on the north side facing south for warmth. Houses were of two storys, but the southern portions of the buildings were kept to one story so as not to keep the

sun's rays from entering the main living spaces.

The houses that Land built for the UN, and the designs on which he is now at work are both attractive and inexpensive. Land believes people should have their own homes at low prices. While he is cautious on prices, he believes that an attractive courtyard house can be constructed for $20,000. If the homeowner were to build the structure himself, then the cost might be about $10,000. In Peru, Land led teams of UN experts who taught villagers in earthquake-devastated villages how to build homes at a cost of from $200 to $400 each. These small homes did not contain electricity or plumbing.

The essence of the high-density, low-rise (HD/LR) concept is low profile urban structure at high densities without elevators. Residential building types may be mostly two story houses with some three and four story walk-up access types. Careful, tight and efficient planning can give very high densities and a great deal of variety.

Writes Land: "In low-rise development solar energy can be utilized very effectively as long as appropriate designs and orientations are used. From the moment the sun appears over the horizon until it disappears in late afternoon, it can light and heat the house. This not only gives the individual house an energy advantage over the traditional high-rise structure, but also contributes psychological and biological benefits.

"Economically, low-rise development is very advantageous. Individual houses can be considerably lower in

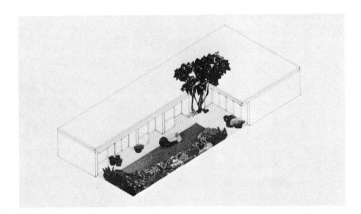

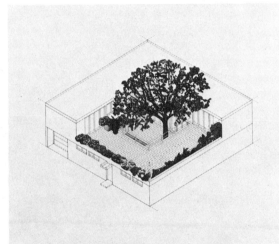

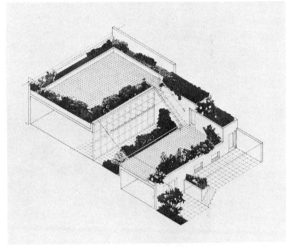

Compact houses would contain small, private gardens. Roofs can have easy access from outside and inside units and be entirely landscaped as terrace gardens using planters, earth and sodded areas which also improve insulation. The entire area of lots will thus be fully utilized and neighborhoods will appear as gardens when seen from above.

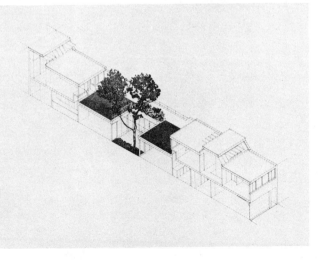

Under the auspices of the United Nations, teams of architects from around the world joined to design a housing development in Lima. The patio concept dominates the design.

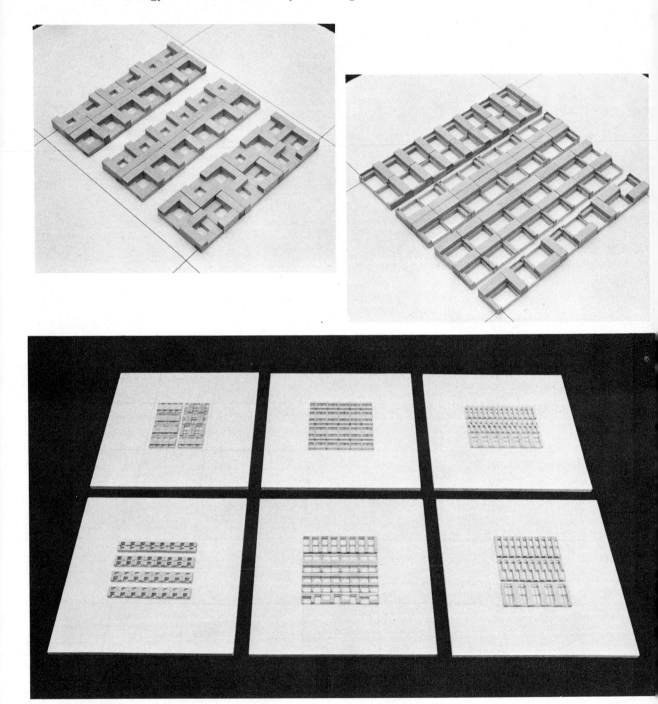

Land works at ways of interlinking courtyard housing so as to preserve diversity and privacy while achieving high-density.

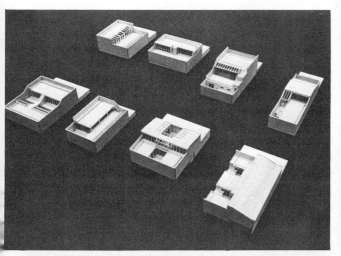

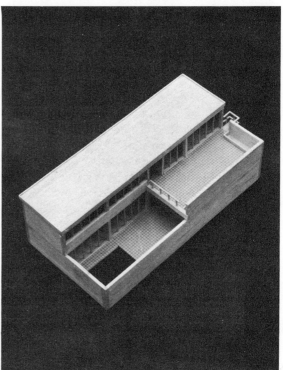

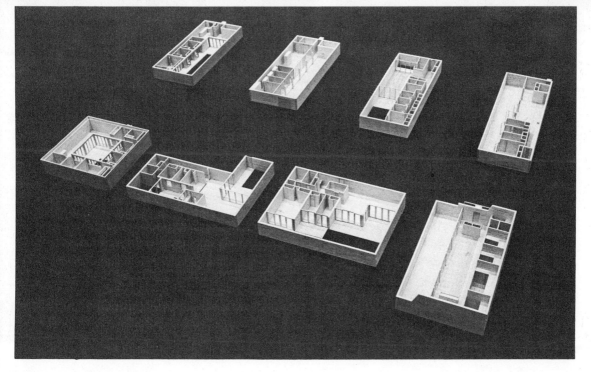

building cost than apartments of comparable area in high-rise structures. Low-rise subdivisions carefully designed with a rational separation between streets for pedestrians and streets for automobiles, and with lot forms of the most appropriate shapes, will permit considerable economies in roads and other servicing infrastructures such as water and sewerage."

What might be the shape and character of an ideal community planned on HD/LR lines with patio houses? It would be distinctly urban but with gardens in evidence, low in profile, compact with the scale of people. Walking could be the main way of movement as distances could be short because densities would be high. Few automobiles would be seen as they are stored in garages within houses. Alongside a busy pedestrian-public, commercial-civic realm of streets and squares, with frequent and open contact between people, is also the realm of inner privacy offered by patio houses.

In small access streets to houses, pedestrians have priority over automobiles, which would move slowly. Streets connect to an extensive, pedestrian necklace of lanes and compact gardens intensively planted, threading through the community and carefully differentiated in scale. Houses would embody private gardens in patios and on roof terraces, etc. Small neighborhood gardens may be walled and others not. Open areas and larger gardens within a community, as distinct from those surrounding it, would be kept to a minimum so as not to fragment the urban structure, and be used to a

maximum. An open space may service the needs of a school, perhaps a walkup apartment building, as well as the individual houses surrounding it. Schools, etc. would not sit in the middle of an open space but nestle on its perimeter and be contiguous with the fabric of houses.

Groups of densely planned communities would be in contrast to the open or tree-surrounded landscape. The macro configuration of communities would be linear aggregations to permit additions of units along communication routes and the growth of units perpendicular to them. The regional pattern is one of dense urban nodes, which maintain a clear distinction between the built environment of cities and the countryside, linked together by rapid transportation lines.

HD/LR is a basis to recover human scale in cities. In contrast, high density high rise (HD/HR) is an opposite strategy which achieves high densities with tall buildings. The resulting type of urban structure loses the scale of people. There is an application for some tall structures in certain urban locations but the first priority at this time is to hold the scale of cities with low profile development.

As reduction in size is the surest way to reduce costs, the houses are by necessity small and compact. However, it is very important that the living/dining area of a house is comparatively generous as this is where most time is spent by a family during the 24 hour cycle. It should be the focus of the home and the hearth, of contact between members of a family. It should be generous enough in area, appropriate in shape and in careful relationship to its garden to fulfill this most important and central role in the house.

A generous living/dining area is obtained by careful overall planning and by keeping the bedrooms small. The bathrooms in most houses are kept to one installation. Bed sitting rooms are included where possible so that parents and grandparents can be accommodated conveniently in a home. These rooms may also be for family, television and study uses. Bedrooms in some cases are equipped with sliding walls so that they can be easily opened or divided according to need. The bedrooms are viewed as having other uses as well, perhaps at a different time, for study, hobbies, etc. Flexibility in these spaces is important. The utilities are in a separate small room which in some cases is also large enough to provide additional storage.

Split-Level

The split-level one story project is a new concept and a house type which offers many advantages and interesting features. Its special features are conservation of energy with respect to the insulation of the lower level of the unit and very efficient land utilization through full coverage of the lots and use of roofs as gardens. The vertical level shift enables the bottom level to be sunk half a story, or to the sill line, thus creating a semi-basement to take advantage of the near constant temperature of the surrounding earth for relative effect of cooling in summer and warming in winter. The split-level enables very easy half-flight access to all roof levels and their full use as gardens with terraces, with the additional insulation which these provide.

The split-level profile lends itself to attached conservatories for interior/exterior covered winter gardens. Several of the projects have this feature and some are designed so that glazed wall and roof sections may open or retract. Others have glazed sections covering and enclosing patios with changeable positions, one for summer and another for winter. In this way tropical and semi-tropical plant types which thrive in summer outside, but which would die in winter, may be enclosed within the house during the inclement months.

Automobile parking is off the actual house lot in the single story units; thus access streets are minimum width and collective covered parking serves and would be attached to groups of houses.

Many of the house types can change position within the lot and most of the types can expand, or be built in a range of sizes. Changes within the lot are done by rotating the plan, or changing the location of the patio, and alternating the position of the second floor. These types offer a range of options in orientation for the entire unit, or ground and second floors separately, with an identical plan type. Thus a high degree of standardization of plans, elements and building components leading to economic production with a wide choice of unit form becomes possible with this new approach. Most house types can expand in stages, or may be initially built in a range of sizes, to suit different needs while maintaining the same plan type.

Gardens

Within each lot form the house is organized and the design generated by several factors, the most important of which are the interior patio garden, the relationship of living spaces to the patio, the shapes and dimensions of bedrooms as determined by beds and light flow and penetration. Other factors are also obviously important, such as bathrooms, kitchens, etc., but less so in articulating the basic geometry of the plan.

The patio garden provides inner privacy for each house and it becomes the focus for the home, which is designed around it. In some cases the spaces and rooms of the house go around it and in others they look frontally into the patio. In some houses there is more than one patio. Some patios are square or nearly square with the house on two, three or four sides; others are long and narrow with the house down the longer side, looking across the patio, or on the narrow side as well, with the living area of the house looking down the long dimension. Toilets, utilities and storage are located within the plans so as not to consume the vital patio wall surface which is ideally reserved for living, dining and bedroom spaces only.

7

Solar Transition

An Economic Analysis

Industrial/Consumer Energy Demand

Employment Projections

Implementation Scenario

Maintained Production Levels

The following analysis of jobs, economic implications and energy policies was prepared by Leonard Rodberg. Rodberg is a member of the Public Resource Center, and prepared this study for the Joint Economic Committee of the Congress.

Since World War II, American consumption of energy has tripled, and advocates of the coal and nuclear route argue that continued energy growth, in spite of its potential costs, is essential for economic growth.[1,2,3,4] As one advocacy group put it, "Growth in energy use is necessary to our national prosperity and to provide the jobs that are needed today . . . the relationship between energy availability and jobs is direct and inevitable."[5] Clearly, many people still believe that continued growth in our consumption of energy, and especially of the nonrenewable fuels—oil, gas, coal and uranium—is still essential if every American is to have a chance at the good life.

What is shown here is that this view is not correct. It will be demonstrated that it is possible to produce the same goods and services, and to achieve a higher GNP, by emphasizing the conservation of energy and conversion to renewable energy sources. Conservation and renewable energy can be major growth industries in the decades ahead, contributing both to the health of our economy and our citizenry. Introduction of a broad range of currently feasible conservation measures can simultaneously cut the consumption of rapidly depleting energy resources and create hundreds of thousands of new jobs. The expansion of solar energy programs can create a permanent substitute for declining reserves of nonrenewable fuels and add millions of new jobs, particularly in urban areas where they are desperately needed. They can also reduce the outflow of dollars for imported oil and curb the inflationary effects of rapidly rising fuel prices.[6]

The United States continues to experience a failure to provide enough jobs for its citizens, especially for minority groups who suffer the highest rates of unemployment. In 1978 the unemployment rate still stood at 6 percent, with black unemployment at 12 percent and teenage unemployment at 16 percent; "disguised unemployment" makes the real situation twice as bad. Economists do not see any prospect for an early improvement in this poor economic performance, and many foresee a downturn in the coming months which will make this situation even worse.

Many analysts argue that energy growth is crucial to a reduction in unemployment. In reality, the purpose of what we commonly call "energy" is to reduce the need for human labor, exacerbating the problem of providing jobs for a growing labor force. Industry has increased its output by drawing on the apparently limitless supplies of fossil fuels while shrinking its labor force. As the Congressional Office of Technology Assessment has commented, "The national energy policy of the last several decades has been to replace human labor as rapidly as possible with petroleum energy."[7] Thus the same practices which are creating the energy shortage have also been responsible for the shortage of jobs.

The ready availability of cheap energy has reduced employment opportunities in the energy-consuming industries and led to a continuing displacement of workers onto an uncertain job market. The energy industry itself cannot take up the slack; it employs a small proportion (historically, about 2 percent) of the labor force, and energy-related employment has not been growing. Both producers and the users of energy have taken advantage of the ready availability of inexpensive energy supplies to introduce highly-automated, energy-consuming production techniques, reducing employment per unit of output first in agriculture, then in manufacturing, and, most recently, in the service sector. The economy has not grown because of rising energy consumption, but in spite of it. Total employment has increased because the total output of goods, and especially, of services has increased and overcome the "labor-saving"—that is, employment-reducing—effects of rising energy usage.

Economists often argue that such "labor-saving" measures increase economic "efficiency" by freeing workers to perform other necessary tasks. However, when the economy is not able to provide jobs for all who need them, and when energy supplies are limited, the opposite is true. If the workers who are displaced cannot find employment, they must be supported by unemployment insurance and welfare while being economically unproductive; those who do find employment will consume additional energy in their new jobs, thus accelerating the depletion of scarce energy resources.[8]

The nation thus faces two difficult but related problems, the continuing shortage of jobs, and the coming shortage of energy. The purpose of this study is to show, with a specific plan, how large-scale investment in conservation and solar energy can contribute to the resolution of both problems. Most projections show only slow growth for the renewable energy technologies. However, these projections tend to be self-fulfilling prophecies. By assuming slow growth, they inhibit investment and thus ensure slow growth. We present a positive scenario that examines the implications of rapid growth, to stimulate discussion and interest in this possibility.

Baseline Projections

Conventional projections of energy consumption assume that the past relation between gross national product and energy consumption will continue into the future. More recently they have been assuming a rise in the price of the non-renewable fuels and, as a consequence, a slightly less rapid rise in demand for energy.

Until about four years ago, most projections of energy demand envisioned an aggregate demand by the year 2000 of 190 quads per year, two and one-half times our current consumption. (We use the common measure of energy output, the "quad", or one quadrillion British thermal units (BTU). A quad is approximately equal to the energy supplied by 172 million barrels of oil, 42 million tons of bituminous coal, 0.98 trillion cubic feet of natural gas, or 293 billion kilowatt-hours of electricity. In 1977 the United States consumed 75.9 quads of primary fuels.) Now, with evident signs of a decline in the rate of energy growth, projections are beginning to show more moderate increases. A "consensus" prepared by the Edison Electric Institute calls for consumption of about 150 quads in the year 2000, twice our current usage.[9] They assume continuing growth at a rate of about 3 percent per year, somewhat less than the pre-1973 growth rate of 3.5 percent but still a continuation of exponential growth. In spite of clear signs of an approaching price and supply crunch, they continue to assume that energy consumption will grow exponentially out to the next century.[10]

These "business as usual" projections of energy consumption assume that past practices will continue into the future and that new supplies of the energy sources we use today—coal, oil, natural gas, and uranium—will be discovered as current sources are depleted. They assume that alternative sources of energy—solar heating and cooling, wind power, etc.—will play a small role during this time period and foresee an ever-growing consumption of the non-renewable energy sources. As oil and natural gas become increasingly scarce and expensive, they forecast a shift to coal and nuclear energy and, especially, to electricity produced by these fuels.

In this study we will use, as our reference base, an energy projection prepared by Data Resources, Inc., for the period 1977-79.[11] DRI assumes that oil prices will rise 7.5 percent per year, to $1.31 per gallon by 1990, while natural gas prices rise 3.5 percent per year to $3.76 per thousand cubic feet. (Here, and throughout this study, we use 1978 dollars.) They then forecast a growth rate of 2.98 percent per year and total consumption of primary fuels in 1990 of 110.7 quads. Extended to the year 2000, this yields a total annual consumption at that point of 148 quads. In the DRI projection, the consumption of energy by sector and fuel type is shown in Table A-1.

Table A-1
Energy Consumption
(quad/yr.)

	Coal		Natural Gas		Petroleum		Nuclear		Hydro		Total	
	1977	1990	1977	1990	1977	1990	1977	1990	1977	1990	1977	1990
Household & Commercial	0.2	0.1	8.3	9.5	6.6	8.8	-	-	-	-	15.1	18.4
Industrial	4.2	6.1	7.2	7.9	7.3	11.3	-	-	-	-	18.7	25.3
Transportation					19.2	21.0	-	-	-	-	19.2	21.0
Electric Utilities	10.3	21.9	2.4	1.2	4.6	5.3	2.2	13.3	3.0	4.3	22.5	46.0
Total	14.7	28.1	17.9	18.6	37.7	46.4	2.2	13.3	3.0	4.3	75.5	110.7

Consumption of every energy source increases, but coal and nuclear power meet most of the increased demand, largely through their use in electricity production. Nevertheless, petroleum and natural gas are assumed to be still available by 2000 and consumed in even greater quantities than today. This is possible only because of the assumption that increasing quantities of these fuels are imported (e.g., 57 percent of the petroleum is imported). However, United States demand will be competing with the increasing demand from other countries, including growing Third World economies, and many analysts foresee a shortfall in world supply between 1985 and 1995. For instance, the report of the MIT Workshop on Alternative Energy Strategies concluded that, even in its moderate growth model, "energy demand growth quickly outpaces plausible projections of potential supply. It follows that historically high growth rates of energy use—rates substantially higher than ours—projected into the future are simply not realistic."[12] As noted in the introduction, this is just one of a number of potential barriers to this scenario.

Over three-fifths of all energy use takes place in the industrial and commercial sectors, where goods and services are produced and workers employed. Yet, the major consumers of energy employ relatively few people. Between 1948 and 1970, energy use by the goods-producing sectors rose 120 percent, while their employment declined 1.4 percent. By contrast, energy use in the provision of services increased 62 percent, but employment gained 75 percent.[12] (In Bureau of Labor Statistics categories, the goods-producing sectors are agriculture, forestry, fisheries, mining, construction, and manufacturing; the service-producing sectors are transportation, communications, utilities, wholesale and retail trade, finance, insurance, real estate, services, and government.)

Six industries have historically consumed the lions' share of the energy used by industry. In 1968 (the year of the most recent detailed study of industrial energy use), the primary metals, chemical, food, paper, stone-clay-glass products, and the petroleum and coal processing industries used 68 percent of all energy used by industry, yet employed only 25 percent of all industrial workers and just 7 percent of the nation's total work force.[13,1] Between 1950 and 1971, their work force increased only 2.5 percent, while their energy consumption increased 106 percent.

These relationships will probably continue in a period when energy prices are rising. The response of business to rising energy prices and the prospect of shortages is difficult to forecast, since we have not encountered such a period before. Economic projections must be made on the basis of the past, but we have evidence only from a period in which energy prices were falling and supplies were plentiful.

Much will depend on the response of public policy to this new situation, as well as on the overall economic environment. Businesses may reduce output, and thus their demand for labor, in the face of higher energy prices (the "income effect"), or they may call upon more labor and capital resources to replace energy (the "substitution effect"). Studies by Jorgenson and his co-workers suggest that the substitution effect will predominate, but only slightly. Using a model driven by cost-minimizing business behavior, they find that an average increase of 54 percent in energy prices will reduce energy consumption in the year 2000 by 38 percent and raise labor demand by 1.5 percent.[14,15]

The Bureau of Labor Statistics of the U.S. Department of Labor carries on a continuing program of economic projections, in order to provide forecasts of labor demand in particular industries and occupations.[16] These projections are based upon expected levels of employment and labor productivity, with price variables playing a secondary role. Thus, though they make use of the DRI projections to ensure that their predicted level of energy production is compatible with such "mainstream" energy forecasts, they do not incorporate the effects of rising energy prices on other categories of consumption. Nevertheless, since these effects are, at this point, uncertain but likely to be small—given sufficient time for adjustment to new patterns of consumption, new transportation modes, etc.—the BLS projections seem quite usable.

The BLS forecasts that the labor force will grow, between 1977 and 1990, from 99.5 million to between 113.5 and 125.6 million.[17] This is an average

growth rate of 1.4 percent, considerably slower than the 2.3 percent growth rate that characterized the 1970-77 period.

Within the BLS projections, the growing consumption of energy is not accompanied by a corresponding rise in employment in the energy industry or in the industries which use that energy. Rather, it leads to a continuing relative shift of employment away from these sectors to the more labor-intensive service sectors. Table 2 shows the projected change in employment shares.

Table A-2

	Increase in Employment 1977-1990	Share of Total Employment (percent)	
		1977	1990
Goods-producing sectors	4,797,000	26.8	25.5
Energy-intensive industries	373,000	4.1	3.6
Service-producing sectors	18,352,000	71.2	72.6
Energy industry	351,000	2.0	1.9
Total	23,500,000	100.0	100.0

More than three out of every four workers entering the labor force in this period will have to find a job in the service sector where, quite frequently, wages are low and jobs provide less than full-time work. In 1976 the average wage in the service-producing sectors was $4.45 per hour, only 79 per-

cent of the average wage in the goods-producing sectors.[1]

Bullard has argued that escalating energy prices will make "planned obsolescence" more expensive and will favor the manufacture of more durable products.[18] Manufactured goods will become more expensive relative to less energy-intensive services, consumers will buy them less frequently, and they will have to last longer and be maintained better. This will result in fewer assembly-line jobs and more maintenance and repair jobs.

The new jobs in the energy industry, which are of primary interest to us in this study, are largely related to the expansion of electricity production. They are jobs constructing the needed electric plants, mining and refining coal and uranium, and operating power plants. It is characteristic of these occupations that large-scale migrations of workers will be required, as fuel sources in particular locales are exploited and then depleted, and as health and safety requirements demand the remote location of power plants. These can impose severe dislocations and social costs on workers and their communities.

In general, this "business as usual" projection envisions an economic environment in which it will be difficult to achieve high levels of employment. With energy prices rising relative to other costs, increasing portions of the consumer's dollar will be taken up with direct and indirect energy costs. Until energy conservation measures can be undertaken, or alternative living modes adopted which can reduce energy consumption, relatively less income will be available for the purchase of other goods and services having a low energy, and high job, content. In this setting, conservation and renewable energy become essential parts of any strategy for full employment.

Toward Conservation and Renewable Energy

To avoid the manifold deleterious consequences of continued reliance on nonrenewable fuels, we must undertake a strong program stressing conservation and renewable energy (CARE). There would be a strong emphasis on conserving energy, that is, on making the most efficient possible use of the energy we do consume, and on conversion of an increasing portion of our energy consumption from nonrenewable fossil fuels and uranium to solar energy in its various direct and indirect forms (solar heating, wind, biomass). Total fuel consumption would be capped and ultimately reduced, and the mix of energy sources would be changed, with an increasing portion coming from renewable sources.

In general, energy consumption can be reduced by (i) performing the same activity in a more energy-efficient manner, (ii) using energy that is now wasted, and (iii) changing behavior to reduce the need for energy. All three should be undertaken, though the last—involving modifications in our housing patterns, our transportation systems, the way we produce goods and services—will require more time to implement and more sweeping social changes. Our present patterns have been developed in an era when energy was cheap and its supply thought to be endless. As we realize that these conditions no longer hold, we may begin making significant changes in the way society organizes its living and working activities.

Very large savings appear possible even without this. With relatively modest efforts in the first two categories, savings approaching one-half of current consumption can be made.[19] There are great opportunities for energy conservation, not just because we have been using energy wastefully, but also because we have been using it inappropriately. We have been using fuels and processes which produce very high temperatures (hundreds or even thousands of degrees) to heat our homes 10 to 20 degrees, with excess heat simply thrown out into the atmosphere. By producing energy that is tailored to its use, and extracting all the useful work from it, we can make significant gains over our past inefficient practices. Furthermore, conservation is not expensive; estimates of the cost of conservation measures range from one-half to one-tenth the cost of adding an equivalent amount of energy from new sources.[20,21,22]

It should be emphasized that, as we (and most analysts) use the concept, "conservation" does not mean the curtailment of energy-using activities. Rather, as the CONAES Demand and Conservation Panel defined it, conservation includes "technological and procedural changes that allow us to reduce demand for energy (or specific scarce fuels) without corresponding reductions in the goods and services we enjoy."[23]

However, we will need some additions to our current supply of energy, not just conservation of what we use, and we will soon have to begin replacing fossil fuels with renewable sources of energy. We have to create an entirely new industry to produce, install, and maintain solar energy units of all kinds—hot water and air collectors and storage units, photovoltaic generators, biomass converters, wind machines, and so on. In the 1950s, a national decision created the massive federal highway system and, in the 1960s, the space program. Each involved investments of billions of dollars and hundreds of thousands of jobs. In the same way, we need to move toward a national program of solar energy production and conversion. Solar energy could be the technology that lifts the economy out of the doldrums of the 1970s into a more prosperous period in the 1980s.

We will look at projections to the year 1990, assuming that such a program is initiated. The year 1990 may be looked on as a typical year in a fifty-year transition from dependence on nonrenewable fuels to nearly complete reliance on renewable energy sources, primarily energy from the sun. Most homes, office buildings, and factories have useful lives on the order of fifty years. Thus, about fifty years are required to replace this building stock and convert it to energy-conserving, renewable sources.

One frequently hears expressions of concern for the employment impact of such alternative energy policies. These reflect doubts over the ability of the alternative approach to provide the energy that industry needs, in order to operate the machines on which many workers depend for their jobs. The approach adopted in this study assumes that no policy will be adopted that does not provide sufficient energy to fuel the economy and, especially, its productive machinery. Thus the approach incorporates ways of substituting, step by step, renewable energy sources for non-renewable ones. It assumes that there will be no reduction in the use of conventional energy sources, and no reduction in the supply of conventional fuels, at whatever price, until an alternative is available in sufficient quantity to meet the demand.

An extensive range of measures can be encompassed within a CARE strategy. Those postulated to be installed and operational by 1990 include the following:

(1) For residential and commercial use:
—Reduction of heat loss through additional insulation, efficiency improvements in the use of heating and cooling units, and careful attention to the flow of heat in the building and through its outer "envelope".
—Improved energy efficiency of equipment and appliances.
—Increased heat absorption from the sun through passive solar designs.

—Solar water- and space-heating through active fluid collection and circulation.

(2) For industrial use:
—More efficient industrial practices, recovery and re-use of waste heat, and use of recycled materials.
—Generation of electricity as a by-product of heat and steam production ("cogeneration").
—Solar energy collectors and solar-powered heat engines.

(3) For transportation:
—Increased automotive efficiency.
—Increased use of urban mass transit and inter-urban rail and other energy-efficient modes of transportation.

(4) For portable fuels, production of methane and alcohol from agricultural and urban wastes.

(5) For electricity production:
—Photovoltaic cells, including concentrators and cogeneration, on homes, commercial and industrial buildings.
—Wind-powered electric generators.
—Solar-powered heat engine-generator systems.

Other uses of solar energy, especially for cooling purposes, have not been included in the estimates made in this study because of the cost and underdeveloped nature of these systems. Similarly, capturing other forms of solar energy, such as ocean thermal energy, has been proposed, but such systems have not yet reached a sufficient stage of development to be able to estimate their energy and employment potential.

The energy savings achieved, and the number of jobs produced by these measures, depend upon the scale of investment in them. For this study we assume a set of national goals, projecting the achievement of a specific level of implementation for each measure by the turn of the century. (With different goals, the results will be scaled up or down proportionately.) The goals we assume are described in Table A-3.

Table A-3

Measure	Goal for Year 2000
Residential Use	
Conservation	50% saving*
Active and passive solar	100% of new homes; 50% of existing homes
Commercial Use	
Conservation	50% saving*
Active solar	50% of all buildings
Industrial Use	
Conservation	40% saving by 1990*
Cogeneration	100% of all usable sites
Active solar	25% of all process heat
Transportation	No specific goal
Portable Fuels	Conversion of 50% of waste products
Solar/Electricity	25% of current electricity production

Energy saving goals refer to the consumption of delivered energy at the site of end use.

These goals are ambitious but achievable with the vigorous support of public policy. To meet them, we assume that investment in conservation and renewable energy builds up over a five-year period preceding 1985, with a constant level of investment thereafter. We find, for the year 1990, the following projections:

Table A-4

	Annual Investment ($ billion, 1978 $)	Direct	Number of Jobs (thousands) Indirect	Total
Residential				
Building conservation	5.7	125	74	199
Appliance conservation	1.4	29	23	52
Passive solar	0.7	15	11	26
Active solar	14.8	266	244	510
Commercial				
Conservation	2.4	52	34	86
Active solar	6.6	119	109	228
Industrial				
Conservation	1.5	20	25	45
Cogeneration	3.8	51	62	113
Active solar	12.1	163	198	361
Transportation	—	—	—	—
Portable Fuels	4.3	89	77	166
Electricity				
Photovoltaics	3.6	69	53	122
Wind	5.3	91	81	172
Heat engines	3.4	31	59	90
Total	65.6	1,120	1,050	2,170

We distinguish the "direct" jobs involved in producing and installing the final products from the "indirect" employment involved in producing raw materials and components. The jobs projected here pay wages and salaries that are typical of the respective industries in 1990, especially manufacturing and construction. One-quarter of the investment and the jobs are in energy conservation, three-quarters in solar energy. About one-third of the investment is in the residential sector; the remainder of the investment must be made by business and government decisionmakers.

For comparison, the BLS projects the gross national product in 1990 to be $3,241 billion, with gross private domestic investment equal to $510 billion. Total employment will be 114,000,000 and total unemployment 5,400,000, with the BLS assumption of an unemployment rate of 4.5 percent.

Construction employment will be 5,574,000 and manufacturing employment 23,872,000. Thus, conservation and solar employment will impose relatively small pressure on the economy as a whole, but it can make a significant dent in unemployment.

These investments lead to very significant savings of non-renewable fuel. Rather than including solar energy in the national energy accounts as contributing positive amounts of energy, there is less ambiguity if it is viewed as a conservation measure, enabling the consumption of non-renewable fuels to be curbed. (The recently-enacted National Energy Conservation Policy Act includes solar energy and wind power devices among the energy conservation measures it promotes.) This method of accounting is especially appropriate for on-site solar techniques, where the energy supplied by solar devices is not transmitted, marketed, or even measured, but simply permits less dependence on external energy sources powered by non-renewable fuels.

Assuming that a strong CARE program is begun in 1980, we find that the fuel consumed in 1990, compared with the DRI business-as-usual projection, is as shown in Table A-5.

The implementation of these CARE measures leads to a saving of 44.9 quads of non-renewable fuels. (It might be thought that we should add the fuel consumed in the course of manufacturing and installing the conservation and solar systems. However, we have no way of knowing whether this production is part of the production already included in the BLS projection, or is an addition to it. In any case, this energy "investment" is "paid back" by these systems in a year or two and thus represents 5-10% of their useful energy delivery).[24]

Projecting forward to the year 2000, with CARE measures implemented according to Table A-4, we obtain a total fuel consumption of 52.7 quads, little more than a third of the 144 quads found if the conventional, business-as-usual path is followed. About half the savings are achieved through conservation measures, half through solar energy.

The conventional method of energy accounting would add to the energy sources shown in Table A-5 the contribution of hydropower and various active solar systems envisioned in this scenario. Using this approach, we find the situation as expressed in Table A-6:

Table A-5
Primary Fuel Consumption
(quad/yr.)

	DRI	CARE
Coal	28.1	14.2
Natural gas	18.6	11.5
Petroleum	46.4	33.6
Nuclear	13.3	2.2
Total	106.4	61.5

Table A-6
Energy Consumption
(quad/yr.)

	DRI	CARE
Non-renewable fuels	106.4	61.5
Hydropower	4.3	4.3
Solar systems	—	10.2
Total	110.7	76.0

Total energy consumption in the CARE scenario is just about equal to total consumption in 1977, that is, there is zero energy growth between 1977 and 1990. Solar systems provide 10.2 quads or 13 percent of the energy in 1990, and they provide 22 quads or 28 percent of the energy in 2000. (This understates the significance of solar sources; to the extent they substitute for electricity produced from non-renewable sources, 1 Btu of solar energy replaces 3.4 Btu of non-renewable fuels.) For comparison, ERDA Report No. 49, the National Solar Energy Research, Development, and Demonstration Program, projected a solar contribution of the order of 10 quads by the turn of the century; the Stanford Research Institute found 15 quads in its "solar emphasis" scenario; the Mitro Corporation projected 6 quads; the Committee on Nuclear and Alternative Energy Systems (CON-AES) of the National Academy of Sciences found a high-solar scenario yielding 14 quads; and the Council on Environmental Quality projected 15-25 quads.[23,25,26,27]

The savings achieved by introducing this wide range of conservation and renewable energy measures allows spending on non-renewable fuels to be reduced by $118.8 billion in 1990. We estimate that this will lead to a reduction of 644,000 jobs operating and supplying facilities that use and distribute nonrenewable fuels and of 493,000 jobs in electric power plant manufacture and construction. Of the total of 1,137,000 jobs, 680,000 are directly in these industries; 457,000 are in industries that are indirectly affected by these energy savings.

By 1990, the money saved by residential, commercial, and industrial consumers from reduced fuel consumption greatly exceeds the amount invested annually in CARE measures. These extra funds can be spent to purchase additional goods and services. For the net savings of $53.2 billion ($118.8 billion less the annual CARE investment of $65.6 billion), there will be an additional 1,870,000 jobs created. The BLS projections assume that the cost of energy rises no faster than the general rate of inflation, which they project at 5.4 percent per year. Since the price of these fuels will very likely rise faster than this, the dollar savings will probably be greater and the number of jobs created by the shift in spending correspondingly larger. Also, to the extent that CARE investments are made out of borrowed funds rather than current income, there would be more disposable income available and, consequently, more jobs produced. On the other hand, if fuel prices are raised by their suppliers in response to the drop in demand, there would be fewer additional jobs.

Keeping in mind these caveats regarding this estimate of the jobs created (and, indeed, the approximate nature of all of the estimates in this study), we have the net job creation in Table A-7.

Table A-7

	Number of Jobs Created (thousands)
Conservation	521
Solar Energy	1,649
Non-renewable fuels	−1,137
Added disposable income	1,870
Total	2,903

These figures do not include the additional jobs that would be created through the multiplier effect (spending of the income earned through this employment) and the accelerator effect (increased investment induced through anticipated growth). Such effects result from a stimulus added to an existing economic situation, whereas many of the jobs envisioned here may be part of the employment growth projected by BLS. To the extent they are not reflected in those projections, but represent additional investment beyond that in the BLS forecast, there would be a roughly-equivalent number of additional jobs created through the multiplier (re-spending) effect.

It is now widely recognized that employment programs must be "targeted" to be effective, that is, they must place funds and jobs in the regions, and among the population groups, suffering the most from unemployment. Jobs in the fuel extraction industries (coal mining, oil and gas exploration, etc.) and in power plant construction tend to be far from the areas suffering the most severe unemployment. On the other hand, energy conservation and solar energy system production and installation will take place largely in settled urban areas where the unemployed reside and where they can easily be trained and hired. Thus, the jobs created in this scenario can make a significant contribution to solving the chronic unemployment problem facing our urban areas. Some jobs, such as those involved in producing photovoltaic arrays and solar heat engines, will be in

more centralized manufacturing facilities; these can replace the jobs displaced by the reduction in conventional energy investment and production.

The jobs will be dispersed as widely across the country as are the dwellings people live in and the sites of their work. It will not require workers to move to remote or temporary construction sites. Energy conserving technologies tend to be decentralized, geographically distributed in roughly the same proportion as the population. Fuel supply technologies, on the other hand, tend to be centralized and located where the fuel sources are, e.g., in Alaska, offshore, in the Rocky Mountains or on the northern plains.

Jobs will be created in insulating and retrofitting homes with solar units, manufacturing and installing more efficient heating and cooling systems, making office buildings more energy efficient, producing and operating mass transit systems, producing and installing cogeneration devices, and recycling valuable materials. The skills required will be similar to those required for conventional construction projects and heating system installation. Work will be provided for sheet metal workers, carpenters, plumbers, pipefitters, construction workers, and production line workers of all kinds. Energy management will be increasingly important and will be a new source of employment for engineers and designers. Also, solar energy technology is suited to community-based enterprise and small business. Expansion of this industry will open up opportunities for ownership and economic development by those who now have little or no role in the multinational energy industries.

As energy conservation and the use of renewable energy become guideposts for community planning, land use and housing density patterns will shift. Higher densities, with a reduction of suburban sprawl, will reduce transportation energy usage and allow more energy-efficient housing construction.[28,29] Compact communities will facilitate the introduction of neighborhood-scale solar units for both heat and electricity generation.[4] Such units have a number of significant advantages, including the possibility of utilizing shared community spaces with protected access to the sun and of incorporating very large storage tanks that can store summer heat for winter usage. Very high densities (especially buildings of four or more stories) will be discouraged, since the solar resource is relatively diffuse (requiring

about 400 square feet per family) and on-site energy supply would then become unfeasible.

Commercial and industrial activities will require more energy planning and more land for access to the sun. (In a solarized society, land becomes an energy resource!) Though these activities may occupy a small fraction of a community's land, their solar energy needs will require several times the space they occupy.[29] There will have to be community- and region-wide planning to ensure that the necessary space is available, whether on buildings or on open spaces. There may also be a tendency for energy-intensive industries to locate in areas having large amounts of annual solar radiation; though increased transportation costs may tend to counter such shifts.

In general, energy considerations will become a predominant consideration in land use planning, community organization, and the location of jobs.

Financing the Solar Transition

Achievement of the scenario envisioned in this study, and of the job creation it would generate, depends on political and economic decisions which induce the necessary investment and make available the necessary funds.

It seems likely that this will not occur unless mandatory federal standards are established governing a broad range of energy conservation and renewable energy measures (similar to the mileage requirements now imposed on

automobile manufacturers). Even though price factors alone would appear to impel the introduction of these measures today, in fact, a great many of those with the ability to introduce them have not done so. The builders of homes and commercial buildings want to keep their initial selling costs down even though, over the lifetime of the building, the purchaser may well end up paying more through high energy usage for heating, cooling, and solar energy, insisting on twice as large a return (about 30 percent per year) from an investment in energy conservation as from an investment that increases productive output.[30]

Many conservation measures are relatively inexpensive and, even at today's fuel prices, would pay for themselves in energy savings in just a few months or years; as prices rise, they will become even more cost-effective. Many solar energy systems make economic sense today when compared with the cost of electricity, though not yet when compared with the cost of oil or gas.[31,32] In all cases, these financial benefits accrue in the future through some substantial investment in the present. Consumers and businesses may prefer other ways of spending their money. Generally, an energy-related investment will not markedly improve current living conditions for the individual consumer or expand sales for the businessman.

In addition, it is characteristic of most CARE measures that they are purchased by the user of energy, rather than by the current producers of energy. Whereas a power plant is purchased, constructed, and operated by an electric utility, a solar heating unit is purchased by the individual homeowner or builder for installation on the individual home. The user's return on this investment depends on the cost of the energy saved, and thus on the average cost of all facilities then producing and distributing energy. A supplier's investment choice, on the other hand, is based on the comparative cost of new facilities currently being built.

New energy production plants tend to be increasingly expensive so that, in general, an investment in conservation or solar energy would save more energy than would be produced by the same expenditure on new facilities using non-renewable fuels.[4,31] Cogeneration equipment costs industrial users more than what they are now paying for electricity, but less than what it would cost a utility to produce equivalent central power plant capacity.[33] Since the user's investment is compared with the average cost of energy, while the supplier deals with replacement cost, the user's decision is weighted against the purchase. To overcome this, some alternative financing arrangement seems to be necessary.

One alternative is to introduce some form of national subsidy, such as the recently-approved tax credit for homeowners and businesses. However, this applies only to particular classes of taxpayers and will not address the general need for making CARE investments attractive to the energy user.

Another possibility would be to have the suppliers, especially the electric utilities, purchase (or loan the money for) conservation and solar installations. These investments would then be incorporated into the internal accounting of the energy producers. However, this would negate some of the main advantages of renewable energy systems, namely, their flexibility and amenability to control by the user. It would seem preferable to set up an alternative financing scheme which would accomplish the same end, that is, introducing a broad societal perspective into the financial arrangement, without transferring control to the current suppliers of energy. Since suppliers' investments will, in any case, be based on borrowed money which is repaid through payments by consumers, it should be possible, in principle, to devise mechanisms which would achieve this.

One would be an energy development bank which could borrow large sums at attractive rates on the private money market and loan these for CARE purchases, either directly or through local banking institutions, to users (including communities for shared, neighborhood-scale facilities). In effect, this federally-backed bank would be borrowing the sums that would otherwise be drawn on by the utilities and other energy suppliers, and making them available to energy users. By loaning them out for long terms at low interest, the monthly cost to users can be reduced below what their energy spending would otherwise be. (Indeed, the San Diego Savings and Loan Association is already making available loans which are extensions of a homeowner's mortgage, so the homeowner may end up with no additional monthly cost for the CARE installation.)

With the introduction of a financing mechanism such as this, with a broad-based education effort, and with the strong support of public officials, it should be possible to launch a national conservation and renewable energy program that would have the very great employment benefits identified in this study.

References

1. Statistical Abstract of the United States, Bureau of the Census, U.S. Dept. of Commerce, Washington, DC, 1977.

2. *Man's Impact on the Global Environment*, Report of the Study of Critical Environmental Problems, MIT Press, Cambridge, 1970.

3. Alvin M. Weinberg, "Can We Do Without Uranium?", in *Future Strategies for Energy Development*, Oak Ridge Associated Universities, Oak Ridge, TN, 1977.

4. Amory B. Lovins, *Soft Energy Paths*, Ballinger, Cambridge, 1977, and "Soft Energy Technologies", *Annual Review of Energy*, 3, 477, 1978.

5. "Jobs and Energy: A Call for Action", Americans for Energy Independence, Washington, DC, 1976.

6. For an excellent summary of the case for conservation and solar energy as an employment-producer, see the booklet "Jobs and Energy" prepared by Environmentalists for Full Employment, 1101 Vermont Ave. NW, Washington, DC, 1977.

7. "Analysis of the Proposed National Energy Plan", Office of Technology Assessment, U.S. Congress, Washington, DC, 1977.

8. For a more detailed examination of the relation between economic growth and energy consumption, see Leonard S. Rodberg, "Energy and Jobs: The Case for CARE", in *Energy and Equity: Some Social Concerns*, Joint Center for Political Studies, Washington, DC, to be published.

9. *Electric Perspectives*, 77/6, Edison Electric Institute, NY.

10. *Energy: Global Prospects, 1985-2000*, Report of the Workshop on Alternative Energy Strategies, McGraw-Hill, NY, 1977.

11. Energy Review, Summer 1977, Data Resources, Inc., and Maria Mahon, Bureau of Labor Statistics, U.S. Dept. of Labor, private communication.

12. Study by Jack Alterman, Bureau of Economic Analysis, U.S. Dept. of Commerce, 1975.

13. "Patterns of Energy Consumption in the United States", prepared by the Stanford Research Institute for the Office of Science and Technology, Executive Office of the President, Washington, DC, 1972.

14. *A Time to Choose: America's Energy Future*, by the Energy Policy Project of the Ford Foundation, Ballinger, 1974.

15. E.A. Hudson and D.W. Jorgenson, "U.S. Energy Policy and Economic Growth, 1975-2000", *Bell Journal of Economics and Management Science*, Autumn, 1974; K.C. Hoffman and D.W. Jorgenson, "Economic and Technological Models for Evaluation of Energy Policy," ibid, Autumn, 1977.

16. The projections used in this study for the period 1977-90 were preliminary results provided by the Office of Economic Growth of BLS, especially Charles T. Bowman. The author is grateful for the assistance of this office. Summaries of the macroeconomic and industry final demand projections have now been published in Norman C. Saunders, "The U.S. Economy to 1990: Two Projections for Growth" and Arthur Andreassen, "Changing Patterns of Demand: BLS Projections to 1990", both appearing in the December, 1978, issue of the *Monthly Labor Review*. The industry output and employment projections are scheduled for publication in the April, 1979, issue of the *Monthly Labor Review*. These will incorporate some minor revisions from the preliminary results used in this study. For descriptions of earlier projections, see "The U.S. Economy in 1985: A Summary of BLS Projections" (Bulletin 1809), "The Structure of the U.S. Economy in 1980 and 1985" (Bulletin 1831), and "Factbook for Estimating the Manpower Needs of Federal Programs" (Bulletin 1832), all published by the Bureau of Labor Statistics, U.S. Dept. of Labor, Washington, DC, 1975."

17. "New Labor Force Projections to 1990: Three Possible Paths," Bureau of Labor Statistics press release, August 16, 1978.

18. Clark W. Bullard, "Energy and Jobs", paper presented at the University of Michigan Conference on Energy Conservation—Path to Progress or Poverty, November 1-2, 1977.

19. Marc H. Ross and Robert H. Williams, "Energy and Economic Growth," prepared for the Joint Economic Committee, U.S. Congress, Washington, DC, 1977.

20. Robert H. Williams (ed.), *The Energy Conservation Papers*, Ballinger, 1975.

21. Denis Hayes, *Rays of Hope*, Norton, NY, 1977.

22. Wilson Clark, in "Creating Jobs through Energy Policy", Hearings before the Subcommittee on Energy of the Joint Economic Committee, U.S. Congress, Washington, DC, March 16-18, 1978.

23. Demand and Conservation Panel of the Committee on Nuclear and Alternative Energy Systems, "U.S. Energy Demand: Some Low Energy Futures", *Science*, April 14, p. 142.

24. John P. Holdren, "Environmental Impacts of Alternative Energy Technologies for California", in "Distributed Energy Systems in California's Future", Interim Report, U.S. Dept. of Energy, Washington, DC, May 1978.

25. "Solar Energy in America's Future: A Preliminary Assessment", Division of Solar Energy, ERDA, Washington, DC, March 1977.

26. "Solar Energy: A Comparative Analysis to the Year 2000", Mitre Corporation, McLean, VA, 1978.

27. "Solar Energy: Progress and Promise", Council on Environmental Quality, Washington, DC, April 1978.

28. M.F. Fels and M.J. Munson, "Energy Thrift in Urban Transportation: Options for the Future", in ref. 20.

29. Owen Carroll and Robert Nathans, "Land Use Configurations and the Utilization of Distributive Energy Technology", in "Distributed Energy Systems in California's Future", Interim Report, U.S. Dept. of Energy, Washington, DC, May 1978; Robert Tw., Pat Smith, and Peter Pollock, "Land Use Implications of a Dispersed Energy System.

30. G.N. Hatsopoulos, E.P. Gyftopoulos, R.W. Sant, and T.F. Widmer, "Capital Investment to Save Energy", *Harvard Business Review*, March/April 1978.

31. Denis Hayes, "The Solar Energy Timetable", Worldwatch Paper 19, Worldwatch Institute, Washington, DC, 1978.

32. "The Economics of Solar Home Heating", study prepared for the Joint Economic Committee, U.S. Congress, Washington, DC, March 13, 1977.

33. R.H. Williams, "Industrial Cogeneration", *Annual Review of Energy*, 3, 1978.

8

A National Energy Plan

Program For Action

Maximum Public Participation

Public Energy Districts

Regional Energy Boards

National Energy Organizations

The plans and programs set forth in the preceding sections are grounded in concrete experience. They represent bold and imaginative thinking by citizens of local communities in different parts of the nation. These communities differ from one another in terms of their population size and makeup, geography and industrial base.

So far these initiatives have been focused on immediate local problems, but as the reader can readily observe, the different communities in one way or another all have begun to relate to regional or even national programs and policies. In Northglenn, ultimate resolution of the water issue involves metropolitan Denver and the communities and farms extending out and along the slopes of the Rockies. The interests of those regional groups in turn are dependent on national water policy, (the policies of the Department of Interior, Environmental Protection Agency,

Department of Agriculture, etc.) In Davis, a major obstacle to developing a new transportation policy is the failure of federal and state agencies to support mass transit that could carry people back and forth between Davis and Sacramento, and between Davis and the Bay area. In Seattle, the central issue in the energy debate was the city's proposed participation in a regional nuclear power pool.

As I argued in the introduction, energy is a national political issue, and over the long run, must be dealt with in a national context. The United States economy is highly centralized. The companies which dominate fossil fuels, and which have become important factors in the expanding alternative energy industry, achieve their power at the national level through the Congress and administration. I believe that over the long term any substantive change for the better in local energy policy will entail a change in policy at the regional and federal level.

Not long ago I joined together with friends from the Public Resource Center and elsewhere to discuss the broad outlines of an overall plan that could change the existing energy system in the United States. We met in the wake of the 1973 Arab oil boycott, and our interests were aimed primarily at fossil fuels, but the plan we came up with has direct bearing on alternative energy. We set forth principles and then a tentative scheme for a new system, actually a network of democratically constituted local, regional and national energy organizations. This system would have the authority to produce, transmit and distribute energy throughout the nation. Its introduction clearly would have major effects on other parts of the political economy as well.

In doing so, we recognized all the dangers inherent in Utopian planning. But it seemed to us important to set forth a vision for the future and also a framework into which various reforms or changes could be fitted. Otherwise, we are likely to go fumbling along, patching up a decrepit system here and there, not driving for any fundamental change.

Proposed Plan

Our plan or system is based on several principles, including:

1. The natural resources of the nation should belong to all the people.
2. Each citizen should be assured a fair share of the energy made available to the American people.
3. Whatever system is developed, it should be firmly rooted in local popular control. Thus, regional and district agencies, created under the plan, should be involved in every stage of the preparation of the national energy plan.
4. All information regarding the activities of every energy agency and all reserve statistics and data on energy consumption should be publicly available on a timely basis, to facilitate the fullest possible participation by the public in the preparation of the plan, and in its subsequent implementation.

5. The prices of energy products should be set at the minimum level consistent with the costs of production and the ecologically sound use of the nation's resources, including not only energy resources but also air, water, land and other natural resources.
6. There should be the minimum possible consumption of non-renewable resources. Where possible, the energy plan should be coordinated with other national planning aimed at reducing the consumption of non-renewable resources.

With these principles in mind, an initial, tentative scheme for actually translating the ideas into a legislative and administrative program is laid out.

Briefly, the concept calls for creation

of public energy districts around the country. There would be several hundred such districts, and the district energy boards would be chosen in general elections. The district boards would plan, control and administer energy production and distribution within their territories. They are the guts of the system. The local districts, in turn, would send representatives to regional energy boards. The regional boards would send representatives to the national energy agency, which would coordinate and develop national energy policy and arrange for international transactions.

This governmental system would plan energy development and execute energy policy. It would dispense research and development funds and administer large portions of the energy apparatus that is now under private control.

The essential aim was to ground an energy system in responsive democratic government at the local level, which would not only govern, but whose constituents would be intimately involved in actual production, distribution and use of energy. The plan would place control of private transportation systems, i.e., oil and gas pipelines and electric transmission systems, in the hands of the national agency. The plan additionally would sever the bonds that link industry and government by removing planning from the industry purview and putting it in the hands of the new system. Research and development functions also would be taken from the federal government and industry, and instead placed directly in

the hands of the district, regional and national energy agencies.

In practice the energy system might work like this: The energy district board of, let's say, Riverhead, Long Island, New York, would meet weekly to debate and develop energy policy that would include a five- to ten-year forward plan. These plans would take into account such factors as the feasibility of introducing solar energy for heating and cooling of buildings, low energy architecture, transportation and industrial patterns. Riverhead's district then would join with other public energy districts making up a Middle Atlantic region, for monthly meetings at New York. At these meetings, the Riverhead representative would work with other regional representatives in hammering out a coordinated energy plan, also involving maximum use of solar and other alternative energy schemes. These meetings would result in a regional plan, which the regional representative would present in Washington to the national agency. The members of the national agency, each one representing a region, would then work up a coordinated national plan that sought to meet the requirements of each region and district.

Suppose, in the case of the middle Atlantic region, including Riverhead, the national plan calls for allocating oil to be used for medicine and gasoline. The national board allots the region an amount of oil production on the outer-continental shelf off Lousiana. Then the Middle Atlantic region contracts with the southern region for production of the oil at rates established by the national board. The oil then is transported from offshore Lousiana to Middle Atlantic refineries via pipelines controlled by the national board, and from the Middle Atlantic refineries to Riverhead, in pipelines controlled by the region.

This system is operated by a popular governmental planning process that is grounded in local constituencies. Private enterprise functions within this system in a circumscribed way, i.e., its methods of operation, rates, etc., are established by the system, treated in effect as a public utility.

Here is a more detailed description of the plan's different aspects:

Public Energy Districts: The heart of the plan involves creation of a new local government unit to administer energy policy—the Public Energy District (PED). This would be a sort of municipal corporation, a political subdivision within a state. The idea is taken in part from Lee Webb's work on a model energy scheme for Vermont. In part it is based on historical experience in the state of Washington. As David Whisnant has described the Washington experience in *People's Appalachia,* "In concept the public utility district is relatively simple. Normally a PUD law authorized a publicly controlled body to issue revenue-producing bonds, receive and disburse funds, acquire real estate (by condemnation if necessary), construct dams and other power generation and distribution facilities, and sell electric power. Many PUDs in the Northwest are distribution facilities only, buying their power from the Bon-

neville Power Administration. All PUDs pay a specified portion of their receipts into the general revenue funds of their counties. As nonprofit enterprises, they are able to supply electricity to their customers at about half the rate charged by private utilities, while paying off their own indebtedness to bondholders.

Directors of the PED would be elected at the polls as part of regularly scheduled elections with standards set for local geographic and worker representation.

A public energy district would have power to eminent domain, but not the power to tax.

The public energy district would be the basic unit within the proposed system of local, regional, and federal energy planning and administrative bodies. It would conduct planning, carry out research and development, produce oil, gas, coal, uranium, etc., design and manufacture solar collectors, build oil refineries, lay pipelines, operate and construct electric generation systems—all of the functions now carried on by the different energy industries or fragmented public or nonprofit bodies.

It is anticipated that the district would continuously debate energy policy and establish and administer policy for the region. It would set utility rates and priorities for end use of fuels.

The district is meant to be a powerful political and economic organization. For example, if an automobile manufacturer sought to open a plant within a public energy district, it must first submit a detailed plan of operations to the PED whereupon the directors would initiate hearings on the advisability of building such a plant, initially taking into account the plan's impact on energy and the environment. But as the PED developed, it might also go further, inquiring into the energy efficiency and usefulness of the end product, i.e., car, truck or bus; the effect of the plant on employment and transportation within the PED, environmental impacts, effect on economic growth policies, and in other ways look into the beneficial and adverse effects of constructing the factory.

Within the different operations of the district, workers would manage and operate the facilities, although the overall policies would be determined by the district board or council, which of course also would include workers.

Regional Energy Boards: Each public energy district would send a representative of its board to a regional energy board. The federal government has developed 10 multistate regions for the purpose of administering its different programs, and while these regions are arbitrary, the plan uses them as a basis, at least, tentatively.

There are several different sorts of federal regions, including six large "depressed areas" defined by the Economic Development Administration; 25 metropolitan administrative areas called Federal Executive Boards, and 10 overall administrative regions which cover the entire nation and its territories. Under Nixon, the major emphasis was to develop the 10 regions, and the Departments of Labor, HUD and HEW all were committed to similar

regional concepts, and often had offices in the same building in the same city, which served as a sort of regional capital: Boston, New York, Philadelphia, Atlanta, Dallas, Denver, Chicago, San Francisco, Seattle, and Kansas City. Nixon set up a regional council where representatives of each involved agency have a seat.

While the public energy district would administer energy resources on a day to day basis, the regional board would allocate resources within the total area.

The Tennessee Valley Authority provides an idea of what a regional organization might be like. Since its origins in 1933, TVA sought to mesh together different aspects of resource planning, electric power, agriculture, industry, fertilizer production, navigation, flood control, recreation, conservation. It conceived of the immediate job as not merely to build dams and reservoirs, but to put people to work. It did not contract for the workers, but hired them directly, building communities for them, attending to their health needs. It was an important force in reinforcing existing state and local governments, by delegating tasks to these governments on a contractual basis. Its free technical services helped raise the level of state and local services.

Even though it was entirely surrounded by hostile corporations and a federal government which reinforced those corporations, TVA became an immensely important economic force, far more so than often is recognized. It should be remembered that TVA's electrical production program initially made possible the nuclear industry.

Without the vast quantities of electricity produced by the combined coal and hydroelectric plants of the Valley Authority, the Atomic Energy Commission's uranium enrichment plants could never have operated. In providing that electricity, TVA literally reorganized the coal industry. It introduced the concept of long term contracts, was an important factor in mechanizing the coal industry, and became the single largest purchaser of coal, a vital factor in the market. It also introduced a modicum of sanity into the electrical utility industry, through its interlinks with other private systems in the south and southeastern mountains, particularly the American Electric Power Company's operations. Despite the vitriolic attacks made upon TVA by private power, the valley authority, through these entities, made the private systems stronger and more stable.

The tragedy of TVA is that because it became so much an instrument of national economic policy, it has been placed in a position of turning against its own constituency on the strip mine issue. Because of its policy of providing low priced electricity, the authority seeks out coal at the lower prices, and hence trades heavily in strip mined coal from Appalachia. Strip mining is runious to the entire region; by buying the stripped coal TVA turns its own constituency against it.

A similar situation developed around nuclear power. TVA reorganized the coal industry to provide the electricity to enrich the uranium necessary for hydrogen bombs and nuclear power plants. In doing so it was answering the dictates of the Pentagon, which was anxious to perpetuate nuclear technology.

Under this new proposal, the possibility of such policy would be greatly lessened by grounding the policies of a TVA-like authority in the local districts, which in this instance would include the strip mined areas. In this case, it could not become an instrument of top-down federal policy.

National Energy Organization: The purpose of this board or agency would be to coordinate the ideas and plans of the different regions. It would be an important organization, providing the point of contact with the federal governmental apparatus and the Congress.

It would have several principal functions. Perhaps the most important would be to act as trustee of the nation's natural resources, allocating scarce resources to regions for distribution to localities.

In principle, all natural resources of the nation ought to be public, and not given solely to any corporation for exploitation on its own terms. But, as with all other aspects of this plan, transitional steps are needed, Here is one good example:

The national agency could take over from the Interior Department administration of those territories already in the public demain; that is, areas specifically removed from commerce by the Congress for the purpose of the general public good. These federal resources include an extensive amount of mineral fuels. The estimates vary. According to a common estimate, over 50 percent of the fossil fuel energy resources of the United States are in the public domain territories. Some estimates place the amounts as high as 80 percent. According to the Ford Foundation's Energy Policy Project report, about one-third of the remaining domestic oil and gas resources are estimated as likely to be found in the outercontinental shalf, which is part of the public domain. In 1972, the outercontinental shelf lands produced 10 percent of the domestic oil and 16 percent of the domestic gas. Oil shale is almost entirely controlled by the federal government. About 85 percent of the strippable low sulphur deposits are in the public domain. About half of the nation's geothermal resources are on public land. An estimated 50 percent of the domestic uranium supply is in the public domain.

These estimates do not include the huge areas of Alaska that already have been leased by the federal government to oil companies, nor the state-controlled lands.

Under one concept, a transitional scheme would be to place these important resources, already in the federal public domain (and in one sense "nationalized") within the control of the national agency, whose regional constituents then could make initial plans and coordinate national policy based on this resource base.

Eventually, the idea would be to widen the concept of public lands so that all natural resources, including mineral fuel resources, were considered public.

In principle then, all energy sources would come under the public control. In addition, the national organization should have a planning staff that functions as a public research and development center serving the different regions. Probably this staff would conduct the mapping and resource estimates that now are carried out by private industry.

The national organization would take over functions of the Federal Energy Regulatory Commission and other regulatory agencies. For instance, it would establish all interstate rates and end use priorities for energy, and arrange for international trade.

As the history of the modern energy industry instructs, again and again large corporate interests—the Standard Oil Trust, its successor companies, the Morgans, Insulls, Rockefellers—dominated different sectors of the industry through control of the transmission facilities. Rockefeller initially built his monopoly through control over transportation. In the 1930's, the Morgans and Rockefellers controlled the natural gas business by dominating the pipelines. In California today, the major companies control the industry by ownership of pipelines. In electricity, brownouts and blackouts are due in large part to the inefficient systems caused because private companies refuse to transmit public power and interlock their systems with public power systems. Tanker fleets, the largest navies in the world, still are controlled by the major oil companies, and so on. Transportation of energy is absolutely crucial to its ultimate control. Therefore, under the plan the major interstate transportation facilities should be placed under the direct control of the national energy board. This is a crucial part of our long range plan.

It would have the national board, through a staged process, aecquire outright control (51 percent) of key sections of major interstate natural gas and oil pipelines, and electrical transmission systems.

During this 10-year period, the national energy board would lease and operate those portions of oil, gas and electrical transmission systems necessary to transmit energy from public domain territories to the different public energy districts. Terms of the leases would be negotiated between the board and the companies.

The lease period would provide an effective test of the systems and the energy board could determine which parts of the transportation lines should be used in its developing inter-regional system.

In the case of interstate commerce in energy that was transported by water, rail, truck or airplane, the energy board would establish rates and prescribe general policy.

While the national board would determine policy and establish rates, the actual work would be carried out at the local level by the PEDs. Neither the national energy board nor the regional boards should maintain sizeable bureaucracies. All work, including planning, bookkeeping, hearings and investigations would be conducted by the PED staff.

The national energy board would also regulate commerce in energy between regions. Commerce within a given region, among the public energy districts, would be governed by the regional board. Commerce within the public energy district would be regulated by that board.

Planning: As the brief history of the oil and coal industries indicates, the crucial element in the industry's control of public resources and of federal governmental policy is planning. Systematically, since the early 1920's, the federal government has given over to industry access to natural resources and has refused to plan these resources.

The central, most important step in breaking apart big capital from the federal government would be to remove planning from industry. The representative federal board as envisioned in this plan would conduct routine, careful mapping of the nation's mineral energy resources, including geophysical assessments, shallow and deep core drilling, environmental tests, aerial and space surveys, mapping and testing of the nation's coal, etc.

As with other parts of the proposed system, the actual work would be carried out within the different energy districts under contract from the federal and regional boards.

Federal money designated for planning would be earmarked for use first by local energy districts, and secondly through contract with not-for-profit groups within the localities.

Where the money was spent on private industry, it would go to locally owned and managed small businesses.

The long range plan set forth above is primarily concerned with existing fossil fuels and the systems for their production, processing and distribution. But obviously as time goes on there probably will be an increasing use of alternative energy. Any political or economic plan must take alternative energy into account. Following are a few ideas for how alternative energy could be included in the long term plan.

To begin with, communities within a given public energy district should be encouraged to develop 10-year community energy plans, concentrating on residential and transportation requirements. These are the two aspects of energy policy that most affect local communities. Such planning might include introduction of bicycles, car pools, minibus setups, etc. A community energy center could be established to provide information for different neighborhoods and individual residents. For example, it could provide information on energy audits.

A major block to widespread introduction of solar energy and other alternatives is refusal of banks and the government to provide inexpensive loans to make the often expensive changes. The community energy plan along with the community energy center could be vehicles for dealing with this situation. Leonard Rodberg suggests that community groups, perhaps through the center, negotiate as a group with local banks for long-term loans under special conditions. One of those conditions would be that any money borrowed for alternative energy systems be repaid under a graduated payment plan. Under such a scheme, loan repayments would start off small, and grow larger as time goes on. Some housing loans are arranged in this manner now.

Secondly, Rodberg would like to see a change in the recently enacted tax credit system. As it stands the government offers a tax credit of up to 20 percent for homeowners who install alternative energy systems or who employ methods of energy conservation, up to $10,000. Rodberg's idea is to change this tax credit into a direct grant and use it as the downpayment against a loan. Under such a plan, the money would move directly from the federal government to the bank making the loan.

The regional energy boards would be of special importance in any widespread introduction of alternative energy, for many of these systems, including solar, depend on the geography of the locale. What works in southern California may very well not work in the Northeast. Such policies as standard-setting would have special relevance at the regional level. And at the regional level, energy extension services could be developed to spread out into local communities.

At the federal level, the national energy organization could sponsor competitions among architects, engineers and planners for alternative energy system designs, and then gradually over time and on the basis of those competitions begin to set certain criteria for design of public buildings. All buildings constructed with federal funds would be required to adhere to the design criteria. So too would buildings leased by the federal government. Over time the design criteria would apply to buildings inhabited by all organizations receiving federal funds for whatever purpose.

9

Check List For Energy Action

Here are a few tips to keep in mind as you think about ways to change the energy system in your community:

1. How to Begin. One quick, simple way to get started, especially in places where there has been little serious thought to changing the energy mix, is to pull together your neighbors as an ad hoc group. Get everyone to help gather existing information—such things as street maps, bus routes, numbers and routes of car pools, demographic information, electric and gas consumption figures, utility costs; find out where people in the neighborhood work and the means of transportation they use—anything and everything that seems to you to bear on the subject. Then stage a week-long charette in the evenings after work.

A charette is a tool of planners and to a lesser extent of architects. It's a kind of brain storming session where the people who will use or be affected by a school addition, a mall or building are invited to come to a meeting and help lay out what the project should look like and what it should contain. Everyone takes a hand, marking up plans that are spread all around the room. In the case of energy, you'll want to concentrate most heavily on transportation and residential systems. The charette should give you a fast education in energy and a rough idea of what can be done in your immediate community.

2. Start a Community Energy Center. Form your neighborhood or community group into a community energy center. No matter how small or makeshift this center is to begin with, it can be an important step in planning for an alternative system. The center can provide information to residents who want to make their own energy audits, or put them in touch with others living in similar style houses who already have conducted audits. Gradually it should become a resource for the entire community, providing details of all sorts on what can, and cannot, be done. It should also be a forum for community discussion and debate, and provide liaison with local government. The center itself can make approaches on behalf of its members to banks and other financial institutions for special loans; it could represent the community before regulatory commissions, conduct studies, and so on.

3. Local Government. Local government can be an important, constructive forum for progressive change in energy policy. In the cases of both

Seattle and Davis, change came as the result of action by the city council which in turn had been influenced by ad hoc citizen groups. Remember, most local governments want and need citizen participation. If your group is willing to put in the effort, you'll probably find the local government will be more than happy to let you do things.

4. Simplicity Counts. As the Davis experiment suggests, simple changes make the biggest impact. A transportation system, for example, which includes safe interconnecting bike grids is crucial if a community is to expand the use of bicycles. Try adding requirements that new buildings take advantage of southern exposure, or a simple requirement that plumbing for new buildings include outlets for future installation of solar equipment.

5. Planning is Crucial. Long term plans are key. In energy, change is slow and costly. You can't change the basic underpinnings of the American system over night. You'll win some battles and lose others. But if you move forward within the general framework of an accepted plan there is much hope for considerable change. Without a plan, defeats can become major setbacks, and victories represent little real progress.

6. Money is Available. Don't despair on this count. Small amounts of planning money are available through the states. Obtain a copy of the state energy plan, required by the federal government, from the state energy office. The plan will spell out different programs and funds available for each one. Often state energy planners are on the lookout for innovative local programs. So don't hesitate to put your ideas forward.

7. Alternative energy can mean more jobs. A growing volume of data, analysis and reportage indicates there are more jobs in this generally less capital intensive area. We have included Leonard Rodberg's study in this book. For more up-to-date information, write him at the Public Resource Center, 1747 Connecticut Ave. NW, Washington DC 20009.

10

From Fossil Fuels to Renewable Alternatives

Changing the energy system of the United States from reliance on fossil fuels to renewable alternatives entails a long, arduous struggle. It entails reorganizing the foundations of the most powerful and flexible industrial economy in the world. No one should ever underestimate the amazing elasticity and flexibility of the United States economy to withstand or absorb major challenge.

All the same, the communities described in this book have begun to move towards major systematic change. In a previous chapter, I have sketched a vision for a future energy system. Communities, in their own concrete, pragmatic fashion have begun to develop the building blocks for a national policy. So far, there are three simple planks to this plan:

The first is reorganization of transportation within the community, and later, the region. It involves bringing the workplace closer to home, and then making it possible to go back and forth by walking, by use of the bicycle, or mini-bus. Regional transport entails buses, railroads and to some extent car pools.

The second is reorganization of housing away from the suburban pattern that has dominated United States residential developments since the end of the Second World War. Land's work is but an indication of what can happen. Housing will almost certainly be more densely clustered and smaller in size. It will also be more environmentally sound.

The third involves the capturing, control and employment of wastes. During the early stages of the industrial revolution, Benthamites and other utilitarians argued that introduction of modern sanitation should be accompanied by a system for the capture and use of wastes. These early technocrats were overwhelmed by expanding capitalism. Now, more than one hundred years after those early struggles within the industrial revolution, their arguments are gaining currency. Northglenn is no mill town, but its waste water program is straight out of a Benthamite text.

On a much more immediate level, the

response of the localities described in this book amounts to a resistance to the arguments of the oil companies and the nuclear industry, which insist that without further development of fossil fuels, synthetic substitutes and nuclear energy, the nation will become reliant on insecure foreign oil that will be ruinously inflationary.

But as Davis and Seattle have begun to show, energy conservation together with judicious introduction of alternative methods can add up to substantial energy reductions. In Davis, savings already have been recorded. In Seattle, the city has adopted a policy that aims to replace the energy scheduled to be produced by nuclear plants with energy gained from conservation. A new energy base is thus being built.

INDEX